Penguin Books

The Second World War

A J P Taylor was one of Britain's most authoritative and popular historians. He wrote definitive works of British and diplomatic history, which also became bestsellers, and he was much admired for the many impromptu television lectures he gave.

Alan John Percivale Taylor was born in Lancashire in 1906. He was educated at Bootham School in York before winning a scholarship to read History at Oriel College, Oxford, where he received a first-class degree. He then became a lecturer in Modern History at Manchester University from 1930 to 1938, and from then until 1976 was a Fellow of Magdalen College, Oxford. He was later made an Honorary Fellow of Magdalen and received honorary doctorates from, among others, Bristol, Warwick and Manchester universities. His books include *The Course of German History*; *The Last of Old Europe*; *How Wars Begin*; *How Wars End*; *The Trouble Makers*; *Beaverbrook*; *Essays in English History*; *Europe: Grandeur and Decline*; and his autobiography, *A Personal History*. His most important works are still in print, of which Penguin publish *Bismarck: The Man and the Statesman*; *The Origins of the Second World War*; *The First World War*; *The Second World War: An Illustrated History*; *The Habsburg Monarchy 1809–1918*; *The War Lords*; and a collection of his essays on nineteenth-century Europe entitled *From Napoleon to the Second International*. *From the Boer War to the Cold War*, a further collection of his essays, is forthcoming in Penguin.

A J P Taylor died in September 1990. In his obituary, *The Times* paid tribute to him as 'probably the most controversial, and certainly the best known, historian in the English-speaking world. In his prime A J P Taylor attracted – and usually bewitched – a wider following than Macaulay ever dreamt of. Prolific and best-selling author, gifted journalist, and *sui generis* as a television star, he attempted to transform the historical understanding of his day.'

A J P Taylor

The Second World War

An illustrated history

Penguin Books

To Len Deighton

PENGUIN BOOKS
Published by the Penguin Group
Penguin Books Ltd, 27 Wrights Lane, London W8 5TZ, England
Penguin Books USA Inc., 375 Hudson Street, New York, New York 10014, USA
Penguin Books Australia Ltd, Ringwood, Victoria, Australia
Penguin Books Canada Ltd, 10 Alcorn Avenue, Toronto, Ontario, Canada M4V 3B2
Penguin Books (NZ) Ltd, 182–90 Wairau Road, Auckland 10, New Zealand
Penguin Books Ltd, Registered Offices: Harmondsworth, Middlesex, England

First published by Hamish Hamilton 1975
Published by Penguin Books 1976
10 9 8 7 6

This book was designed and produced by George Rainbird Ltd
Marble Arch House, 44 Edgeware Road, London W2

House Editor: Penelope Miller   Picture researcher: Patricia Vaughan
Designer: Alan Bartram   Maps: John R. Flower and Tom Stalker Miller

This edition printed and bound by Toppan Printing Co. (S) PTE, Singapore

Contents

Colour plates

Maps

Acknowledgments for illustrations

The following abbreviations are used in the list:

APN   Novosti Press Agency, London
CP   Camera Press Ltd, London
IWM   By courtesy of the Trustees of the Imperial War Museum, London
KPA   Keystone Press Agency Ltd, London
NA   National Archives, Washington, D.C.
RTHPL   Radio Times Hulton Picture Library, London
RvO   By courtesy of the Rijksinstituut voor Oorlogsdocumentatie, Amsterdam
USN   By courtesy of the US Navy

Pictures are listed top to bottom and left to right.

Page numbers marked with an asterisk* indicate colour illustrations.

Title page: German reinforcements bound for El Alamein, Oct. 1942. *IWM*; and captured German equipment near Sevastopol, 1944. *APN*

13   German army manœuvres, 1931. *IWM*

14   Nazi rally in prewar Germany. *CP*

15   Hitler at the Reichs Party Day, Nuremberg, 1934. *CP*

16   Chicago soup kitchen, 1930s. *NA*

19   Mussolini and Victor Emanuel, Nov. 1923. *RTHPL*

20   Graffiti on a shuttered Jewish store. *IWM*

22   Meeting in Berlin, Sept. 1937. *RTHPL*

23   Members of the Japanese War Cabinet. *IWM*

24a   Churchill in May 1940. *RTHPL*

24b   Stalin. *CP*

25   President Roosevelt after his election, 1932. *NA*

27a   Submarines in Krupp's yard. *IWM*

27b   Prewar army exercise in France. *IWM*

28a   Lord Mayor of London inspecting guns. *RTHPL*

28b   A machine gunner practising for war. *RTHPL*

30   Japanese victory march through Shanghai. *RTHPL*

31   Hitler's victory parade through Vienna. *KPA*

34   German troops at the Polish border, 1 Sept. 1939. *KPA*

35   German troops enter Poland. *IWM*

37a   A London policeman, 3 Sept. 1939. *RTHPL*

37b   Anti-gas training in Britain. *RTHPL*

38   Announcement of mobilization in France. *RTHPL*

39   German and Russian soldiers in Poland. *RTHPL*

43   British and French ministers meeting in Paris, Feb. 1940. *Photo: Harlingue-Viollet*

44   The *Admiral Graf Spee* off Montevideo. *IWM*

46   Russian T-26 tank captured by Finns, 1940. *CP*

47   German troops in Oslo, May 1940. *RTHPL*

49   Members of the BEF in France. *IWM*

51   MPs in the Local Defence Volunteers, London. *RTHPL*

53   German troops crossing the Meuse, 1940. *IWM*

54   German troops milking a French cow. *Photo: G. Sirot*

55   Heinz Guderian at Le Quitteur, France, 1940. *IWM*

56   Philippe Pétain. *Photo: Harlingue-Viollet*

57   Dunkirk. *CP*

58   Dunkirk beach after the evacuation. *Photo: G. Sirot*

59   Germans in Paris, 1940. *Photo: Harlingue-Viollet*

61   Cover of *Kölnische Illustrierte Zeitung*, Dec. 1940. *CP*

62   Charles de Gaulle, June 1940. *RTHPL*

64   German poster of 1940: 'Help, I'm starving – there are still no bananas.' *IWM*

67   A German army exercise near Calais. *IWM*

70a   Air battle over London, 6 Sept. 1940. *RTHPL*

70b   London bus in a bomb crater. *RTHPL*

71a   Clearing bomb damage at Bank tube station. *RTHPL*

71b   German Dornier Do. 215 bombers over London. *IWM*

72   View from St Paul's Cathedral of London ruins. *RTHPL*

73*   C. R. W. Nevinson: *Anti-Aircraft Defences. Photo: Derrick Witty. IWM*

74–5*   Paul Nash: *Battle of Britain, Aug.–Oct. 1940. Photo: Derrick Witty. IWM*

76*   Dame Laura Knight: *Take Off: Interior of a bomber aircraft. Photo: Derrick Witty. IWM*

77   Civilians sleeping in the Underground. *IWM*

78   The *Bismarck* sails for the last time. *CP*

79   British convoy caught in a German periscope. *Associated Press*

82   Molotov *left* and Hitler in discussion. *IWM*

85   RAF rounding up Bedouin Arabs in Iraq, 1941. *IWM*

86   Gen. O'Connor in Derna, Libya. *IWM*

87a   Italian troops surrendering to Australians. *IWM*

87b   Column of Italian prisoners in Western Desert. *IWM*

88   First German landing in North Africa. *IWM*

89   Erwin Rommel and Afrika Korps staff. *IWM*

90a   German soldiers in Yugoslavia. *KPA*

90b   British troops in Greece, 3 May 1941. *IWM*

91   Emp. Haile Selassie in Addis Ababa, May 1941. *IWM*

93   German parachute troops over Crete. *IWM*

96   Vichy casualties outside Sarda, Syria. *IWM*

99   Spanish volunteers in Russia. *KPA*

100   German transport train. *KPA*

101   T-34 tanks. *APN*

103   Snapshot found on body of Nazi soldier. *IWM*

105   Atlantic Charter meeting, 10–12 Aug. 1941. *USN*

107   Life-line to Leningrad. *APN*

108a   Buildings burned by fleeing Russians. *KPA*

108b   Blazing houses in Vitebsk, Aug. 1941. *KPA*

109*   A. A. Gorpenko: *Battle at the Kryukovo Railway Station* (detail). Central Museum of the USSR Armed Forces, Moscow. *APN*

110–11*   I. Krivonogov: *Korsun-Shevchenkovsky Battle*. Central Museum of the USSR Armed Forces, Moscow. *APN*

Preface

I have been composing this book for more than thirty years. During the war I gave monthly commentaries in Oxford and other towns, surveying the events of the previous month and sometimes speculating on what was likely to happen next. At the end of the war I summarized its history in a series of radio talks for the Danish service of the BBC, talks no doubt irretrievably lost. Ever since then I have been increasing my knowledge and deepening my understanding. Now I begin to think that I have something useful to say.

Thirty years afterwards is about the right time to look at the Second World War with detachment. Interest in it is still strong, as the flow of war books shows, and we are far enough away to shake off some of the contemporary passions and illusions. I do not write as a partisan of any group or country, though I happen to think that my country fought on the right side, and where I make a judgment on controversial topics, it is after careful consideration of all the available evidence.

The Second World War was fought in three seas or oceans (the Mediterranean, the Atlantic and the Pacific) and in four major land campaigns (Russia, North Africa and the Mediterranean, western Europe, and the Far East). Each of these wars had a different character, and historians have often treated them in independent narratives. I have tried to bind them together: to remember that when Pearl Harbor was attacked, the Germans had been halted in front of Moscow; that when Stalingrad was besieged, the British were winning the Battle of El Alamein;

and that when the Anglo-Americans landed in Sicily, the Russians were winning the Battle of Kursk. The victory of 1945 was an Allied victory, to which all three great Allies contributed to the best of their ability and resources.

I express my gratitude to the audiences at Aylesbury, Banbury, Oxford, Reading, Wolverton and elsewhere, who first encouraged me to think historically about the Second World War. I also express my gratitude to the University of London for enabling me to give the substance of the first chapter as the Creighton Lecture for 1973.

A.J.P.T.

1

World war

In the first half of the twentieth century mankind experienced two great wars – the first mainly confined to Europe despite being dignified afterwards with the name of world war, the second truly world wide. In both wars Germany and her associates fought roughly the same coalition of Powers. Both wars were bloody and prolonged. In many ways their differences were greater than their similarities.

The outbreak of the First World War was clear cut. At the beginning of July 1914 the Great European Powers were at peace with each other as they had been ever since 1871. A month later all except Italy were at war. There were changes among the participants as the war went on – Italy and the United States joined in, Russia fell out. But no one can doubt that war began on a great scale in August 1914 and continued on much the same scale until November 1918.

But when did the Second World War begin? Many historians, conditioned to think of Europe as the centre of the world, date the war from 1 September 1939 when Germany attacked Poland. This is not an answer that would satisfy the Abyssinians or the Chinese for whom the war began earlier. It would not satisfy the Russians and Americans for whom the war began later. In any case this European war virtually ended in June 1940 with Germany dominating the entire Continent west of Russia. If a formal declaration of war marks the starting point, the Second World War began in April 1932 when Mao Tse-tung and Chou Teh declared war against Japan in the name of the Kiangsi Soviet. (It is a historical curiosity that the Republic of China did not declare war against Japan until after Pearl Harbor.) If we wait until the war was being fought in every continent except the two Americas, the date must be 1942 or even 1944.

A number of small wars gradually coalesced into a great one. They did not coalesce fully, so much so that it is almost possible to write about the war in Europe and the Mediterranean without mentioning the Far East and about that in the Far East without mentioning Europe and the Mediterranean. Almost possible but not quite. In the prewar years Great Britain might have taken a firmer line with Germany if it had not been for her anxieties in the Far East. Contrariwise she might well have compromised with Japan in the Far East if she had not needed American economic and later military support in order to maintain her position as a European Great Power. In 1940 Hitler's conquest of France and Holland tempted the Japanese to turn south. In 1941 the Japanese action at Pearl Harbor tempted Hitler into declaring war on the United States. Thereafter the American campaign in the Pacific did more than that in the Mediterranean to delay the Allied landings in northern France.

In wartime the respective alliances never fully coalesced. Though Mussolini grandiosely presented the association between Germany and Italy as the Axis round which European affairs revolved, in fact he conducted an independent campaign in the Mediterranean until he ran into trouble, and Hitler then intervened solely to rescue his fellow dictator, not to pursue a strategy of his own. Germany and Japan did not cooperate at all. One ocean-going Japanese submarine reached Bordeaux with supplies for Germany. That was all their partnership amounted to. The signatories of the Tripartite Pact (Germany, Italy and Japan) did not even find a common name. Their opponents called them the Aggressors, the Militarists, or the Fascists, none of them an accurate description.

On the other side, there was never a formal alliance between the United States and Great Britain, though their economic and military affairs became closely intertwined. The alliance between Soviet Russia and Great Britain was indeed formal and not much else. In practice Great Britain ran an independent campaign against Italy with some support from the United States; the United States ran an independent campaign against Japan with some participation by Great Britain; and Soviet Russia ran an independent campaign against Germany until the last year of the war. These associates, too, did not find a common name except as signatories to the declaration of the United Nations. Great Britain and the United States called themselves the democratic or, more straightforwardly, the Anglo-Saxon Powers. Soviet Russia preferred 'the peace-loving nations'. The Grand Alliance was sometimes used for the three Great Powers (Great Britain, Soviet Russia and the United States). More often they were simply the Big Three.

The First World War was fought throughout in much the same place and in much the same way. The prospective combatants had long foreseen that the decisive battle would be fought on the plains of Flanders and northeast France. So it was, though four years instead of the expected six weeks were needed to reach the decision. The other campaigns – on the Eastern and Italian fronts, at sea and in Asiatic Turkey – were peripheral to the prolonged battle in France. The methods of war also remained much the same. Though tanks played some part before the end, the outcome depended mainly on masses of infantry flung against each other, much as they had been in the days of Napoleon or the Romans.

The Second World War, though also expected, repeatedly changed its character and field of decisive action while it wore on. A Swiss historian has called it 'one of the most gigantic improvisations in history, far above the usual measure'. Only the British Air Staff had planned their strategy in advance, and this turned out to be irrelevant, for the Royal Air Force long proved incapable of carrying it out. Otherwise every campaign was run up while the war was on. Who could have foretold that the decisive battles of the Second World War would be fought at Stalingrad and Midway Island, El Alamein and Caen? Equally the decisive weapons were not foreseen. Aircraft carriers eclipsed battleships. Mass bombing that had been expected to work wonders made only a marginal contribution to the result. Landing craft and jeeps – instruments that no one had envisaged, at any rate as weapons of war – counted for far more. Tanks certainly played a full part. But few foresaw that, with the coming of the anti-tank gun, the infantry would go in first and the tanks follow, instead of the other way round. The war ended with the explosion of two atomic bombs. Before the war hardly anyone believed that nuclear fission would ever have a practical application.

The nature of the First World War is easy to define. It was a conflict between two alliances or power blocs – the Triple Entente (France, Great Britain and Russia) on one side, the Central Powers (Austria-Hungary and Germany) on the other. The war was within a single society. The combatants had similar social and political systems. All were capitalistic with trade unions playing a subsidiary part. All had constitutions, though the Russian constitution was rather a sham. Despite attempts to discover deep moral issues – against German barbarism, for German *Kultur*, for or against self-determination – the war was fought for the sake of winning it, and the aim was an adjustment of the Balance of Power, not the mastery of the world. If Germany had won there would have been some territorial changes in her favour, and she would have emerged stronger than before. As it was some territorial changes were made to her disadvantage, though she was not basically weakened. The dismemberment of the Habsburg and Ottoman empires, the Bolshevik Revolution in Russia and the establishment of a League of Nations were consequences of the war, not its causes either beforehand or while it was on.

Historians still debate the causes of the First World War and find no easy answers. Who planned it? Was it even planned at all? Or did the European Powers, as Lloyd George said, 'muddle into war'? With the Second World War, the causes are embarrassingly many.

The most obvious division in the interwar years was that between victors and vanquished, or in more practical terms between France and Germany with Great Britain and, until the last years of peace, Italy trailing along reluctantly on the French side. Nearly all Germans believed that their country had been unfairly treated in 1919. They had expected that, when Germany accepted the Fourteen Points and became a democratic republic, the war would be forgotten and Germany would return at once to the comity of nations. Instead a peace treaty was imposed on her. She had to pay reparations; she was compulsorily disarmed; some of her territory

was lost and other parts of it were occupied by Allied troops. Nearly all Germans wished to overthrow the Versailles settlement, and few distinguished between undoing the terms of the Versailles treaty and restoring Germany to the dominant position she had held in Europe before her defeat.

Germany was not alone in her grievances. Hungary also railed against the peace settlement, though not to much effect. Italy, despite being ostensibly among the victors, had come off almost empty-handed or thought she had, and her dictator Mussolini, a former socialist, described her as a 'proletarian' nation. In the Far East Japan, also numbered among the victors, increasingly girded against the superior position of the British Empire and the United States. For that matter Soviet Russia, though ultimately joining the defenders of the *status quo*, was aggrieved by her territorial losses at the end of the First World War. German grievances, however, provided most of the driving force, and Adolf Hitler voiced them from the moment he became a political agitator.

These various grievances remained harmless during the 1920s when there was a brief restoration of the prewar economic order – more or

The German army on manœuvres with wooden tanks

The Nazis and their Führer

The great Depression: a soup kitchen in Chicago

less unrestricted world trade, stable currencies, and private enterprise little affected by state interference. This restoration was shattered by the great economic depression that first struck the world in the autumn of 1929. World trade declined catastrophically. There was mass un-employment – over two million in Great Britain, six million in Germany, fifteen million in the United States. Currencies rocked. In 1931 the sacred pound sterling was forced off the gold standard. Faced with this storm, countries retreated within their own national systems, and the more industrialized the country, the greater was its withdrawal from the world. In 1931 Germany ended the mark as a free currency and moved towards international trade by barter. In 1932 Great Britain, the traditional home of Free Trade, adopted protective tariffs and soon extended them to her colonies. In 1933 the newly elected President Roosevelt devalued the dollar and set out on a policy of economic recovery regardless of other countries.

Economic warfare started largely unawares. At first a war of all against all, it soon changed its character and reinforced the division of the world. Soviet Russia had always been a closed economic system, though this did not enable her to escape the effects of the Depression. Of the others, some Great Powers – the United States most of all but also the British and the French empires – could, if pressed, make do on their own resources. Germany and Japan lost out. Though they, too, were great industrial nations, they could not provide for themselves. They needed raw materials from the rest of the world, yet the Depression made it impossible for them to obtain these by the normal methods of international trade. Their economic leaders felt, no doubt with some exaggeration, that their countries were being strangled and that they must create their own economic empires. The Japanese took the simplest course and extended their military power, first into Manchuria and then over the maritime areas of China. Germany, still hampered in the early 1930s by the restraints of Versailles, had no such easy way out. She had to use economic weapons and thus intensified the isolation or autarky that events had forced upon her.

At first the rulers of Germany did this reluctantly. When Hitler became ruler of Germany in January 1933, he embraced autarky as a positive good. Men debated later whether Hitler and the National Socialist movement that he led were created by Versailles or by the Depression. The answer is by both. Economic discontent carried Hitler to power, but he had already established his reputation by his campaign against Versailles. In his view, the German Depression was the legacy of defeat, and the instruments for overcoming the Depression would also carry Germany to political victory. Autarky would strengthen Germany for political conquests, and these would in turn enable her to carry autarky further.

Here was the underlying conflict in the years before the Second World War. For the United States, and less wholeheartedly for Great Britain, economic warfare was a regrettable and temporary expedient. For the Japanese and Germans, it was a permanent measure and their only way to greatness. This had a paradoxical result. Usually the aggressive or restless Power is the stronger, pushed on by a conviction that it can seize more than it holds. It has been argued that this was the situation before the Second World War. The Balance of Power, it is said, had broken down. Germany overshadowed Europe; Japan overshadowed the Far East. This was true if their immediate neighbours alone were considered – the European states adjacent to Germany, or China in the Far East. It ceased to be true once the World Powers were thrown into the scale.

Both Hitler and the rulers of Japan were acutely aware of this. Far from planning a world war, as they were often credited with doing, they were convinced that a world war would be their ruin. But this did not make them retreat towards peace. Both Hitler and the Japanese planned to make a series of small gains without war or at any rate without serious fighting. They counted rightly on the reluctance of the World Powers to go to war and, less justifiably, on their own ingenuity. They intended to creep forward, as it were, unobserved or at least unchecked until they emerged as World Powers too strong to be challenged. They almost succeeded. Hitler secured the mastery of Europe at dawn on 14 May 1940 when German tanks crossed the Meuse at Sedan; Japan secured the mastery of the Far East in a couple of hours at Pearl Harbor on 7 December 1941. German losses in the French campaign of 1940 were not much greater than those of the British army in a single day on the Somme in 1916; the Japanese lost twenty-nine aircraft at Pearl Harbor. Never were decisive victories won so cheaply. What would have happened if these victories had been consolidated? Hitler sometimes talked of Germany's conquering the world, though he usually added that this would only take place a hundred years after his death. The Japanese might have been content with dominance in the Far East. However, Germany and Japan were arrested before their transformation into World

Powers was complete, and the question of their further intentions was therefore never asked, let alone answered.

In retrospect this conflict between the Powers who were more or less content with the world as it was and those who wished to change it gave the Second World War its basic pattern. At the time conflict of political ideas and principles attracted more attention. This was in part a legacy of the First World War. At the end of the war the Allies and their great associate, the United States, were convinced that they had been fighting for ideal causes – democracy, self-determination and a League of Nations. Collective security was to prevent war in the future. The doctrine never operated effectively. The Japanese disregarded the League in 1931 when they occupied Manchuria, though their offence was less flagrant than was depicted later. Mussolini defied the League in 1935 when he led Italy into war against Abyssinia. Hitler defied the entire system of international relations when he repudiated the Versailles system in 1935 and the Treaty of Locarno in 1936. Though Great Britain and France were the only Great Powers loyal to the League throughout – at any rate nominally – Soviet Russia joined it belatedly, and the United States, despite their own policy of isolation, deplored the disregard of international obligations. Here was a moral cleavage between those who respected international obligations and those who did not. It was no accident that the cleavage corresponded to that between the satisfied and the disatisfied Powers.

The League of Nations was a rather remote affair, causing a stir principally among diplomats and enthusiasts for collective security. The Bolshevik Revolution, however, rent European civilization asunder and divided Europe more deeply than the Reformation had divided it in the sixteenth century or the French Revolution at the end of the eighteenth. Soviet Russia, Marxist in doctrine and dedicated to world revolution, seemed to threaten the capitalist world in one way or another. That world retaliated by boycotting Soviet Russia and in the Wars of Intervention sought her downfall by military means. In the 1920s many people, and especially the Communists themselves, expected that the Wars of Intervention would be repeated and that in the next great war the capitalist Powers would gang up against 'the workers' state'.

This expectation was not fulfilled. But mutual suspicions cut deep. The belief that Germany was a bulwark against Communism led the former victors to regard her with less distrust and to make more concessions to her than they might otherwise have done. Russia, previously a Great Power in both Europe and the Far East, ceased to count in either and was never seriously included in diplomatic calculations. The Franco-Soviet Pact of 1935, for instance, was on paper as firm as the old Franco-Russian Alliance. Yet when in 1939 the French, in association with the British, sought alliance with Soviet Russia, they negotiated as though the Pact of 1935 had never existed – it was something best forgotten or wished away. The alliance negotiations of 1939 themselves provide a further example. It is clear in retrospect that none of the three parties involved in them expected them to succeed or wished them to do so.

During the 1930s anti-Bolshevism was partially eclipsed by another cleavage in European civilization: that between Fascism and capitalist democracy. When Mussolini set up Fascism in Italy few people except leftwing socialists took alarm. Indeed he was supposed to have saved Italy from Bolshevism. He took on the appearance of a respectable statesman, was solemnly consulted by British and French statesmen, and as late as April 1935 stood forth at Stresa as the champion of collective security and the sanctity of treaties.

National Socialism, the German variety of Fascism, was a threat on a quite different scale. Statesmen in other countries were well aware of what was happening in Germany and what National Socialism stood for. Nazi barbarities were fully reported in the world press and by foreign ambassadors. The political parties and

Duce and King

the trade unions had been destroyed. Freedom of speech had ceased to exist. The Jews were being driven out of public life, and only the more fortunate managed to emigrate. The principles of European civilization were being repudiated. The Nazi rulers from Hitler downwards were 'gangsters' as the British Ambassador called them.

What lesson were the statesmen of democratic countries to draw from their knowledge of conditions in Germany? Protests made Nazi behaviour worse. An international boycott of German goods, in the unlikely event that it were effective, would increase Germany's economic difficulties, and it was the general belief, by no means unfounded, that these difficulties had brought Hitler and the Nazis to power. French statesmen gave up the problem in despair. At each step in Germany's advance, they protested and did nothing. British statesmen settled for the idea that if Germany's grievances were redressed and her prosperity restored, Nazi behaviour might become less barbarous. The British accepted the German system of bilateral trade and tried to make autarky tolerable. Neville Chamberlain, who became British Prime Minister in 1937, sought to appease Germany by the active redress of her political grievances. Some, including probably Chamberlain himself, believed that appeasement would succeed. Others accepted it for the time being while British rearmament was in train.

Soviet Russia and the United States, the two World Powers, stood aside. The Soviet rulers often proposed collective resistance to the aggressor. Their words fell on stony ground. Western statesmen thought that the Russians wished to stir up trouble in Europe; Soviet

Jewish shops closed for the duration

statesmen thought that the Western Powers were seeking to entrap Russia in a war from which they themselves would stand aside. Neither of these suspicions was without foundation. In addition, Western statesmen, and perhaps Soviet statesmen also, were quite unable to gauge Soviet Russia's military strength, particularly after Stalin's great purge of 1937 eliminated practically all the Soviet high command.

There was no such doubt about American military strength: apart from the navy it did not exist. Nor was there any will to remedy this.

As a legacy of the First World War, whether justified or not, the American people were almost totally dedicated to a policy of isolation. President Roosevelt may have wished to change this, more perhaps against Japan than against Germany, and even attempted to give a lead in 1937 when he advocated a quarantine of any aggressor. The public response was not encouraging, and he retreated into cautious isolation until after the outbreak of war in Europe.

Under such circumstances Western statesmen shrank from an anti-Fascist crusade, even when the Spanish Civil War seemed to offer the opening for one in 1936. The British and French governments tolerated aid to the Spanish rebels by the two Fascist Powers, Germany and Italy, and finally even welcomed a rebel victory as the only means of ending the civil war. Certainly volunteers from Great Britain and France, as well as from many other countries, fought on the Republican side, and for them the Second World War began in 1936. But they were a minority. In the autumn of 1944, shortly after the liberation of France, General de Gaulle visited Toulouse. He inspected the partisan forces of the district. Stopping before one raggedly dressed man, he asked, 'And when did you join the Resistance, my friend?' The partisan replied, 'Bien avant vous, mon général' – he had fought in the Spanish Civil War. For once General de Gaulle was disconcerted.

The general and the partisan saw the war in different terms. De Gaulle saw a war of national liberation, the partisan a war against Fascism. Both were right. The two causes were mixed up, often in the same person. Ostensibly the Second World War was, like the first, a war between sovereign states. Simple patriotism was for many people the sole motive and for many more the predominant one. Patriotism appeared in unexpected places. The Russians had been the most strenuous before the war in calling for united action against Fascism. Yet when Russia was invaded, the war became the Great Patriotic War or, in an alternative translation, the Great War for the Fatherland, and the principal historic figure invoked was Suvorov, not Lenin. Communists elsewhere became the most resolute and wholehearted in the Resistance from the moment Russia was invaded. But they, too, fought in the name of national liberation – whether in the Resistance in France and Italy or more openly under Tito in Yugoslavia.

Nevertheless the war was also unmistakably a war of creeds. The Germans were fighting consciously for National Socialism. German victories did not merely lead to changes of frontiers in Germany's favour. They brought the assertion of National Socialist principles and practices: Germans as the master race, the degradation of all other peoples and the physical extermination of some. The opponents of Germany were fighting less consciously to defeat everything that National Socialism stood for. Starting with the aim of national liberation, they moved inevitably to the restoration of democracy also, though the Russians interpreted this word very differently from the way in which it was interpreted in the West. As the war proceeded, the anti-German coalition came to stand for the simple cause of humanity. The full record of German crimes was not known while the war was on. It only became clear afterwards that the gas chambers of Oświęcim (Auschwitz) represented National Socialist civilization as truly as Gothic cathedrals represented the civilization of the Middle Ages. Even so, enough was known to rule out any ending except unconditional surrender and to make the Second World War that very rare thing – a just war.

Germany's associates did not really fit into this pattern. Though Fascism had been invented in Italy, its crimes were on a small scale like Italy's activities during the war, and it never ate into the heart of the people. Only the Ustaše government of Croatia committed crimes approaching those of the Germans. Japan was not Fascist at all. The Japanese were oldfashioned nationalists, possessing and indeed operating an oldfashioned constitution. Their crimes sprang from a disregard of human life and not from any principle. Nevertheless the pattern was imposed on them also. They, too, became Fascists and enemies of democracy.

The First World War had already been described as a war of the masses. This was true in the sense that millions of men became combatants. But the Front was still remote from the Home. Civilians changed their jobs rather than their way of life. There was still room for discussion as to what the war was about and whether it should be continued. There were often manifestations of civilian discontent. In the Second World War everyone was involved. The distinction between Front and Home almost disappeared under the impact of indiscriminate bombing. In Great Britain, for instance, until 1942 a serving soldier was more likely to receive a telegram that his wife had been killed by a bomb than his wife was likely to receive one that her husband had been killed in battle. Conscientious objectors serving in ARP (air raid precautions) were in greater danger than if they had been in the armed forces.

National solidarity in the principal belligerent countries was beyond all precedent. Before the war the British government had anticipated that bombing would cause a breakdown in civilian order and actually enlisted a former Indian police officer, experienced in the control of panic-stricken crowds. His services were not required. The endurance of the masses – the British during the Blitz, the inhabitants of Leningrad during its long siege, the Germans in the last months before their final defeat, and the Japanese even after the two atomic bombs – was never in question.

This was rightly called a People's War. But it was not created or shaped by popular feelings as, to some extent, the First World War had been. In 1914 excited public opinion pushed the governments towards war, and demagogic jingoism later had a powerful influence on strategy. Before and during the Second World War, the statesmen led and the peoples followed. The British government was the only one pushed into war by public opinion, and even that opinion was voiced in the House of Commons, not in the streets. Hitler may have calculated that victories would increase his hold over the German people, but he alone decided where and when the victories should be won. There was for instance no popular campaign of anti-Bolshevism before the German invasion of Soviet Russia. Rather there was a dead silence, and the invasion was sprung on the German people unawares. In the United States President Roosevelt believed, until the actual moment of America's entry into the war, that he was ahead of public opinion. He may have been wrong, but his belief shaped American policy.

The statesmen counted for far more in the second war than they had done in the first. Who remembers the names of the French premiers before Clemenceau or of the German chancellors after Bethmann Hollweg (and Bethmann had only a marginal influence on events)? Lloyd George ostensibly became a sort of war dictator in December 1916, but even he, according to his own account, was principally distinguished by rarely getting his own way. The popular heroes were generals – Kitchener, Hindenburg, Joffre – demigods who ran the war in the light of their own inspiration or lack of it.

In the Second World War the generals were administrators with little more popular appeal than if they had been civil servants. Rommel was built up into a romantic figure, more by the British than by the Germans. Montgomery created a legend about himself, but twice escaped dismissal only by a humble apology. Essentially only the political leaders counted. When the German generals, or some of them, tried to overthrow Hitler, they discovered that they had no followers. Churchill dismissed such formidable figures as Wavell and Auchinleck. Stalin dismissed his generals by the dozen, and even Zhukov trembled before him. It is hardly an exaggeration to say that four men – Hitler, Churchill, Roosevelt and Stalin – made every important decision of the war personally, with Mussolini feebly trying to imitate them. Only Japan continued to be run by a more or less anonymous committee.

The Axis: Mussolini and Ciano, Hitler and Goering

The great men all had previous experience of war. Hitler and Mussolini had been frontline soldiers; Churchill and Roosevelt had held office during the First World War, and Churchill had also served in the trenches; Stalin had held high command during the Russian civil war. They understood war as well as their advisers, if not better. Of course they listened to their advisers, though Hitler listened impatiently. Of course they weighed, if they did not always observe, the limits of the practical. All the same they determined where the campaigns should be fought

Prime Minister Tojo and his Cabinet

and how they should be conducted. They determined the foreign and economic policies of their respective countries except on trivial issues. Churchill was sometimes blown off course by romantic impulses. Hitler lost, as someone has to do in war, and has therefore been written off as a psychopath. To a detached view, the statesmen of the Second World War acted on rational principles in the pursuit of victory. The Second World War was a record of slaughter and brutality, but, unlike the First World War, it was not a confused muddle.

The four men differed greatly in their individual characters. Hitler was the most revolutionary in outlook and method, disregarding preconceived ideas and ready to turn the world upside down for good or ill. He was probably also the most unscrupulous. Churchill was the most oldfashioned and the most humane – reliving a British Empire that had vanished and deeply stirred by generous emotions. Stalin was undoubtedly the most singleminded: his only thought was to preserve the Soviet Union and his own dictatorial power therein. Roosevelt

First day at No. 10

The other dictator

was the most enigmatic. Expedients and high principles, day-to-day calculations and distant aims were inextricably mixed together in him. Of the four he was the most successful, but it is impossible to say whether even this was deliberate. Despite their many differences the four men had one thing in common that marked them off from everyone else: each was uniquely powerful in his own country.

Each of the four had come to power differently and exercised it in different ways. Roosevelt was an elected president, sole executive by virtue of the American constitution. Though Commander-in-Chief, he rarely interfered in the conduct of the war except to make the great decisions. Churchill was a constitutional prime minister, theoretically sharing power with the War Cabinet and responsible to Parliament. As Minister of Defence he supervised the Chiefs of Staff and got his way by argument, not by order. In his own inimitable phrase, 'All I wanted was compliance with my wishes after reasonable discussion.' Stalin and Hitler were dictators, ostensibly leading their respective parties, Com-

'We have nothing to fear except fear itself.' Roosevelt's first
appearance as President

munist and National Socialist. Stalin was Prime
Minister and Commander-in-Chief and throughout directed the day-to-day running of the war
much as any ordinary commander-in-chief
would have done. Hitler began as a more or less
theoretical head of the armed forces and gradually took over the position of Commander-
in-Chief, particularly on the Eastern Front. But
in one way or another these four determined
the politics and strategy of the Second World
War.

The great men had their troubles. There were
ineffective conspiracies against Hitler; Churchill
was often criticized in the House of Commons;
Roosevelt had to face two presidential elections
while the war was on; perhaps even Stalin was
occasionally harassed by the Politburo. None
of them was ever seriously endangered. These
four alone commanded the allegiance of the
masses. The People's War had as its corollary
rule by dictators. The four great men embodied,
each in his own way, the National Will – a
strange conclusion to the age of Nationalism
and Democracy that had started with Rousseau.

2

The beginnings

The run towards war started in 1936 so far as it can be pinned to any precise time. The instruments of collective security had been shattered. Germany had shaken off the restrictions imposed upon her by the Treaty of Versailles and had also repudiated those she had voluntarily accepted in the Treaty of Locarno. The League of Nations was moribund after its failure to protect Abyssinia from Mussolini. The only remaining international arrangement of any weight was the Anglo-French alliance. This had operated unofficially since the end of the First World War and acquired more formal existence when the British gave France a guarantee during the turmoil that followed Hitler's repudiation of Locarno in March 1936. The guarantee was intended to be a temporary affair until a new agreement with Hitler had been negotiated. None was, and the guarantee thus became permanent. It was a guarantee of principle only. The British did not possess the means with which to fulfil it. Though they were now increasing their expenditure on armaments, most of the money went on the navy and the air force, very little on the army, and, as British rearmament advanced, British isolation with its emphasis on a 'limited liability' army advanced with it.

Serious rearmament began in 1936 in Germany, Great Britain and France. It had a different character on the opposing sides. Hitler, relying on threats or small wars, prepared everything for the front line, and disregarded the provision of reserves, either military or economic. The British and French devised a rearmament in depth which, even if the plans were accomplished – and the French were not – would take years to mature. A confused situation followed. Hitler was better placed for a conflict that would take a few weeks. Great Britain and even France, if she could survive the initial blow, would grow stronger during the course of a long war. Time was on their side, though they made poor use of it.

The two Western Powers appreciated their present weakness more than they did their future strength. The years immediately before the outbreak of war in Europe were overshadowed by persistent exaggerations of Germany's military power. The British intelligence services, deriving much of their information from German generals allegedly opposed to Hitler, consistently estimated German rearmament at over twice its true rate. In 1938, for instance, the British Air Staff reported that German frontline strength in the air was twice that of the British, and future German production would be twice the British also. The civilian authorities anticipated that 600,000 people would be killed during the first two months of a war. In fact German frontline aircraft strength in 1938 was only 60 per cent higher than the British, and reserves were less. British production of aircraft surpassed German in the course of 1939. The total of British people killed by air attack throughout the Second World War was 60,000.

The Germans had no aircraft or strategy for independent bombing. Their air force was designed solely for cooperation with the ground forces. The British were frightened by a ghost

Rearmament, German-style: U-boats at
Kiel; British-style: tanks on the move in
France

27

of their own making. The Royal Air Force, and the Royal Air Force alone among European air forces, believed in strategic bombing, though until 1944 it did not possess aircraft sufficiently well-equipped and numerous to carry it out. Hence the British lived under the apprehension of a German threat that did not exist and relied on an equally non-existent threat of their own. In the years before the war it was the German threat that mattered.

In November 1936 Germany and Japan signed the Anti-Comintern Pact, the first coming together of the potential aggressors. This was no more than a gesture of common aims. It was not an effective alliance even against Soviet Russia. The two signatories never coordinated their actions either at the time or later. The only practical result was that Germany gradually cut down the military aid that she had hitherto been giving to China. Still, the pact looked formidable as a gesture, and still more so when Mussolini, anxious to join what he expected to be the winning side, also signed it in the following year. Here, too, there was no coordination of policy. Hitler went on his way without consulting Mussolini and vaguely assumed that Italy would make trouble for the British and French in the Mediterranean.

Maybe the Anti-Comintern Pact encouraged the Japanese to go ahead in China. It seems more probable that their move was made without premeditation. There had been an uneasy truce in the Far East since 1933 – the Japanese consolidating their hold on Manchuria and northern China as far as Peking, Chiang Kai-shek trying to create a more effective army, and the Chinese Communists prodding Chiang towards resistance. On 7 July 1937 there was a clash between Japanese and Chinese troops at the Marco Polo bridge near Peking. The Japanese struck back, more, it seems, at the impulse of junior officers than under guidance from on high. They took Shanghai after seven weeks of fighting. In December 1937 they occupied Nanking, Chiang Kai-shek's capital. In the course of 1938 they took Hankow and Canton, thus controlling the

entire Chinese coast. Chiang Kai-shek withdrew to remote Chungking near the border of Tibet. The fighting died away. It had cost the lives of perhaps 800,000 Chinese and 50,000 Japanese. Some 50 million Chinese were driven from their homes. There was again deadlock. The Japanese tried in vain to find a puppet Chinese government. Chiang, with the bulk of his armies destroyed, waited for American aid.

In November 1937 the Powers with interests in the Far East held a conference at Brussels in an attempt to stop the fighting. Nothing came of it. Nevertheless there was a change of sentiment. British businessmen, hitherto sympathetic to the Japanese, now regarded them as bandits and destroyers of Chinese trade. The British government looked forward to the day when they could send a fleet to the Far East – hence their desire to have done with European distractions. American opinion, though still resolutely neutral, also began to turn against Japan. President Roosevelt hoped to arrest the Japanese advance, if only by economic pressure. This accorded with American strategic ideas so far as these existed. The United States, though virtually without an army, had a great navy, whose chosen field of action was the Pacific.

There was a more practical change in the Far East at this time. The Japanese tried to strengthen their position in Manchuria by destroying the Soviet forces across the frontier. In July 1938 and again in May 1939 the Japanese took the offensive. On both occasions they were defeated, the second time at Nomonhan with heavy loss. Hitherto war against Russia had been their army's favoured cause. Now, especially after the outbreak of war in Europe, the Japanese decided to leave Russia alone. The Russians, themselves preoccupied with Europe, reciprocated. The decision was not made consciously until 1941, but in reality a Russo-Japanese war had been ruled out two years earlier. Henceforth there was only one way of expansion for Japan to follow – south into the Pacific whenever British and still more American difficulties elsewhere opened the door. There she would find

Japanese troops on the march at Shanghai

the oil, rubber and tin for her economy.

In 1938 few people in Europe except the experts bothered about the Sino-Japanese conflict. All eyes were turned on Hitler. It was said at the time and has often been said since that he had a defined programme for his march to world power. It seems rather that he was an opportunist who took gains as they came. His aim was no doubt clear: to transform Germany into a World Power. The means were to be provided by events. Hitler counted confidently, over-confidently as it proved, on Western inaction. In 1938 he even received Western encouragement. This came from Neville Chamberlain, who had succeeded Baldwin as British Prime Minister in May 1937.

Chamberlain believed that France was secure behind the Maginot line, and Great Britain equally so under the protection of the Royal Navy; both could draw unlimited supplies from the United States in case of war. But just as they were safe from Germany, she was safe from them. With the fortification of Germany's western frontier, there was nothing Great Britain and France could do to impede the extension of German power in eastern Europe. Nor did Chamberlain greatly wish to impede it. In his view, Germany even under Hitler was a lesser evil than Soviet Russia, and German predominance in eastern Europe, however unwelcome, would be a barrier against Communism. Therefore Germany should be encouraged to proceed in an orderly manner. This was the message that Lord Halifax, Chamberlain's close associate, took to Germany in November 1937. The questions of Danzig, Austria and Czechoslovakia, he told Hitler, could be settled in Germany's favour, provided there were 'no far-reaching disturbances'.

During 1938 Hitler applied this programme.

Enthusiastic Austrians welcome Hitler to Vienna

In March, after the Austrian government had attempted to control the local Nazis, he sent his armed forces into Austria and incorporated it into Germany. There was no fighting. Many, perhaps at that time most, Austrians welcomed their transformation into German nationals. Hitler's occupation of Austria was characteristic of his methods: he moved into a fortress only when the walls had already fallen down. Nevertheless his move was in a sense the beginning of the Second World War in Europe. For the first time since the end of the First World War the army of a Great Power had crossed a European frontier and imposed a territorial change by force.

Hitler did not need to consult his timetable, even if he had one, for his next move. Czechoslovakia was the obvious target – a democratic state allied with France and less closely with Soviet Russia, almost encircled now by German territory, and with over three million German-speaking citizens. Neville Chamberlain determined to act first and to satisfy Hitler's demands before they were made. This was the policy of appeasement, a policy fully applied only during the summer of 1938. Throughout that summer Chamberlain and his associates laboured to ensure that the Czechoslovak government would yield to Hitler's demands and that the French would abandon their Czechoslovak ally. Chamberlain succeeded, though only just and not without war's alarms. At the Munich Conference on 29 September 1938 the German-speaking areas of Czechoslovakia, generously interpreted, were handed over to Germany. Ostensibly there was agreement between the four European Great Powers – France, Germany, Great Britain and Italy – with Soviet Russia safely excluded from European affairs. But the agreement was far from being freely negotiated.

The Czechs and the French had yielded solely from fear of war, and Chamberlain had difficulty convincing the British public that this had not been his motive also. Hitler on his side was confirmed in his belief that threats would continue to prevail.

Chamberlain had promised peace for our time. There was peace for six months, Chamberlain obstinately hoping that appeasement had done the trick, Hitler waiting for another opportunity to turn up. On 15 March 1939 one did. Czecho-Slovakia, hyphenated since October 1938, broke up. Slovakia became a nominally independent state. Bohemia, or Czechia, became a German protectorate. Hitler himself spent a night in Prague. Here again he seemed to be operating to a prepared timetable, where perhaps he was merely taking advantage of events. The question has only academic interest. What mattered was the reaction of British opinion, and this held that Hitler had been exposed as an aggressor. Next time, it was held, he must be resisted.

The next time was not long in coming. It came over Poland. This was almost certainly not according to Hitler's intention. His first aim, as shown in his book *Mein Kampf*, was to destroy French hegemony in Europe. He originally assumed that Great Britain and Italy would remain neutral or even support him. During the Czech crisis or after it he began to change his mind and to anticipate that he might encounter British opposition also. He did not take this danger seriously. The British had no army of any size, and Hitler expected them to give up once France was defeated. Confident of this he made few preparations for war against Great Britain. He neglected the German navy and even the building of U-boats. Grand Admiral Raeder told him that Germany needed 300 U-boats for a war against Great Britain. When that war broke out she had only 23 fit for Atlantic service.

Poland, however, was important for Hitler. Obsessed with memories of the First World War, he was determined to avoid a war on two fronts. He had sought to secure this by the Non-Aggression Pact with Poland which he signed in 1934. Poland, Hitler believed, was dominated by fear of Soviet Russia and would happily become a German satellite as Hungary and Romania were to do. There was an obstacle: grievances far more deeply implanted in German minds than independent Austria or the German-speaking inhabitants of Czechoslovakia had been. By the Treaty of Versailles, Danzig, inhabited by Germans, had become a Free City, and the so-called Polish Corridor separated East Prussia from the Reich. Hitler had to redress these grievances in order to maintain his prestige, particularly with the German generals. He anticipated that the Poles would yield willingly in the hope of acquiring the Ukraine from Russia later. In this he totally misunderstood the outlook of the Polish rulers. Imagining that Poland was a Great Power, they were determined to remain independent of both Germany and Soviet Russia and would yield nothing to either. When the Poles proved obstinate Hitler tried to help negotiations along in his usual way by vague threat of some military action.

This threw the British government into a panic. During the winter of 1938–9 they had gradually come to fear some German action in the west, against Holland, against France or perhaps even against Great Britain. Reluctantly they recognized that France must be strengthened. On 22 February 1939 they agreed to Anglo-French staff talks, though to no great purpose. Now Poland became important for the British also. Previously, as late as December 1938, they had accepted that Poland would become a German satellite. Once France had to be strengthened, Poland was needed in order to provide a second front. If she fell out, France would be gravely weakened, at any rate in appearance. Still worse, the French might seek an alternative second front by turning their pact with Soviet Russia into a reality. The British Chiefs of Staff reported that nothing could be done to aid Poland. They also reported that Soviet Russia would be more valuable as an ally. Chamberlain ignored these opinions. On 30 March he wrote out a guarantee to Poland with his own hand. Colonel Joseph Beck, the Polish Foreign Minister, accepted the guarantee, as he said, 'between two flicks of the ash off his cigarette'.

The British guarantee to Poland led directly to the outbreak of war in Europe. Hitler, far from being deterred, was provoked. At the end of April he denounced both his Non-Aggression Pact with Poland and the Anglo-German naval agreement of 1935. He told the German generals to prepare a campaign against Poland for 1 September. Even this may have been a bluff: some of the generals at once carried the news to the British and French ambassadors, as Hitler no doubt knew they would. Hitler also consolidated his international position. Ribbentrop, the German Foreign Minister, had been trying for some time to transform the Anti-Comintern Pact into an effective alliance. The Japanese were evasive. They had received no aid from Germany during their frontier clashes with Soviet Russia and now kept a free hand to exploit in the Far East any difficulties Hitler created for the Western Powers in Europe. Ribbentrop achieved only the Pact of Steel with Italy, signed on 22 May. He intended this to frighten the Western Powers. Mussolini had exactly the opposite intention of using the pact to postpone war for three or four years, when he imagined that Italy would be better prepared.

After this Hitler withdrew into ominous silence. He made no further demands on Poland. He delivered no public speeches. He waited confidently for the two Western Powers to impose concessions on the Poles as they had done with Czechoslovakia in the previous year. This time he waited in vain. The Western Powers were willing enough: not only were they still anxious to appease Hitler, they actually agreed this time with the justice of his claims. The Poles, however, would not yield an inch, drawing from the Czech crisis the moral that the only way to avoid making too many concessions was to make none. No doubt the Poles had an exaggerated idea of their own strength. By a more pardonable error they also exaggerated that of the Western Powers. They could not grasp that Great Britain and France were no longer the triumphant victors of 1918. Surely, the Poles thought, the Western Powers would honour their guarantee and, if they did, would again prove victorious.

Great Britain and France encouraged this Polish delusion. They recognized, in their more rational moments, that they could do nothing to aid Poland. They were embarrassed by her obstinacy. But they could not repudiate their pledged word without losing all prestige as Great Powers. Moreover, if they abandoned Poland, she would either yield to Hitler's demands without a fight or be conquered after a brief conflict. In either case the second front would disappear. Hence the British and French statesmen wilfully lured Poland into disaster, or maybe dreamed that Hitler would be impressed by a bluff in which they did not believe themselves.

There was one other resource: an alliance of the Western Powers with Soviet Russia. Negotiations for such an alliance were halfheartedly pursued throughout the summer of 1939. Again the British guarantee to Poland stood in the way. In 1921, at the end of the Soviet-Polish war, the Poles had acquired territory in the east inhabited predominantly by Ukrainians and White Russians. The Poles believed rightly that if Soviet troops once entered this territory they would never leave it. Hence they refused to accept Soviet aid, and the British could not threaten to leave them in the lurch. Once more a bluff was pursued: something that would deter Hitler without alarming the Poles.

The British proposed that Russia should go to war 'if desired' – by the Poles, by one of the little Baltic states, by the Western Powers, by anyone except themselves. This was a humiliating, indeed an impossible, proposal to make to a Great Power. The Russians answered by proposing a simple triple alliance with Great Britain and France whereby each of the signatories would be pledged to act if any one of them were involved in war with Germany for whatever reason. The British started back from this proposal with horror: a war in which they were simply fighting on Soviet Russia's side against Germany was inconceivable. It would offend large sections of British opinion, particularly among the supporters of the National government. It would offend General Franco. It would offend the Pope. The negotiations reached deadlock.

Military conversations were then tried in an attempt to get round the political difficulties. They produced new difficulties of their own. Stalin told Churchill later that the Russians would have had to provide 300 divisions against Germany while the British would have provided four. The geographical situation made this inevitable as Stalin was to discover when Russia was finally involved in war. The obstacle

in 1939 was still Poland. The Russians asked to be allowed to enter Polish territory. The Poles refused permission. Under the circumstances there was nothing the Russians could do except remain neutral.

Hitler appreciated this. Earlier in the summer he had talked of attacking Poland even if Soviet Russia aided her. The breakdown of the Anglo-French-Soviet negotiations opened an easier way for him. On 23 August Ribbentrop flew to Moscow and reached agreement with Stalin the same day. The Nazi-Soviet Pact, as it came to be called, was not an alliance: it simply exchanged promises of mutual non-aggression and neutrality. A secret protocol defined spheres of interest, a form of agreement that Stalin was to favour with others later. Finland, Estonia and Latvia were within the Soviet sphere, Lithuania in the German. If, as it was euphemistically

Poland: German troops break down the frontier barriers

expressed, changes took place in Poland, the division between the Soviet and German spheres of interest was to follow roughly the ethnic line as the Russians saw it. There was an outcry in the West against Soviet Russia's wickedness in making an agreement with the leading Fascist Power. The reproach came ill from British and French statesmen who had actively promoted the partition of Czechoslovakia and were even now striving for a fresh agreement with Hitler at the expense of Poland.

Hitler seems to have believed that the resistance of the two Western Powers would collapse now that they had lost all hope of Soviet aid. In the excitement of success he advanced the date for an attack on Poland to 26 August, even though the German military preparations would not then be complete. On 25 August he drew back. Perhaps he was deterred by an announce-

ment of neutrality by Mussolini, perhaps by the formal signature of the Anglo-Polish Alliance. More probably he merely appreciated that his army was not ready. There followed six days of desperate negotiations, the British trying to extract concessions from the Poles, the Poles refusing to budge. On 31 August Hitler could wait no longer. Once the army was ready, it had to move at once. Otherwise its impetus would run down. With no sign of yielding by the Poles, Hitler ordered the invasion to begin at dawn on the following day.

In eastern Europe dawn came on 1 September 1939 at 4.45 a.m. With the dawn German troops crossed the frontier of Poland. An hour later German aircraft bombed Warsaw and destroyed more than half the Polish air force on the ground. There was no ultimatum or declaration of war. At 10 a.m. Hitler addressed the Reichstag. As

Hitler watches the advance of his horse-drawn forces

London: air raid precautions in full blast
right and *right, below* postal workers
taking cover

usual he was aggrieved. He had sought a negotiated settlement with the Poles. They had ignored his offers. Germans were being massacred in Poland. During the preceding night Polish regulars had fired on German territory. No evidence of this was ever forthcoming, though according to one story SS men – the Blackshirt terrorist police – faked an attack on a German radio station by condemned criminals dressed in Polish uniforms, whose dead bodies were left on the ground. However, the National Socialists in the Reichstag needed no convincing. They duly applauded. In the streets of Berlin and other German cities there was a dull silence, far from the enthusiasm that had marked the outbreak of the First World War.

Poland appealed at once to her allies. She received a dusty answer. The two Western Powers addressed a pained protest to Berlin – not, they insisted, that this should be regarded as an ultimatum. They looked expectantly to Mussolini, and they did not look in vain. Mussolini was willing to propose a conference that should dismember Poland as Czechoslovakia had been dismembered at Munich in the previous year. Bonnet, the French Foreign Minister, eagerly accepted the offer and threw in the further argument for delay that the French generals wished to conduct mobilization undisturbed by German air attacks – attacks that, with most of the German air force engaged in Poland, would not take place in any case. Halifax, now British Foreign Secretary, seconded Bonnet's line. The French army proceeded with its laborious mobilization which, it was reckoned, would take three weeks to complete. In Great Britain nearly two million women and children were evacuated from the areas supposedly threatened by aerial attack.

There was little open display of popular feeling, no crowds marching down Whitehall with the cry 'Stand by Poland', such as there had been crying 'Stand by the Czechs' a year before. But the House of Commons was deeply disturbed. Its members, or most of them, recognized clearly the British pledge to Poland. They did not appreciate that this had been merely a diplomatic gesture. They did not understand that there was no way of aiding Poland. They only knew that British honour was involved. By the evening of 2 September it was clear that the government would fall the next day unless war were declared. When Henry Channon, one of the few remaining appeasers, expostulated with the Conservative Chief Whip, he was told: 'It must be war, Chips, old boy, there's no other way out.' Members of the Cabinet shared the feeling of the House of Commons. Later in the evening they staged a sit-down strike, refusing to disperse until a decision had been taken. Chamberlain said quietly: 'Right, gentlemen, this means war.' Halifax noted sourly in his diary: 'The whole thing, to my mind, showed democratic assemblies at their worst.' The Chamberlain government, in order to remain in power, bowed to the will of Parliament and probably of the country.

At nine o'clock on the morning of 3 September the British Ambassador in Berlin presented an ultimatum demanding an answer within two hours. No answer was received. A state of war automatically followed as Chamberlain lugubriously announced in a broadcast speech. As he finished speaking, sirens gave warning of an air raid. Londoners trooped to the shelters, dutifully carrying their gas masks. It was a false alarm. The French were dragged into war by their British ally. A French ultimatum was delivered at noon and expired, also unanswered, at 5 p.m. Thus Great Britain and France went to war for that part of the peace settlement that they regarded as least defensible. There was no sign of popular excitement. Men accepted war as a bureaucratic necessity. In England they said: 'Let's get it over with', and in France: 'Il faut en finir.'

The declarations of war were diplomatic gestures like so much that had gone before. Nothing was done to aid Poland. The Royal Air Force attempted to attack the German fleet at Wilhelmshafen. It suffered heavy loss, inflicted virtually no damage, and did not repeat the

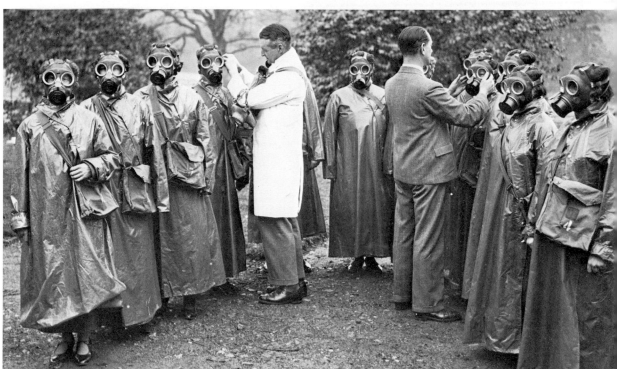

attempt. The French leisurely reinforced the Maginot line. In theory they had a crushing superiority. The Germans had 33 divisions in the west, mostly composed of elderly veterans from the First World War. They had no tanks and 300 guns. The French had 110 divisions, 3286 tanks and 1600 guns. But 10 divisions were on the Italian frontier, 15 in North Africa, and 40 on the Belgian frontier. This left only 45 divisions in the Maginot line, with tanks untrained for independent action. Some French

General mobilization in France

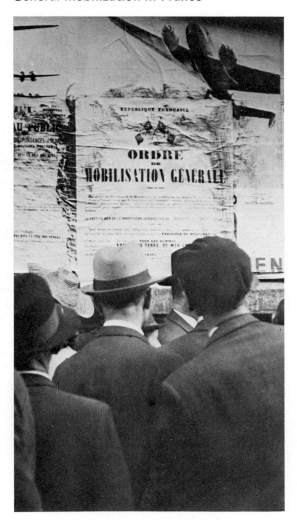

forces crept into a corner of the Saar from which the Germans had withdrawn. Booby traps were the only obstacle they encountered. When German forces began to move west after the Polish collapse on 17 September, the French pulled back. Daladier, the French Premier, boasted how little French blood had been shed.

Thus the Poles were left to fight alone. On paper they were not unequally matched with the Germans: 40 Polish divisions against 52 German. But, thanks to the delays in mobilization imposed to please the Western Powers, not much more than half the Polish divisions were ever embodied. Moreover six of the German divisions were armoured. The Poles had few tanks and had lost most of their air force. They had established their armies in advanced positions – partly to defend the industrial areas of Poland which were all in the west, partly with the fantastic hope of invading Germany. Two German armies, one from East Prussia and the other from Silesia, cut in behind the Polish positions and disrupted their communications. The German armoured divisions pushed ahead on their own, relying more on their speed than on firepower. The infantry merely consolidated what had been won. The Polish armies collapsed into chaos.

There was one break in the gloom. On 8 September Polish forces retreating eastwards ran into the German flank on the river Bzura. There was heavy fighting for six days, the biggest battle in Europe until the German invasion of Soviet Russia in 1941. The German commanders were considerably alarmed – an indication of how a tank offensive could go wrong if it lost momentum. On 14 September the exhausted Polish survivors withdrew into Warsaw which was then besieged. The shattered remnants of the Polish armies fell back to the remote southeast, their commander still dreaming that he might receive fresh supplies through Romania or even the greater aid of an Allied offensive in the west. Instead Soviet forces entered Poland from the east. With this, all fighting in the field ceased. The Polish government escaped into

Romania where it was interned. A government of exiles was set up in Paris. About 70,000 Polish troops also escaped, along with three Polish destroyers and two submarines. Warsaw held out until 28 September. The last Polish fortress surrendered on 5 October.

A total of 694,000 Polish soldiers became prisoners of the Germans, 217,000 of the Russians. The Germans lost 8400 killed. When the fighting ended, the Germans had come to the end of their supplies. If the French had taken the offensive the Germans would have had nothing with which to resist it. Here was a clear indication, unknown of course in the West, that Hitler, far from preparing for a great war, operated on a narrow margin and counted on quick victories achieved at little cost.

The German victories had taken the Russians completely by surprise. Molotov, the Commissar for Foreign Affairs, complained to the German Ambassador on 10 September: 'The Red Army had counted on several weeks which has

Poland: German and Russian soldiers fraternize

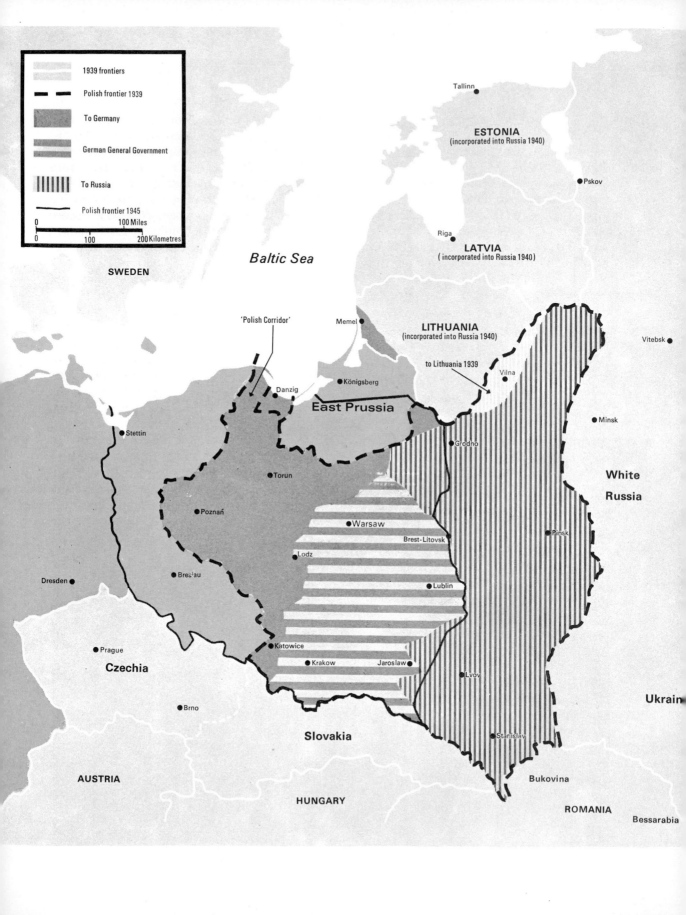

	1939 frontiers
	Polish frontier 1939
	To Germany
	German General Government
	To Russia
	Polish frontier 1945

0   100 Miles

0   100   200 Kilometres

Baltic Sea

SWEDEN

ESTONIA
(incorporated into Russia 1940)

● Tallinn

● Pskov

● Riga

LATVIA
(incorporated into Russia 1940)

'Polish Corridor'

Memel

LITHUANIA
(incorporated into Russia 1940)

● Vitebsk

to Lithuania 1939

● Vilna

Danzig

● Königsberg

East Prussia

● Minsk

● Stettin

Grodno

White
Russia

● Torun

● Poznań

● Warsaw

● Pinsk

Brest-Litovsk

● Lodz

● Dresden

● Breslau

● Lublin

Czechia

Katowice

● Prague

● Krakow   Jaroslaw

● Lvov

Ukrain

● Brno

Slovakia

● Stanislav

AUSTRIA

Bukovina

HUNGARY

ROMANIA

Bessarabia

now shrunk to a few days.' Moreover Molotov needed an excuse with which to justify Soviet action in the eyes of the world. He wanted to say that the Red Army was advancing to protect the Ukrainians and White Russians 'threatened' by Germany. Finally, to meet German objections, he compromised with the public statement that 'the Soviet Union felt obliged to intervene to protect its Ukrainian and White Russian brothers'. The Soviet advance on 17 September met with little resistance. Indeed, many Poles thought that the Russians were coming to save them. Only 737 Soviet soldiers were killed.

On 28 September Ribbentrop went again to Moscow. The original line of partition was adjusted. Lithuania was allotted to Russia. Germany was left with the whole of ethnic Poland – much the line that Empress Catherine had drawn a century and a half before. Originally Hitler seems to have intended to set up a rump Poland as a sort of German satellite. Stalin vetoed this. The two parties agreed 'not to tolerate any Polish agitation' in their territories. Great consequences followed. Hitler was debarred from making even the slightest pretence of concessions to the Poles, and his so-called peace offensive towards the Western Powers was therefore doomed in advance. More sinister, the Poles, and still more the Jews, now subjected to German rule in the anonymous General government, became the first victims of the Nazi policy of racial extermination. Soviet rule was harsh; German rule was mass murder. In two years the Soviet authorities arrested about one-fifth of the Poles in their area. In five years the Germans killed about the same proportion of their Poles.

The British government had watched the Soviet intervention with helpless indignation. The General Staff assumed that Great Britain must declare war on Soviet Russia, adding that 'our strategic situation though serious would not be desperate'. They were corrected by the Foreign Office which pointed out that the Anglo-Polish Alliance applied only to aggression by Germany. Moreover, as the Foreign Office also observed,

the territory that Soviet forces now occupied had been judged to be rightfully Russian by the British government when they drew the Curzon Line in 1920. But the British could not join in dismembering Poland just when they had failed to save her. The opportunity for acknowledging the justice of Soviet Russia's advance passed, and the question continued to haunt relations between Soviet Russia and the Western Powers until the end of the Second World War.

Churchill, though once the principal champion of military intervention against the Bolsheviks, now took the lead in advocating a more realistic policy. He wrote on 25 September, 'In mortal war anger must be subordinated to defeating the enemy.' On 1 October he said in a broadcast, 'We could have wished that the Russian armies should be standing on their present lines as the friends and allies of Poland instead of as invaders. . . . At any rate the line is there and an eastern front has been created which Nazi Germany does not dare assail.' Here was the first announcement of the policy that Churchill was to follow from 22 June 1941 until the end of the war. Hitler had attacked Poland in order to remove the danger of a second front. The elimination of Poland brought into being a second front that was ultimately to destroy him.

3

The European war 1939-40

The Polish war was over. Hitler had won a complete victory. Great Britain and France, once so powerful, had stood helplessly by. On 6 October 1939 Hitler told the Reichstag that he was anxious to make peace. He had, he said, no claims against France. He wanted friendship with England. He would welcome a conference to discuss the future of Poland and of the Jews. After some delay the British and French governments publicly rejected Hitler's offer. In private the British were not so firm. The Foreign Office suggested that it might be possible to acquiesce in Germany's conquests if the Czechs and Poles were allowed some domestic autonomy. But there was one insuperable obstacle: no one any longer trusted Hitler. He must somehow disappear – relegated to St Helena or an architect's office – and be replaced by Goering.

On this absurd basis the British negotiated secretly by means of the Swedish businessman, Dahlerus, who had played a similar role before the outbreak of war. Hitler, to whom the proposals were of course communicated, was much amused by them, Goering perhaps less so. In any case Hitler had already made up his mind to defeat France and expel Great Britain from the Continent. The war, he told his generals on 23 October, was 'not being fought to secure the triumph of National Socialist Germany, but to decide the domination of Europe', and he instructed them to prepare for an invasion of France.

The Allies assumed the postures of war, starting again where they had left off in 1918. The lessons of the last war, it appeared, had been learned. Chamberlain set up a War Cabinet just like Lloyd George's; Daladier a government of National Defence just like Clemenceau's. These two war governments were the same old faces under new names. Churchill at the Admiralty was the only recruit of any significance. The various ministries of the previous war were also revived – shipping, information, food and so on. Controls and directions started on the first day of the war instead of in the third year. There was to be an Allied Supreme Council – Chamberlain and Daladier in yet another guise. There was a blackout in the streets. Ships sailed in convoy. Official news and propaganda were provided by the two ministries of information. A few aliens were interned. Reservists were called up. The upper age limit for compulsory military service was gradually raised. All the sensations of war, in fact, except the fighting.

The Allied leaders were not perturbed by this inaction. Time, they thought, was working for them – a view with which Hitler concurred, though he drew a different moral from it. Halifax remarked, 'The pause suits us well enough, both us and the French, for we shall be a good deal stronger in the spring.' The British were unshakably convinced that the Nazi economic system was at its last gasp. Everything, it was supposed, had been sacrificed to the production of armaments, and Germany lacked virtually all the raw materials necessary for war. The Chiefs of Staff reported: 'The Germans are already an exhausted and dispirited nation.' Great Britain and France only needed to hold their defensive lines and maintain their blockade.

Then Germany would collapse without further fighting. Chamberlain said, 'I do not believe that holocausts are required.'

These views, which the British continued to hold for much of the war, were totally wrong. Germany had rearmed without any lowering of the standard of life. The Germans were well fed and highly contented with Hitler's easy victory. It was the British, not the Germans, who had to make sacrifices. By 1940 British

not be controlled at all. The Germans acquired from Soviet Russia the reserves of raw materials that they had failed to build up before the war. In addition trains across Siberia brought supplies from the rest of the world.

The British, not the Germans, were hit by economic difficulties. The few U-boats caused some damage; German magnetic mines, not mastered until the end of the year, much more. Great Britain lost 800,000 tons of shipping

The Allied Supreme War Council: a funereal meeting

production, though still lackadaisical, outstripped that of Germany in aircraft, tanks and heavy guns, in everything in fact except equipment for a large army. From 1939 to 1942 British estimates overstated the average level of German armament expenditures by more than 100 per cent and the rise in expenditure by nearly 100 per cent. For Hitler did not want unlimited armaments. He only wanted armaments for immediate use. The Allied blockade had little existence except on paper. Italy provided a leak difficult to control; Soviet Russia one that could

before the real U-boat campaign started. Imports fell from a prewar yearly average of 55 million tons to 45 million. Food rationing was introduced in January 1940. The U-boats also sank warships: the aircraft carrier *Courageous* in September 1939, the battleship *Royal Oak* at its moorings in Scapa Flow in November. The one redeeming feature came in December, when a British force caught the German pocket battleship *Graf Spee* in the South Atlantic. The British ships, though less heavily armed, inflicted considerable damage. *Graf Spee* sought

The end of the *Graf Spee*

refuge in Montevideo and was then scuttled on Hitler's order.

Despite reliance on the blockade, the Allies felt that they must do something more positive. The French particularly were anxious to start some faraway action so as to avert fighting on their own front. Before the war the Allies had planned to begin the war by a campaign against Italy, an antagonist of their own weight. A French army of the Levant, some 80,000 men, under Weygand was stationed in Syria. There was a smaller British force under Wavell in

Egypt and powerful elements of the British fleet at Alexandria. Unfortunately Mussolini remained neutral or at any rate 'non-belligerent' and thus failed to present the Allies with a supposedly easy target. The French insisted that something must be done. A second front should be created by drawing Turkey, Greece, Romania and Yugoslavia into a great coalition against Germany. Weygand talked of reaching Vienna with a hundred Balkan divisions. And what would the Allies provide? Fifty thousand French troops, whose transport from Syria to Salonika would take three months. The Balkan states were not attracted by this proposal.

The French were not dismayed. They came up with an even more ambitious project: the bombing of Baku on the Caspian, which, they claimed, would end the war. German supplies of oil from the Caucasus would be cut off; Soviet Russia would collapse. The French had only 117 transport aircraft and 324 tons of bombs. The aircraft would have to fly over neutral Turkey and bomb Baku at night without any precise maps. Even so it was assumed that after a single attack the Caucasus oilfields would be out of use for six months. One French reconnaissance aircraft flew over Baku. Otherwise nothing came of this grotesque proposal.

The British were not interested in these farfetched schemes. They were anxious to conciliate Mussolini and to safeguard the Suez Canal. British attention turned northwards. No sooner was Churchill back at the Admiralty than he revived one of his favoured plans of the First World War and proposed to send the Home Fleet into the Baltic. Professional opinion was too strong for him. He then hit on a more modest plan. Germany was heavily dependent on iron ore from the north of Sweden. During the winter, when the Baltic was frozen, this iron ore was shipped through the Norwegian port of Narvik. If Norwegian waters were mined or Narvik itself seized, the iron-ore ships could not move. Churchill disregarded Norwegian neutrality: 'Small nations must not tie our hands when we are fighting for their rights and freedom. . . . Humanity, rather than legality, must be our guide.' The Cabinet rejected his proposal.

A new opening presented itself unexpectedly. Soviet Russia, still apprehensive of a German attack despite their apparent friendship, was establishing her military control over the Baltic states. Latvia, Estonia and Lithuania acquiesced in the Soviet demands. Finland refused them. On 30 November Soviet troops invaded Finland. Stalin seems to have assumed that a Communist government could be established in Finland without serious fighting. The Soviet troops were ill-prepared for a winter war or indeed for war at all. The Finns at first defended themselves successfully. In the West there was almost universal admiration for the gallant little Finns. The French government was particularly enthusiastic. Communists in both Great Britain and France had opposed the war from the beginning. The British Communists hardly counted. The French ones were formidable. Their party had been declared illegal. Here was a chance of discrediting them for good and all. Moreover the rightwing forces in France which disliked war against Germany would welcome one against Russia. Daladier, the French Premier, would be at last a true national leader. As a final bonus the naval side of any expedition would fall on the British who would thus no longer escape their share of the burdens of war.

The British government was swept along by the current. On 14 December Soviet Russia was formally expelled from the League of Nations. On 19 December the Anglo-French Supreme War Council resolved to aid Finland. But how to get there? Daladier had an easy answer. Norway and Sweden should be asked to act as loyal members of the League of Nations and be assured that the Western Powers would protect them against any Russian or German retaliation. Norway and Sweden did not oblige. They asserted their neutrality. The two Western governments were undismayed. If they could not obtain Norwegian and Swedish cooperation, they would go through without it. An expedition should go to Narvik at once. Then difficulties arose. It would take three weeks to land at Narvik and a further eleven to move the Allied force from Narvik to the Swedish frontier. There the Swedes could stop it by cutting off the electricity. The answer was to occupy Trondheim, Bergen and Stavanger as well. By January 1940 the needs of the expeditionary force had swelled to 100,000 men. Churchill was in despair. The lesser project of cutting the iron-ore route had faded away. Yet it was the prospect of doing this that had led the British government to acquiesce

The winter war: Finnish soldiers with a captured Soviet tank

in the larger French scheme. Certainly the British government, unlike the French, had no desire to be involved in war with Russia.

The Allied governments took their time. Supplies and naval forces had to be accumulated. Troops had to be moved. On 12 March the expedition for Narvik was ready: 4 cruiser squadrons and 4 destroyer flotillas, 14,000 troops about to embark. Chamberlain asked the general who was to take command, 'What will you do if the way is barred?' The general shuffled. Halifax said, 'Well, if we can't get in except at the loss of a lot of Norwegian lives, I am not for it – ore or no ore.' Chamberlain shook hands with the general and said, 'Goodbye, and good luck to you – if you go.' That evening the news arrived that the Finns, hopelessly defeated, had accepted the Soviet terms and made peace. The commanding general did not go to Glasgow, let alone Narvik.

The Allies were discredited once more. They had declared their intention to aid Finland and had failed to do so. In France Daladier was overthrown and was succeeded by Paul Reynaud, a more energetic figure though without a political following. On 28 March he travelled to London for a meeting of the Allied Supreme Council, insisting on some immediate action. The British responded by reviving the plan of mining the Norwegian waters and thus cutting the iron-ore route. If Germany retaliated, so much the better. Churchill said, 'We have more to gain than to lose by a German attack upon Sweden and Norway.' Chamberlain added on 4 April: 'Hitler has missed the bus.' The mines were to be laid on 5 April. The expeditionary force would sail only if Germany intervened. Then there was a delay. Churchill wished to float mines down the Rhine also. The French objected for fear of German retaliation – a similar retaliation in

German troops bicycle into Oslo

Norway did not worry them. The difference was sorted out. On 8 April minelaying began. Thus the British were technically the first to violate Norwegian neutrality.

They were not, however, alone. At the beginning of the war Hitler had been anxious to preserve the neutrality of Norway which would benefit him, as that of Sweden was to do. In January 1940 he grew anxious at the rumours of Anglo-French intervention on behalf of Finland, and still more anxious on 16 February when a British destroyer pursued a German ship, the *Altmark*, into Norwegian territorial waters and liberated the British prisoners of war she was carrying. On 1 March he gave orders to prepare an invasion of Norway. His military advisers proposed a laborious advance by land. Hitler ruled this out as too slow: British sea power would have time to take effect. Hitler insisted on a seaborne attack, supplemented by the dropping of parachute troops. Thus the power weaker at sea actually used the sea against the stronger one. This was Hitler's first direct intervention in strategy. It proved highly successful and a presage of greater successes to come.

From 5 April German warships and merchant vessels, carrying some 10,000 troops, moved up the coast of Norway. The British, thinking only of their own forthcoming action, took precautions against a German naval attack; they took none against a German invasion of Norway. By an astonishing stroke of luck rather than of prevision, Hitler struck his blow within twenty-four hours of the British striking theirs. On 9 April German troops entered Denmark and their seaborne troops seized Oslo, Bergen, Trondheim and Narvik. Denmark, being virtually defenceless, surrendered without a conflict and became a German protectorate for the duration of the war. At Oslo the Norwegians, though taken by surprise, resisted and sank the cruiser *Blücher*. The King of Norway managed to escape and set up his standard in the country.

At first the Allies rejoiced. Hitler was supposed to have committed a supreme blunder. Churchill announced: 'Every German ship using the Skagerrak and the Kattegat will be sunk.' Total confusion followed. Under Admiralty instructions the British navy ran after imaginary German cruisers instead of preparing for a landing. The land forces, when they were sent, consisted largely of half-trained Territorials and were not equipped for an opposed landing. There were contradictory ideas about where to land. Churchill wanted to recover Narvik. The War Cabinet insisted on Trondheim as a political demonstration. The Chiefs of Staff ruled this out as too dangerous and fell back on a pincer movement from Namsos and Åndalsnes, two fishing ports that could hardly handle even small landings. The British discovered, to their surprise, that, with most of the Norwegian airfields in German hands, their army and navy could not operate within range of the German air force. The campaign was a disastrous failure. The troops landed at Namsos and Åndalsnes had to be withdrawn again on 2 May. Narvik was indeed taken by the British on 28 May. By then this was eclipsed by the greater events in France. Narvik was evacuated on 8 June. The aircraft carrier *Glorious* and two destroyers were sunk during the evacuation.

There were compensations, little noticed at the time. The King of Norway and his government escaped to England, adding over a million tons of shipping to British resources. The German navy suffered heavily: 3 cruisers and 10 destroyers were lost, 2 heavy cruisers and 1 pocket battleship put temporarily out of action. In the summer of 1940 the German navy hardly existed: an 8-inch cruiser, 2 light cruisers and 4 destroyers. This was not without relevance when Hitler attempted an invasion of Great Britain. At the time British people saw only the humiliation and failure. Their wrath turned against Chamberlain; their enthusiasm towards Churchill. In fact Chamberlain, though approving the Norwegian campaign, had had little to do with it. It had been conducted with a combination of Churchillian impulses and logistic muddles. However, men thought in terms of the past. Chamberlain paid the price for appeasement. Churchill reaped the reward for his years in the wilderness. By an ironic twist failure in a campaign, directed largely by Churchill, brought Chamberlain down and raised Churchill up.

On 7 and 8 May there was a debate on the Norwegian campaign in the House of Commons. Leo Amery, addressing the government, said, 'In the name of God, go!' Lloyd George told Chamberlain to set an example of sacrifice by sacrificing the seals of office. At the end of the debate forty-one of the government's supporters voted with the Opposition and some sixty more abstained. Chamberlain attempted to reconstruct his government. Labour, somewhat hesitantly, refused to serve under him. On the afternoon of 9 May Chamberlain, Churchill and Halifax discussed what should happen. Halifax modestly remarked that it would be difficult for a member of the House of Lords to be Prime Minister 'in such a war as this'. Churchill took up the burden gladly. On the afternoon of 10 May 1940 he became Prime Minister. It was the appropriate moment. A real war had begun that morning: German armies had invaded Holland and Belgium.

Churchill rose to the challenge. He told the House of Commons on 13 May:

I have nothing to offer but blood, toil, tears and sweat. . . . You ask, what is our policy? I will say: It is to wage war, by sea, land, and air, with all our might and with all the strength that God can give us. . . . You ask, What is our aim? I can answer in one word: Victory – victory at all costs, victory in spite of all terror; victory, however long and hard the road may be.

His speech is supposed to have opened the period of national unity. This was by no means the case. The Conservatives did not forgive so easily. In the House of Commons they rose and cheered

Chamberlain. Cheers for Churchill came only from the Labour benches until the sinking of the French battleships at Oran. Halifax and perhaps Chamberlain still hankered after a compromise peace. National unity came only after the evacuation from Dunkirk and the Battle of Britain, when the British people stood triumphantly alone.

It was even more obvious in 1939 than in 1914 that serious fighting between Germany and the Allies, if and when it came, would be in Belgium. The Maginot line along the Franco-German frontier provided effective security for France and also, though this was less noticed, for Germany. The French treated the line as purely defensive and had no means of sallying out from it as, say, the Romans had sallied out from their wall in the north of Britain. So confident of this were the Germans that they took fewer defensive precautions on their side of the frontier and allotted to it only a third of the forces that the French allotted to theirs – 19 divisions against 59. In this absurd way the Maginot line benefited the Germans and weakened the French.

The line acted as a breakwater or groin, diverting the German current with all the greater force through Belgium. The Belgian fortifications were poor stuff compared with the Maginot line. Until 1936 the French had an alliance with Belgium and could thus count at least on Franco-Belgian military cooperation. Then Belgium withdrew into neutrality. The frontier between France and Belgium was longer than the Maginot line. Its fortification would be impossibly expensive and the French did not attempt it. Hence Belgian neutrality was their only security against Hitler. It was hardly an adequate one.

On the outbreak of war the British Expeditionary Force – at first 4 divisions, swelling to 10 before fighting broke out – crossed to France and was stationed along the Belgian frontier. Loyally observing the lessons of the First World War, the British government put the BEF under the French Supreme Commander, Gamelin. This was a less satisfactory arrangement than it

A peaceful day in the Flanders trenches

sounded. Gamelin delegated his authority to the commander of the French armies on the Western Front, General Georges, who in his turn delegated it to the French general in the northeast. Viscount Gort, the commander of the BEF, did not know where he must look for orders. The British threw up some rudimentary field fortifications. When Hore-Belisha, the Secretary for War, criticized these as inadequate, he was dismissed from his post. Throughout the winter the Belgian frontier and the Maginot line slumbered.

Gamelin tried to coordinate plans with the Belgians. They refused to be drawn. Indeed they moved some forces to the French frontier in order to resist any Anglo-French incursion. Churchill stormed against Belgian neutrality, but clearly the Allies with their high principles could not violate it. Yet they could not stand idly by during a German invasion, if only for reasons of political prestige. Moreover entry into Belgium, it was held, would shorten the Allied line. Gamelin at first projected only an advance to the Schelde. Soon he became more ambitious. Such an advance would not make it possible to aid Holland which also seemed threatened. Gamelin devised a much larger advance to the Dyle and then beyond it to Breda in Holland. Georges and other French generals who doubted the wisdom of this advance were told by Gamelin that it was politically necessary. Gort, though also doubtful, did not reveal his doubts to the British government.

Gamelin allotted virtually all his active divisions and the entire BEF to the advance. In this way, he was confident, a decisive battle would be provoked, as indeed it was, though not in the way that he expected. Gamelin also hoped to add the 22 Belgian and 10 Dutch divisions to his own. His plan assumed that coordination could actually take place on the battlefield without any previous discussion and that the Allied forces could cover 145 miles while the Germans had to cover only 70. All depended on the Belgian fortifications.

Gamelin took it for granted that the Germans would advance on their extreme right wing as they had done in 1914. In this he was at first correct. In October 1939, when Hitler announced his determination to attack in the west, the German generals expressed strong doubts. One of them said, 'France is not Poland.' Hitler insisted and the General Staff reluctantly produced exactly the plan that Gamelin foresaw. There was no thought of a decisive victory, merely an occupation of territory that would push the Allies out of Holland and Belgium and so make the Ruhr more secure. Hitler grumbled

at the plan's inadequacy. He pointed further south to the Ardennes and asked, 'Can I get through here?' The generals answered that this was impossible unless they could be sure that the Allied striking force would advance into Belgium, as indeed Gamelin proposed to do. Hitler laid the idea aside. It was taken up and developed by Manstein, Chief of Staff to the A group of armies in the centre. Manstein's plans did not reach Hitler.

The German attack was fixed for 12 November. Bad weather forced a postponement. After further delays it was fixed again for 17 January 1940. Fate took a hand. On 10 January a German officer in Cologne was late for an appointment. A friend offered to take him by air. The aircraft lost its way and was forced down in Belgium. The officer was carrying the invasion plans and failed to destroy them. The Belgians communicated the plans to the Allies. Here was exactly the confirmation that Gamelin wanted: he allotted still more forces for the advance into Belgium. In Germany the attack was called off. Manstein, who had incurred the displeasure of the General Staff by his urgings, was ordered to eastern Germany. On his way through Berlin he called on Hitler and revealed his plans. Hitler was entranced. The General Staff under Halder yielded and worked out the details. Thus Hitler, Manstein and Halder all contributed. It was Hitler's taste for the unusual and unconventional that counted most.

The Germans would attack in the centre. Bock with 30 infantry and 3 armoured divisions would lure the Allies northwards. Leeb with 19 infantry divisions would make gestures along the Rhine. Rundstedt with 50 infantry and 7 armoured divisions would win the campaign. Opposing him at Sedan, the vital point of the breakthrough, were 3 French divisions of inferior quality. The French refused to believe that an advance was possible through the Ardennes. They even refused to erect any barriers so as not to obstruct the operations of their own cavalry. In case of need they could always move in reserves – if any were to be found.

It was often said later that the Allies were grossly inferior in equipment. This is not altogether true. The Allies had 3200 tanks, the Germans about 2700, and some of the French tanks were more powerful than any German ones. But the French tanks were scattered throughout the armies; the German were in armoured divisions and at the critical points. The German were markedly superior in the air. Their air force was designed strictly for cooperation with the land forces. They alone possessed divebombers. The British, though fairly well equipped with bombers, proposed to attack the Ruhr and other 'strategic' targets, not to take part in the battle. Many of the British fighters were kept at home for the defence of Great Britain.

The Germans did not use two novel weapons attributed to them by popular report among their enemies. The Fifth Column of supposed traitors was the product of panic-stricken imaginations. It did not exist in reality. Nor did the Germans rely on innumerable parachutists dropping from the skies. Their entire force of 4000 parachutists was exhausted in seizing Dutch bridges and airfields. Yet before the end of May many hundred thousand Englishmen were enrolling in the Local Defence Volunteers for the defence of their villages against German parachutists who were expected to arrive at any moment. The Germans did not need such devices. They won by moving faster in both thought and action against generals who still observed the measured tread of the First World War.

The campaign opened on 10 May with the German invasion of Holland and Belgium. The Dutch army fell back at once. On 13 May the Queen and the government left for England along with most of the Dutch navy. On 14 May Rotterdam surrendered. The Germans bombed it in error while the surrender was being negotiated. Some 900 civilians were killed, a figure swelled by the Dutch Foreign Minister to 30,000. This legendary figure is still often repeated. On 15 May the fighting in Holland ceased. The

Home Guard: the church militant

French forces advancing to the aid of Holland never made contact with the Dutch.

The Belgians relied on their great fortress at Eben Emael. German pioneers took it by the simple expedient of landing from gliders on its roof and thrusting explosives through the air shafts. On 12 May the Belgians abandoned the line of the Meuse. Two days later British and French forces made contact with the Belgians and began to coordinate their defence. On 15 May the Allies had a more pressing concern: not how to defend Belgium, but how to get out

France: the German advance to the sea

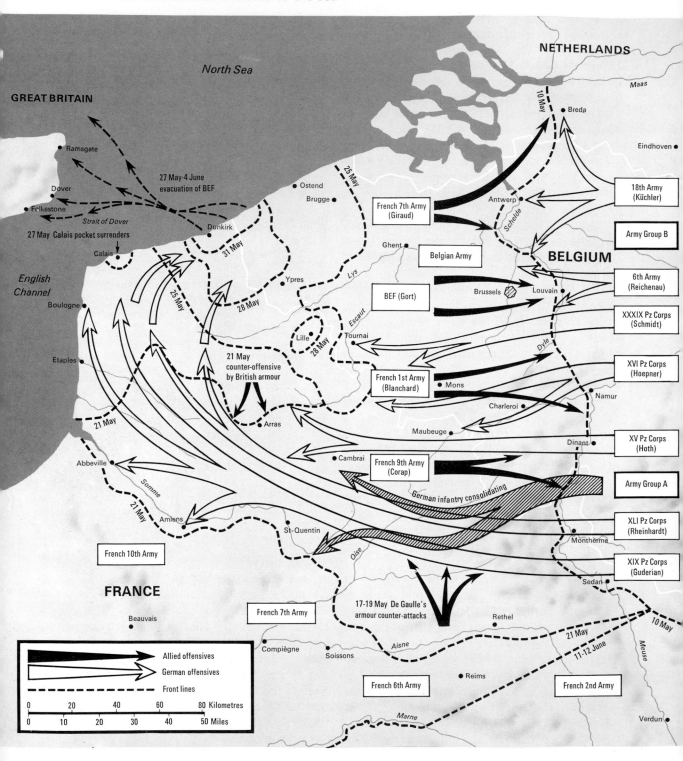

NETHERLANDS

North Sea

GREAT BRITAIN

Maas

Eindhoven

Ramsgate

27 May–4 June
evacuation of BEF

Dover

Breda

10 May

Folkestone

Strait of Dover

27 May Calais pocket surrenders

Ostend

25 May

Brugge

Antwerp

18th Army
(Küchler)

Calais

Dunkirk

31 May

Army Group B

English
Channel

28 May

Ghent

Belgian Army

BELGIUM

6th Army
(Reichenau)

Ypres

Lys

Louvain

XXXIX Pz Corps
(Schmidt)

Boulogne

25 May

BEF (Gort)

Brussels

Escaut

Dyle

XVI Pz Corps
(Hoepner)

Etaples

21 May
counter-offensive
by British armour

Lille

Tournai

28 May

French 1st Army
(Blanchard)

Mons

Charleroi

Namur

XV Pz Corps
(Hoth)

Abbeville

Arras

Maubeuge

Dinant

Army Group A

Somme

21 May

Cambrai

French 9th Army
(Corap)

German infantry consolidating

XLI Pz Corps
(Rheinhardt)

21 May

Amiens

St-Quentin

Montherme

XIX Pz Corps
(Guderian)

French 10th Army

Oise

Sedan

FRANCE

Beauvais

French 7th Army

17–19 May De Gaulle's
armour counter-attacks

Rethel

10 May

21 May

Meuse

Compiègne

Aisne

11–12 June

Soissons

Reims

French 6th Army

French 2nd Army

Verdun

Marne

	Allied offensives
	German offensives
- - - - -	Front lines

| 0 | 20 | 40 | 60 | 80 Kilometres |
| 0 | 10 | 20 | 30 | 40 | 50 Miles |

of it. The Germans had broken through further south on the Meuse at Sedan. The entire active force of the Allies was in danger of being cut off.

This was the great stroke, initiated by Hitler, advocated by Manstein, designed in detail by Halder, and now to be executed by Guderian who commanded the German armour. More than any other general Guderian believed in speed. This was shown at once. The German and French General Staffs had calculated that it would take nine days for the Germans to reach the Meuse. Guderian said four. He reached it in two. One can fix with precise accuracy the moment when France was defeated and ceased to be a Great Power for the duration of the war. At 1500 hours on 13 May, the first German soldiers crossed the Meuse. French resistance was feeble and uncoordinated. German tanks crossed at dawn the next day, and by 15 May Guderian's way was clear. He swept forward, disregarding orders to halt from his army commander and even evading similar orders from Hitler who for a moment lost his nerve. The German tanks drove unimpeded along the open roads. When they ran out of petrol, the crews stopped at the nearest pump, filled up without paying and drove on. Occasionally they stopped to milk a cow.

Further north Rommel's tanks also crossed the Meuse by cable ferry and pushed forward to Avesnes. Though this was a less decisive blow, it meant that Guderian had no worries on his right flank. The German high command worried more about his left. Here the speed of the German infantry carried the day. The Germans had three motorized infantry divisions. Otherwise the infantry plodded along on their feet just as they had done in 1914, their supplies following in horsedrawn wagons. They kept up

The decisive moment: German troops cross the Meuse

the same rate as they had done then: forty miles a day for nearly a week. On 17 May when the French attempted to counter-attack, they were met with a solid defence on Guderian's left flank. One of these attacks was led by de Gaulle, then a little-known brigadier. It was held up later as an example of what the French could have done if their generals had been imbued with de Gaulle's offensive spirit. In fact de Gaulle was stopped by air attack before he came to grips and Guderian did not even report the

'We are beaten; we have lost the battle.' Churchill refused to believe him and ascertained that both Gamelin and Georges were unruffled. That evening Gamelin's nerve broke. He declared, 'It means the destruction of the French army.' On 16 May Churchill flew to Paris. He was told that the Germans would arrive within a couple of days. The smoke of burning documents rose up from the garden of the Foreign Ministry. Parisians were fleeing from Paris, blocking every road to the south. Churchill asked Gamelin,

Kind German soldiers relieve an unmilked cow

affair to headquarters. Alistair Horne justly, if rather unkindly, quotes Dr Johnson's saying: 'A fly, Sir, may sting a stately horse and make him wince; but one is but an insect, and the other is a horse still.' The time for cutting off the German spearhead had passed.

Reynaud was the first to realize what had happened. Early on 15 May he rang up Churchill:

'Where is the strategic reserve?' Gamelin replied, 'Aucune – there is none.' Churchill persisted: 'When and where are you going to counter-attack?' Gamelin said, 'Inferiority of numbers, inferiority of equipment, inferiority of method.' With this he shrugged his shoulders and passed out of history.

Churchill attempted to inspire the French.

He promised that ten more fighter squadrons would be sent to France. The War Cabinet, consulted by telephone, agreed. Back home Churchill encountered resistance. Sir Hugh Dowding, head of Fighter Command, insisted that he needed 52 squadrons to ensure the defence of Great Britain. Even now he was down to 36. If more squadrons were sent to France, he would soon be down to none. Dowding appealed to the War Cabinet. He showed the graph of past wastage and projected it into the future. The War Cabinet were convinced. They agreed only that squadrons should operate over France from British bases. In a day or two the Germans overran most of the bases from which the British could operate in France and the dispute became pointless. All the same, Dowding's graph was the first step towards victory in the Battle of Britain.

The Germans did not enter Paris on 18 May. They had no intention of doing so. Guderian's eyes were set on the sea. On 20 May his tanks took Amiens and then Abbeville. That evening they reached the coast at Noyelles. They had come two hundred miles in ten days. Further north in Belgium the Allies were falling back – the British behind the Schelde, the French south of Lille. On 19 May Gort discussed the situation with Billotte, his French superior. Billotte said they must retreat to the Somme. Gort looked longingly at Dunkirk and the Channel ports. In any case, suppose they could not get through to the Somme? Gort was not a brilliant soldier. He had been out of place as Chief of the Imperial General Staff and had been appointed to command the BEF simply as the best fighting general in the army. Now he took a brave and independent decision: he resolved to save his army. On the evening of 19 May he told the War Office that he might have to consider evacuating the BEF. The next day Ironside, the CIGS, arrived with a formal order that Gort must force his way through to the south. Gort refused. Seven of his nine divisions were fighting the German Army Group B in the north and could not disengage. Ironside com-

Guderian, master of tank warfare

mented, 'Situation desperate. God help the BEF. Brought to this state by the incompetence of the French Command.'

This incompetence now reached its climax of confusion. On 19 May Gamelin at last bestirred himself and drafted an academic observation that the German spearhead must be cut off. He sent this observation to Georges who took no

Pétain, man of Vichy

empty. Weygand cancelled Gamelin's instruction for a combined offensive and then, weary after his air journey from Syria, went to bed for twenty-four hours. On 21 May he flew to Flanders. He failed to meet Gort. King Leopold told him that the Belgian army could not hold out much longer. Billotte, the French commander, was killed in a road accident soon after leaving Weygand.

Unknown to the French, Gort loyally attempted to break through the German encirclement, though he could only raise two tank battalions with sixteen tanks in all. On 21 May this small force attacked the Germans at Arras. The Germans, though much the stronger, were considerably alarmed. Rommel claimed that he was being attacked by five tank divisions. By the evening the British were exhausted and in danger of being surrounded. They were compelled to fall back. On 22 May a French force made a similar attempt with even less effect. On 24 May the French attacked in the south with no effect at all. The German spearhead was now a firm defensive line, too strong to be broken. The Allied armies in the north were irremediably cut off.

At this critical moment the German advance stopped for some days. Rundstedt, still regarding the French army as the formidable force it had been in the First World War, worried about his southern flank and determined to conserve his tanks for the second phase of the campaign. Hitler, also anxious about the French army, endorsed his decision. Goering, who had been out of the picture, declared that his air force could finish off the British unaided. After the war ingenious speculators suggested that Hitler deliberately spared the British in order to make a soft peace with them. There was nothing in this idea. The Germans simply did not grasp the full extent of their victory.

On 25 May Gort decided that the French were incapable of any counter-attack and that he must save his own army. His resolve stiffened on 27 May when the Belgian army surrendered. The Belgian government withdrew, first to

notice. A few hours later Gamelin learned from Reynaud that he had been dismissed. Reynaud called in the two surviving heroes of the First World War, Pétain and Weygand. Pétain joined the government; he was eighty-four. Weygand became Commander-in-Chief; he was seventy-three. He tapped his briefcase, saying, 'I have the secrets of Marshal Foch.' The briefcase was

British troops in Dunkirk

France, then to London. Leopold remained as a prisoner of war, a decision for which he received much unmerited criticism. He had in fact performed a great service. The courageous resistance of the Belgian army enabled the British to consolidate their defensive lines round Dunkirk. The evacuation of the BEF began on 27 May. It was expected that only some ten thousand men would be saved. Churchill warned the House of Commons to prepare itself for hard and heavy tidings.

The evacuation succeeded beyond all hopes. Goering's boast was not fulfilled. British fighters inflicted heavy loss on the German bombers, which were also hampered for part of the time by low-lying cloud. Destroyers, which brought off most of the men, were aided by 860 vessels of one sort and another – pleasure boats, fishing smacks, river ferries. By 4 June, when the evacuation ended, 200,000 British and 140,000 French troops had been brought to England. There was a heavy price to pay. Six destroyers and 177 fighter aircraft had been lost. The BEF had lost all its tanks, guns and motor transport. Many of the men had lost their rifles. Only the Guards were unruffled: at Dover they marched off the boat washed and shaved with their buttons shining and their boots polished.

The evacuation from Dunkirk was hailed in Great Britain as a wonderful accomplishment, almost as a victory. In France it caused bitter feelings. Evacuation in face of defeat had always been the British way – at Walcheren in 1809, at Gallipoli in 1915, now in Norway and at Dunkirk. The French way was to fall back into a fortress, as Bazaine had done at Metz in 1870. They therefore took part in the evacuation reluctantly and late. Churchill had promised that British and French should be evacuated arm in arm, *bras dessus, bras dessous*. Did this mean that, since most of the British troops had gone, no more should be moved until the number of French evacuated caught up with them? That they should be moved according to the numbers remaining in the salient – a proportion of five to one? Or merely that French and British should go in equal numbers? General Alexander, who took over command when Gort was ordered to leave, had no clear instructions from London and accepted this last interpretation. As a result 150,000 French troops remained behind. Indeed it was their obstinate defence that enabled the British to evacuate so successfully. These French troops became prisoners of war, an outcome

German soldiers on the beach at Dunkirk

that did not increase French cordiality towards the British.

The rest of the campaign was little more than an epilogue. Weygand, true to the methods of the First World War, proposed to hold the line of the Somme with 50 divisions – all that remained to him. On 5 June the Germans opened their offensive. Two days later they broke through. One German force swept through Normandy into Brittany. Another went through Champagne and took the Maginot line in the rear. A third advanced south to beyond Lyons. The French government withdrew to Tours and then to Bordeaux. On 14 June the Germans entered Paris and marched down the Champs-Élysées. Two British divisions had been sent to Normandy under General Sir Alan Brooke. He soon grasped that the campaign was lost, and on 15 June his force was evacuated, bring-

ing 10,000 Poles with them. It was almost four years before British troops campaigned on French soil again.

On 10 June Mussolini declared war. The Italian army was poorly equipped: its only good guns were those it had captured from the Austrians at the end of the First World War. Mussolini cared nothing for this. He believed that the war was coming to an end and that he would miss his place at the conference table if he did not declare war at once. The Italian army, though three times as strong as the French forces opposed to it, advanced only a few hundred yards into Menton before the fighting ended.

These days saw the death agony of the Anglo-French alliance which had seemed to direct international affairs during the preceding twenty years. Churchill crossed twice to meet Reynaud

German victory parade down the Champs-Élysées

in an attempt to revive his flagging spirits. Wild schemes were aired: the establishment of a fortified redoubt in Brittany; appeals to President Roosevelt which would bring the New World to the rescue of the Old. There was a fundamental divergence of views between the two Allies. The French believed that only the defence of France mattered and that the BEF and the British fighters should be sacrificed. They resented the way in which the British had, as they thought, abandoned them. The British were concerned to keep the war going. They held that the French government should leave France and go into exile as other governments had done. Above all they wished to secure the French fleet. With it they could still dominate the seas; without it they would be in great danger; if it actually fell into German hands the war might well be lost. They demanded that the French fleet should sail to British ports, though they deeply resented a similar demand from Roosevelt a few weeks later that their fleet should sail to American ones.

On 13 June Churchill, Halifax and Beaverbrook met Reynaud for the last time at Tours. Churchill talked of securing the French fleet. Reynaud pleaded to be allowed to conclude an armistice. The British statesmen went out in the garden to debate their answer. Beaverbrook said, 'We are doing no good here. Let's go home.' Without further words, the British left. It was the end of the Anglo-French alliance. In the ensuing hugger-mugger the British demand for moving the French fleet to safety was never laid clearly before the French government. On 16 June it was put aside in favour of a proposal for an indissoluble union of the two countries – the last flicker of an alliance that was already dead. The French rejected the proposal scornfully. Reynaud resigned. Pétain became French Premier and at once asked for an armistice.

Hitler displayed moderation and political skill, just as he had become German Chancellor with seeming moderation in January 1933. He was anxious to keep a government going in France. He was even more anxious to prevent the French fleet and colonial empire from going over to the British side. When the negotiators met in Foch's railway coach at Rethondes, where the armistice of 11 November 1918 had been signed, they were offered reasonable terms. Though northern France and the entire coast down to the Spanish frontier would remain in German occupation, France south of the Loire would be free, and the French government, soon established at Vichy, would exercise civil authority throughout the country. The French fleet was to be disarmed in its home ports, but Hitler promised not to lay hands on it. The armistice was signed on 22 June. German victory over France was complete. It cost the Germans 28,000 soldiers killed – not a great deal more than the British lost on the first day of the Somme battle in 1916. German reserves of munitions were exhausted. But Hitler did not mind. As he foresaw, they had been just enough. His strategical vision had been vindicated. He was hailed as 'the greatest field commander of all time', and no German general successfully challenged his directions again.

For the overwhelming majority of French people the war was over, or so it seemed. Pétain's government at Vichy followed a policy of loyal collaboration with the Germans, apart from feeble and ineffective protests against the excessive charges that the Germans levied for the army of occupation. After some hesitation almost the entire French colonial empire acknowledged Pétain's authority. There was one tiny breach in this unity. At the last minute Charles de Gaulle escaped from Bordeaux to London. He was a very junior officer. There was none more senior to give a lead. On 18 June he appealed to the French people to continue the war. He declared, 'France has lost a battle. She has not lost the war.' Only a few hundred Frenchmen responded to his appeal. The British government recognized him as the chief of the Free French. This was far from being a government, even in exile.

There remained the menace of the French fleet. On 24 June Darlan, head of the French

Preis **20** Pfg.
5. Dezember 1940
Nummer 49 / 15. Jahrg.
Druck und Verlag von M.
DuMont Schauberg, Köln
Auslandspreise siehe Fuß der Rückseite

Kölnische
Illustrierte Zeitung

navy, instructed his captains to sink their ships if there were any danger of their falling into German hands. This signal was not known to the British. In any case they could not rely on Darlan's word, still less on that of Hitler. The few French ships in British ports were easily disarmed, though with the deaths of some French sailors. At Alexandria the French disarmed their own ships after an agreement between the British and French admirals. The most powerful force was at Mers-el-Kebir near Oran. On 3 July Admiral Somerville executed what Churchill called 'a most hateful decision, the most unnatural and painful in which I have ever been associated'. Somerville presented an ultimatum: the French ships must sail to a British port or to the New World or scuttle themselves within six hours. The French admiral refused these demands. At six in the evening Somerville opened fire. One French battleship escaped to Toulon. Two battleships and one battlecruiser were crippled or destroyed; 1300 French sailors were killed. In England and the United States the British action was hailed as a gesture of resolution and defiance. In the House of Commons the Conservatives cheered Churchill unreservedly for the first time: 'All joined in solemn stentorian accord.' The French saw things differently. Once again they had been the victims of British selfishness. The French government broke off diplomatic relations with Great Britain, though they did not declare war. It was a sad end to the old partnership.

France in London: de Gaulle after his first broadcast

4

War at long range 1940-1

Hitler's triumph had no equal in European history. Napoleon, who came nearest to it, needed ten years to establish his empire. He had to fight three campaigns, the last of them, which culminated with the Battle of Austerlitz, causing heavy casualties. Moreover his empire was never complete: Prussia retained a little independence and Austria a good deal. Germany won domination over the entire Continent west of Soviet Russia within less than a year and at a trifling cost in men and materials. Victory in France paid for itself many times over. The Germans found in the French storage depots enough oil for both the Battle of Britain and the first great campaign in Russia. Occupation costs levied on the French would have been enough to pay for an army of eighteen million men.

The means of German domination ranged from annexation or direct rule to an ostensibly equal partnership with Italy. Before the war Germany had annexed Austria and the Sudeten area of Czechoslovakia. She annexed Danzig and western Poland after her first victories, and Eupen and Malmédy in eastern Belgium after her later one. Luxembourg and Alsace and Lorraine were also annexed in practice though not in theory. Alsatians were conscripted into the German army and committed one of the worst crimes of the war when they massacred the entire population of the French village Oradour-sur-Glane. The fragment of Poland not annexed by either Germany or Soviet Russia fell under direct German rule – surprisingly the only area of Europe to do so, until joined later by the occupied territory of Russia. It

became the anonymous General government under the Nazi tyrant Hans Frank, and here the Nazi doctrines of racial superiority and geno-cide were applied from the first. Belgium and the occupied zone of France were under German military administration, in theory only until after the conquest of Great Britain. The Germans had also one tiny overseas possession: the Channel Islands, administered by the Germans in the name of King George VI. At the time of liberation some of the islanders, imprisoned for offences against the Germans, were actually sent to complete their sentences in Winchester jail.

Bohemia and Moravia, sometimes called Czechia, were ostensibly a German protectorate with a Czech president, Hacha, who held office throughout the war, and Czech ministers. In reality they were at the mercy of the German protector – Neurath, then Heydrich the SS terrorist, finally Frick. In 1942 two Czecho-slovak paratroopers, sent by Beneš from England, assassinated Heydrich. This provoked savage reprisals, including the notorious destruction of Lidice and the less-remembered destruction of Lezaky, another village near Prague.

Holland and Norway had slightly more independent governments under the supervision of Reich Commissioners, whose control increased as the war went on. Both countries produced collaborators – the National Socialist Mussert in Holland, the original Quisling in Norway. Neither received much welcome from the Nazi authorities. Indeed, despite the fact that this was hailed as the age of Fascism, no countries other than Italy, Spain and Croatia took on a fully Fascist character. Denmark and the unoccupied zone of France had a genuine measure of internal independence which diminished later and finally vanished.

Of Germany's so-called allies, Slovakia was a blatant satellite, though curiously this did not prevent her remaining theoretically neutral throughout the war. Hungary and Romania were more nearly allies of Germany, competing against each other for the possession of Transylvania, and both took part in the Russian campaign. Bulgaria, though eager enough to join in the attack on Yugoslavia, refused to declare war on Soviet Russia, insisting that the Slav sentiment in Bulgaria was too strong. Italy enjoyed full treatment as an ally, with Hitler recognizing Mussolini as his only equal.

Sweden and Switzerland held to their demo-cratic institutions and even tried to follow an independent course. In practice they were tied to the German economic system and, being safe from British bombing, were of more use to Germany than if they had been conquered. Germany derived her iron ore from Sweden and her precision instruments from Switzerland. Without these she could not have continued the war. The only countries that were really free to choose their own policy were those that had access to the outer world – Spain and Portugal at one end of Europe, Turkey at the other – and the neutrality of Spain and even of Portugal was for long not above suspicion. Eire also enjoyed a rather fictitious neutrality, thanks to the patience of the British government.

The instruments of German power penetrated into almost every European country, whatever measure of independence it theoretically pos-

German housewife has no bananas

sessed. Sometimes the instrument was the secret police and the SS, sometimes the military, sometimes German businessmen armed with the authority of the Reich. Greater Germany after her military victory dominated Europe simply by applying the principles of autarky without restraint. Europe became an economic community, run for Germany's exclusive benefit. A mercantilist system grew up, dignified with the name of the New Order. Some German authorities aimed to reduce all Europe outside Germany to a purely agricultural level. Others, with the immediate needs of the war in mind, worked to exploit the industries of Europe for Germany's war machine. Others were only interested in plunder. Whichever aim was followed, the European countries were transformed into colonies, supplying Germany with foodstuffs, industrial goods, and ultimately labour. Sometimes these exploited countries received a few German goods in exchange. More often they were paid in credits that the Germans proposed to redeem after the war. Even Soviet Russia accepted these paper promises. When the war ended, only Hungary, it is said, had managed to accumulate a debit balance in Berlin.

The conquered countries paid for the privilege of having been conquered, and the Germans took the profits. Life in Germany was little affected by the war. German living standards actually rose in the second half of 1940. The losses in military equipment were easily replaced by the normal workings of industry. There was no need for economic mobilization or the direction of labour. Some fifteen divisions were disbanded. Twenty-five more were put on a peacetime footing. The production of munitions was cut down in the autumn of 1940 and again in the late summer of 1941. The building of motor roads went on. A beginning was made with the execution of Hitler's grandiose plans for the creation of a new Berlin.

The German people may have thought that the war was over. Hitler did not. The impetus of war carried him forward of itself. The German people had been involved in war twice in a lifetime, and Hitler doubted whether even he could lead them into a third war if he allowed this one to run down. Far better to keep going with the tried method of easy success. Moreover Hitler still insisted that time was not on Germany's side. Interpreting others by himself, he foretold that Soviet Russia and the United States would one day strike against Germany unless he struck at them first.

Hitler's obvious target was Great Britain, still at war and still defiant. Hitler had not expected this or made any plans to deal with it. He had assumed, like Ludendorff before him, that Great Britain would make peace once her continental sword, France, had been struck from her hand. The conquest of Great Britain, even if it were possible, would bring Hitler more disadvantages than rewards. The British Empire would be partitioned between Japan and the United States – or so Hitler believed. At any rate Germany would get nothing. The British fleet would go to the New World, and the United States would be invulnerable while preparing for war on a great scale.

Peace with Great Britain was what Hitler wanted. This would actually transform her into a buffer against an American attack. All danger on Germany's Western Front would be removed, and Hitler would be free to turn against Soviet Russia. But he had only one tactic with which to create a situation favourable to himself: to wait until his opponent's nerve cracked. He had followed this tactic before he became Chancellor in Germany. He had followed it with Czechoslovakia and tried to follow it with Poland. He followed it now with Great Britain. During the armistice negotiations with the French Hitler said to Jodl, 'The British have lost the war, but they don't know it; one must give them time, and they will come round.' Hitler gave the British time. He remained silent until 19 July. Then he addressed the Reichstag. He made a final appeal to 'reason and common sense'. But he offered no moderate terms. He merely denounced Churchill and threatened 'unending suffering and misery' for the British unless they made peace.

There was a moment when the British, or at any rate some members of the War Cabinet, had contemplated making peace. On 27 May, before the evacuation from Dunkirk began, the War Cabinet discussed the possibility of negotiations with Mussolini as intermediary. Halifax, the Foreign Secretary, recommended concessions to Mussolini in the Mediterranean – Malta and Cyprus to become Italian, and Egypt a condominium. As to Germany, Halifax was prepared to discuss terms 'if he were satisfied that matters vital to the independence of this country were unaffected'. Chamberlain supported Halifax. Attlee spoke scathingly against the prospect of becoming a suitor for Mussolini's patronage; Arthur Greenwood, the other Labour member of the War Cabinet, called it 'a step towards ultimate capitulation'. Churchill at first brushed the idea aside and then said grudgingly that if Herr Hitler was prepared to make peace on the terms of the restoration of the German colonies and the overlordship of central Europe, that was one thing. But it was quite unlikely that he would make any such offer.

The next day Churchill, sustained by the two Labour ministers, had second thoughts. Summoning all ministers of Cabinet rank, he remarked, 'Of course whatever happens at Dunkirk, we shall fight on.' Ministers shouted, 'Well done, Prime Minister!' Some burst into tears. Others slapped Churchill on the back. Unwittingly this was a demonstration against Chamberlain and Halifax as well as against Hitler.

After Hitler's speech of 19 July Churchill wanted to set down formal motions of rejection in both Houses of Parliament. Chamberlain and Attlee, the two party leaders, thought that this was 'making too much fuss about it', and Halifax was appropriately given the task of brushing Hitler's peace offer aside on the radio. In private Halifax was still assuring the Swedish minister that the time for negotiations would soon come. But his day had passed. Early in August Churchill defined the aims that Great Britain was to follow until the end of the war.

The Germans must relinquish all their gains and give 'effective guarantees by deeds, not words,' that nothing of the kind would ever happen again, before the British would condescend even to negotiate with them. The door was firmly closed against a negotiated peace. 'Unconditional surrender' became the British programme.

This was a remarkable demand to make when Great Britain was alone and apparently on the eve of being invaded. On paper she had many allies. The governments of Norway, Holland, Belgium and Poland took refuge in London. Beneš was recognized as head of a Czechoslovak government in exile, and de Gaulle represented Free France. Holland and Belgium had great colonial resources, and de Gaulle later acquired some. There was a considerable Polish army and air force. But none of the exiled governments had any power in Europe. Their countries were held firmly under German control, and there was at first little resistance. Even when the resistance started, it could only provide centres of secret information. It could not resist in any effective sense.

The world outside Europe was Great Britain's resource as it had been during the war against Napoleon. The British Dominions, other than Eire, were already in the war. Canadian industry worked to supply Great Britain's military needs and did so on more generous terms than those granted by the United States later. Canadian troops came over for the defence of Great Britain and took part in the invasion of northern France. South African troops fought in Abyssinia and Egypt. New Zealand troops suffered greatly during the battle for Crete. Australian troops held Tobruk in North Africa.

The United States offered the prospect of economic aid on a far larger scale, though the British did not know how to pay for it. Shortly after the formation of the National government, Randolph Churchill called on his father and said something about the difficulties of the position. Churchill replied, 'I can see only one resource. We must get the Americans in' – and so he ultimately did, though thanks more to the Japanese than to his own efforts.

Churchill and his advisers were not content to wait for America's entry into the war. In a confused and contradictory way they entertained the idea that Great Britain might win the war all on her own if she survived the perils of the coming summer. Misled partly by memories of the First World War, partly by reports from anti-Nazi exiles, and partly by their own strategical misjudgments, they exaggerated the effects of the British blockade: they believed, quite wrongly, that German economy was on the point of collapse; and expected decisive results, belied in the event, from long-range bombing.

These were remote calculations. In June 1940, after the successful evacuation from Dunkirk, the British did not have the feel of a defeated people. They thought that they had a good chance of survival, and events proved them right. From this it was easy to drift into the belief that, if they survived, they would somehow again emerge victorious as they had done at the end of the First World War. The memory inspired them and sometimes weighed on the Germans. When the Germans occupied Warsaw, one of their officers remarked, 'Last time I was disarmed by a washerwoman. I wonder who will disarm me this time.' The British made much the same reflection the other way round. Few German officers in eastern Europe were lucky enough, however, to be disarmed by a washerwoman. Most of those not killed found their way to Russian labour camps where they remained for many years.

Hitler had now to fulfil his threats whether he wished to or not. On 21 July he met representa-

German invasion barges that were never used

tives of the three services in Berlin. Sea Lion, the invasion of Great Britain, was resolved on in principle. Ten days later, after further discussion, the invasion date was fixed for 15 September. Hitler doubted from the start whether the invasion was 'technically feasible'. He would decide, he said, only a few days beforehand whether or not it should take place. The invasion was a mixture of improvisation and bluff. Perhaps it would prove practicable as it worked out. If not, the nerve of the British might crack at the fearsome prospect. Either way it was worth trying.

Hitler was always halfhearted about the projected invasion. He was a land animal, and a great campaign against Russia was already in his mind. Even before the British evacuation from Dunkirk ended, he had told Rundstedt that his hands were now free for his 'great essential task: the mortal conflict with Russia'. British obstinacy provided him with a fresh argument. At the meeting on 21 July he turned with relief from the invasion of Great Britain to a campaign against Russia – a project both more rewarding and, as he believed, easier. Russia, not France, he announced, was Great Britain's continental sword, and 'with Russia smashed, Britain's last hope would be shattered'. The invasion of Great Britain was for Hitler a minor operation, something with which to fill up time until his really great operation was ready. He did not direct the campaign personally as he had done and was to do with all others. He retired to his mountain retreat, the Berghof, and watched the proceedings with detached curiosity.

Hence there was no coordination between the three armed forces. Brauchitsch, the Commander-in-Chief, and Halder, the Chief of Staff, were at Fontainebleau; Grand Admiral Raeder was in Berlin; Goering, the head of the air force, remained at his house, Karinhall, forty miles outside Berlin until he set up advanced headquarters at Beauvais in September. The army chiefs loyally prepared for Sea Lion with landings on a wide front from Deal to Weymouth.

They regarded the English Channel as an anti-tank ditch that had nothing to do with them. Someone else would put them across the Channel, and then they would conduct a successful campaign.

This was not at all Raeder's idea. The German fleet was so reduced after its losses in Norway that even the advanced British striking force at Harwich would be too much for it. Raeder wanted a long-term strategy: hundreds of U-boats with which to dominate the Atlantic by the end of 1941 and a large surface fleet that could challenge the British in the Mediterranean by 1942 or 1943. This was too slow for Hitler. Only 5 per cent of German steel production was allotted to naval work, and throughout 1940 the Germans operated with fewer U-boats than they had possessed at the beginning of the war. Thus, as a by-product of the Battle of Britain, the Germans lost the Battle of the Atlantic, though only just.

To outward appearance Raeder loyally conformed to Sea Lion, once he had ensured that it should be postponed until 15 September. River barges and coastal steamers were assembled in the projected invasion ports, much to the detriment of German industry which depended largely on supply by water. Over one essential point Raeder got his way. When the army plans were submitted to him, he insisted that invasion on a broad front was impossible. The navy could at most put the army ashore at Dover. The generals had to conform. They made a revised plan for landings from Deal to Brighton. But they did not believe that such a limited operation could succeed. In fact Raeder and the army chiefs were really agreed that an invasion would be possible only if the British had already surrendered.

Thus all turned on the German air force. Goering was delighted to undertake the task. Like Baldwin and the Italian general Douhet before him, he believed that the air weapon was irresistible: the bomber would always get through. He was confident that the Luftwaffe could conquer Great Britain all on its own.

Eagle, the German air offensive, and Sea Lion had nothing in common. Hitler's instruction, issued on 1 August, was 'to establish conditions favourable to the conquest of Britain'. But according to Eagle, fleets of bombers, escorted by fighters, would simply sail over England and pulverize the British into surrender – Guernica on a larger scale. During the Battle of Britain, the Luftwaffe never considered the needs of the other services. It made hardly any attempt to bomb British warships and often bombed harbours and airfields that the army would need in case of invasion. Eagle was miscalculated even within its own terms of reference. It did not allow for the British fighters. This proved to be a mistake.

The British people were in a state of high exultation in the two months after Dunkirk. They believed that they now stood in the front line. Forgetting the Channel almost as much as the German generals did, they foresaw German tanks rolling through the English countryside, while swarms of parachutists descended from the skies. Bands of Home Guards, armed with pikes or with rifles without ammunition, set up primitive road blocks and prepared to die literally in the village ditches. If the Germans came, Churchill proposed to launch the slogan: 'You can always take one with you.' On a more mundane level, the army chiefs doubted whether the few ill-equipped divisions could defeat an invasion force once it landed; and the navy chiefs, anxious to preserve their capital ships for future combats, doubted whether they could prevent a landing. As the Chiefs of Staff reported, 'all depends on the air force'.

On paper the German air force was much the stronger with a superiority in aircraft of more than two to one. This superiority was misleading. Bombers could operate successfully only if secure from attacks by fighters, and in fighter aircraft the two opposing forces were about equal. Moreover the British had larger reserves than the Germans and, thanks to Beaverbrook's drive at the Ministry of Aircraft Production, actually increased their fighter strength during the battle. The British were operating on their home ground, the German fighters at the limit of their range. The British had also the inestimable asset of radar which enabled them to follow and forecast the movements of aircraft. (Though the Germans had a form of radar, too, it was used only to detect ships.)

Above all, the British knew what they were doing; the Germans did not. The German air chiefs never made up their minds whether the Luftwaffe should proceed with bombing, regardless of fighter attacks, or whether it should destroy the British fighters first. Hence they failed in both. Sir Hugh Dowding, the chief of Fighter Command, had no such doubts. His sole aim was to cripple the German bomber force. Dowding husbanded his fighters with the utmost economy, refusing to be drawn into romantic combats with the German fighters when this could be avoided. The results spoke for themselves. In direct fighter comparison, the British lost more than the Germans. This was eclipsed by the enormous losses in German bombers.

Eagle was officially launched on 13 August. Bad weather delayed the attack for two days, and the Battle of Britain, as it came to be called, ran from 15 August to 15 September. The battle had three phases. In the first the Germans came over with no precise targets and suffered heavy losses. On 15 August alone they lost 75 aircraft to 34. In the second phase the Germans concentrated against the advanced airfields in Kent. They achieved considerable success. British losses were more than the German, and the RAF was in danger of being forced back. There followed a curious diversion. On 24 August a German aircraft that had lost its way dropped bombs on London by mistake. The next day the RAF bombed Berlin in retaliation – an ineffective gesture but one that enraged Hitler. He retaliated in turn, or maybe Goering thought that the time had come for a direct onslaught on British morale. On 7 September the Germans turned aside to bomb London. This began the third phase. It also began, though no one

Below **The battle in the skies,
September 1940**

Right and opposite, left **The Blitz on London**

appreciated this, the indiscriminate bombing of
cities that was to continue throughout the war.

The British thought that the crisis was upon
them. On the night of 7 September the signal
'Cromwell' for 'invasion imminent' was sent
out. The Home Guard stood to arms. In some
districts the ringing of church bells announced
that German parachutists had actually landed.
It was a false alarm. The Germans bombed
London again on 9 September, though with
less effect than on the first occasion: less than
half the bombers got through. On 15 September

Above German bombers over London

the Germans made their last great effort. This time all went well for the RAF. The British lost 26 aircraft; they destroyed 60 German aircraft and were the more inspirited by the erroneous belief that they had destroyed 185. Even the correct figure was enough. The Luftwaffe had failed to establish air superiority. In all, the Germans lost 1733 aircraft during the Battle of Britain; the British lost 915 and had 665 fighters in service as against 656 in July.

The way for Sea Lion had not been cleared. Still less had the British been battered into sur-

render. On 17 September Hitler postponed Sea Lion 'until further notice'. On 12 October he cancelled it for the winter. The Germans kept up some preparations until March 1942, and the British maintained their defences, particularly with a greatly strengthened Home Guard, until long after that. But 15 September was the day of decision. Great Britain was safe from invasion for the duration of the Second World War. Victory in the Battle of Britain completed what the evacuation from Dunkirk had begun: it restored British spirits. Thereafter there was often discontent at particular grievances and sometimes sharp criticism when the war was being run badly or at least not successfully. But so far as the historian can tell, the British people never questioned that they should go on until victory was complete.

All the same it was a strange war in which the British were now engaged: two mortal antagonists committed to the destruction of each other and unable to do anything about it. The Germans had failed to invade Great Britain. The British had no forces with which to invade the Continent. No British and German troops exchanged shots between mid-June 1940 and the last day of March 1941 except for a few British commando raids on the French coast. Both sides were forced back to war at long range: bombing and blockade.

The German bomber offensive at night against Great Britain grew more or less accidentally out of the Battle of Britain and was continued as much in retaliation for British bombing as for any other reason. The Germans had no aircraft designed for long-range bombing and no pilots trained for night operations. They had no clear idea of what they wanted to do. Sometimes they tried to disrupt British communications by bombing ports and railway centres. Sometimes they tried to break British morale by devastating the centres of cities with high explosive and incendiary bombs. Sometimes they merely dropped bombs. The Blitz, as it was incorrectly called, did much damage. Three and a half million homes were damaged or destroyed. The

Below Improvised shelter in London's
Underground

***Bismarck* puts to sea on her last voyage**

House of Commons was destroyed. Buckingham Palace was hit. The City of London, the East End, and many provincial cities were devastated. The loss of life was less serious than had been feared. Some 30,000 people were killed during the Blitz, most of them in London. The effect on production was less serious still. Even in Coventry, which suffered one of the most notorious raids, all the factories were in full production again only five days afterwards. Morale was unshaken after the first few days of panic, and the British people became a united nation in the face of perils which all shared. In May 1941 the Germans broke off the Blitz in preparation for their attack on Russia, and there-after precautions against air raids were more of a burden than the raids themselves.

The British bomber offensive was at this time little more than nominal. The RAF had in theory a strategic aim: to destroy the synthetic-oil plants and other vital industries on which German military strength depended. Precision bombing of this kind was possible only by day, and the British soon learned that, without fighter cover, day raids were out of the question. No senior RAF leader sought the answer of long-range fighters, just as no senior British general of the First World War sought the answer of tanks to the problem of trench warfare. Instead, the British resorted to night bombing. Incapable of hitting precise targets, or indeed any targets at all, the British fell back on indiscriminate bombing in the mistaken belief that German morale was inferior to their own. In fact the British bomber offensive was pursued simply because it was the only way of showing that Great Britain was still at war with Germany.

The effect on German production was negligible. On British production it was profound. During 1941 the RAF lost a bomber for every ten tons of bombs dropped, and its bomber offensive killed more members of the RAF than German civilians. Add to this the manpower, industrial resources and raw materials devoted to producing bombers, and it is clear that the offensive was more expensive for Great Britain than damaging to Germany. In November 1941 the bomber offensive was broken off – a formal admission that the results were not worth the casualties being suffered. But the British continued to believe that strategic bombing could be decisive if it were powerful enough. Throughout the war the resources of British industry, and soon of much American industry also, were concentrated on the production of heavy bombers. This was a fateful legacy of the year when Great Britain stood alone.

Blockade proved a more dangerous weapon, at any rate on the German side. With all Europe at Germany's disposal and supplies flowing lavishly into Germany from Soviet Russia, there was little the British could do except control the dispatch of goods from such distant places as South America and southeast Asia. Grand Admiral Raeder, however, was more or less free to conduct the long-term strategy he had always favoured. He operated within narrow limits. Hitler regarded the big surface ships as precious possessions and grudged risking them at sea. In May 1941 Raeder sent *Bismarck*, the heaviest ship afloat, on a rather pointless expedition into the Atlantic. The combined forces of the Royal Navy sank her after losing the battlecruiser *Hood*, thus confirming Hitler's reluctance to send the remaining big ships out.

Hitler also grudged the use of German

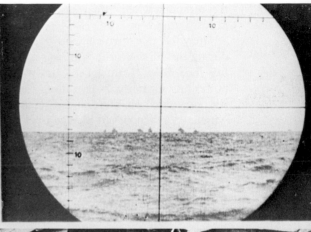

German U-boat commander sights a British convoy

resources for the production of U-boats, and Raeder had to operate with those he had. The German U-boats did not reach their prewar strength until the summer of 1941. Even so their attacks were alarmingly effective. The Germans now had the use of the French Atlantic ports and so could strike far out into the ocean. The British had a corresponding disadvantage: the three naval ports in Ireland were now denied to them, and not even Churchill's threats of military action could shift Eire from her implacable neutrality. In April 1941 alone nearly 700,000 tons of shipping were sunk – far more than British shipyards could replace. The scale of rations had to be reduced. This was probably the moment when Great Britain came nearest to losing the war.

Then the tide turned. Convoy, rediscovered during the First World War, was again successful. The RAF turned reluctantly aside from bombing Germany to patrolling the sea lanes. American aid was increasingly forthcoming. In August 1940 Roosevelt handed over 50 obsolete destroyers. Only 9 proved fit for early service, and the gift was more a symbol for the future than of use in the present. Roosevelt was more forthcoming after his election as President for a third term in November 1940. American warships took over patrol in the western Atlantic. American troops relieved British troops in Iceland, the main staging post for the Anglo-American convoys. At first the American ships merely signalled the presence of U-boats to the British. By the autumn of 1941 they were sinking U-boats themselves and being sunk by them. Though the number of U-boats increased, the number of ships sunk diminished. As a further alleviation some 50 U-boats were transferred to the Mediterranean where they soon wrought a change most unfavourable to the British. But the first phase of the Battle of the Atlantic had been won by the Anglo-American forces. Roosevelt continued to insist that the more supplies reached the British the less likely American involvement in the war became. Churchill seconded him, declaring, 'Give us the tools and we will finish the job' – a most hazardous speculation. In fact the United States was conducting an undeclared war at sea against Germany. War itself was averted only by Hitler's determination not to be provoked by the American actions.

The U-boat campaign was too slow for Hitler even when it was being successful. He wanted to sustain the momentum of war, not to let it run down while he waited for news from the Atlantic. For a little while he played with the idea of attacking Gibraltar and breaking into North Africa. Raeder wanted this in order to shake the British hold on the Mediterranean; the German generals wanted it in order to put their great army to some immediate and, as they thought, easy use. In October 1940 Hitler met Franco, the Spanish dictator, at Hendaye and Pétain at Montoire. To both he displayed the delights of a Moroccan campaign. Franco refused to be drawn. Pétain expected high rewards if France became an ally of Germany's instead of a defeated and largely occupied country. Hitler foresaw only difficulties. Franco, Pétain and even Mussolini would quarrel over the spoils of North Africa, and he could not satisfy them all. The Spanish Canary Islands and the Portuguese Azores would fall into British or American hands, and Germany's naval position would be worse than before. The assault on Gibraltar was never pursued, though the General Staff went on planning for it almost until the attack on Russia.

If the western Mediterranean were ruled out, the eastern Mediterranean might be more profitable. Again Raeder and the generals were in favour. Conquest of Egypt and the Middle East would end British power in the Mediterranean and open the way to the oil of Iraq and Persia. For a few weeks Hitler was tempted. Though he insisted that the Mediterranean was Italy's sphere, he welcomed the Italian advance to Sidi Barrani and even at first the Italian attack on Greece. In November he changed his mind. Maybe he thought that Italy was an ineffective instrument; maybe he became obsessed with the Russian shadow in his rear. Basically he could not take the Middle East seriously. Though he acted there defensively later – in order to ward off a British landing at Salonika – he lost interest in any positive German action. As a land animal, Hitler thought in terms of continents, not of strategic points, and the Middle East seemed to him a trumpery affair.

Thus Hitler always came back to the great idea that had been in his mind since June 1940 and more vaguely since the beginning of his career: the decisive campaign against Soviet Russia. He assumed that the war against Great Britain would somehow solve itself, particularly when Russia had been conquered. In the meantime the British could do him no harm, or so he thought. He anticipated that at some time in the future the United States might challenge German predominance. He even fixed on 1942 as the year when the Americans would be ready for war – 1944 would have been a better guess. This was another argument for finishing with Soviet Russia quickly. Hitler did what he could to postpone American entry into the war. He ignored the American breaches of neutrality – the destroyer deal, lend-lease, and even the participation of the American fleet in the Battle of the Atlantic.

Hitler made one diplomatic move that was to have profound consequences. Hitherto the Japanese, though members of the Anti-Comintern Pact, had held out against a formal alliance. After Hitler's conquest of Europe they were tempted. On 27 September 1940 Germany, Italy and Japan signed the Tripartite Pact, promising entry into war if any of the three was attacked by a fresh enemy. Hitler was not interested in Japanese aid against Russia. He hoped that the alliance would increase their confidence against the United States. If a Far Eastern war followed, the United States would be too busy to have time for European affairs. Germany's Western Front would be secure.

Japan was certainly on the move in the Far East, and not only because of the newly signed alliance. Hitler's victories created a vacuum in the Far East into which the Japanese were inevitably drawn. French Indo-China and the Dutch East Indies were defenceless, the British at Singapore not much less so. Here, it seemed, was a way of cutting off supplies from Chungking and thus breaking the deadlock that had lasted for over a year. The French agreed to close their supply lines to Chungking. The British agreed to close the Burma road, though only for three months, and that during the rainy season when the road was in any case unusable. The Japanese also wanted a guarantee of oil supplies from the Dutch East Indies. The exiled Dutch government in London would have liked to agree. They were restrained by fear of offending the United States. The antagonism between Japan and the United States seemed to be developing much as Hitler hoped.

This was a misreading of the situation. Neither Japan nor the United States wanted war in the Far East; they wanted agreement. Of course they wanted it on entirely different terms, and the means they used in trying to attain it brought war nearer instead of staving it off. The Japanese, reversing Hitler's outlook, reckoned that the United States would soon be too busy in the Atlantic to have time or resources for Far Eastern affairs. Therefore if Japan strengthened her position and made herself more secure against American economic pressure, the Americans would be ready for a compromise that would give Japan practical hegemony over China. Whenever the Americans proved obstinate, Japan pushed up her gains in the Far East, always in the conviction that the Americans would finally yield.

President Roosevelt and his military advisers certainly put the European war first. This decision had a long history, going back to the period just after the First World War when the Americans contemplated a possible, even if unlikely, war against Great Britain and Japan. The American strategists then argued that they must defeat the stronger naval power, Great Britain, before going on to deal with Japan. They continued to put the Atlantic ahead of the Pacific even when their possible enemies had changed to Germany and Japan, though Germany had no navy worth speaking of. The German danger was swelled out by alarms that the Germans intended to invade South America and from there march on Washington – a fantasy that Hitler never harboured. On a more practical basis the Americans judged that the maintenance of Great Britain as an independent power was essential to their own security in both the Atlantic and the Pacific. The British had to put the European war first and the Americans automatically followed their lead.

This is not to say that Roosevelt deliberately planned to involve the United States in war anywhere. The supreme improviser in the most improvised of all wars, Roosevelt did not decide on the future until it became the present. During his campaign for re-election as President in the autumn of 1940, he said, 'Your boys are not going to be sent into any foreign wars.' At the time he meant it, even though he added in private, 'If we are attacked we shall have no choice.' Even in the autumn of 1941 he seems to have assumed that German hegemony would ultimately be reduced somehow so long as American aid kept Great Britain going. With his mind turned towards Europe Roosevelt certainly wanted an agreement with Japan. But the agreement he contemplated involved Japanese withdrawal from all China except Manchuria and the restoration of the 'Open Door'. The means he used for promoting agreement were those of the Japanese in reverse. With each

Japanese advance in the Far East Roosevelt tightened financial and economic pressure in the conviction that they would back down.

Thus there was deadlock in the Far East, matching the corresponding deadlock in the European sphere. In November Hitler took a curious diplomatic initiative, or perhaps Ribbentrop took it and Hitler acquiesced. The Germans proposed that Soviet Russia should make a fourth in the Anti-Comintern Pact. The partners would divide the world: Europe for Germany, the Mediterranean for Italy, the Far East for Japan, and Persia and India for Soviet Russia. This indeed would be a Continental League on a grand scale. Stalin appeared to be interested. Molotov came to Berlin, the first of his many diplomatic excursions. He proved to have only one word in negotiations: No. Far from being dazzled by the glories of the Orient, he asked

Molotov in Berlin: he said, 'No'

embarrassing questions about German troops in Finland and Romania. He demanded Soviet control of the Straits. When a British air raid drove the negotiators into the shelter, he remarked: 'If Britain is already defeated, why are we here?' Though Soviet Russia continued to supply Germany with essential raw materials, it was clear that she would not become a German satellite. Stalin intended to remain neutral in the 'imperialist' war and maybe to intervene when the combatants were exhausted. Hitler returned with relief to his plans for destroying Soviet Russia once and for all.

During these negotiations and manœuvres, the war was kindled into a surprising flame by the least of the Great Powers whom everyone else had forgotten. Mussolini had played a sorry role during the few days of his war against France. He resented his exclusion from the limelight and resolved to strike out on his own. He already had two wars on his hands. In Abyssinia an Italian army of 200,000 men, cut off from their homeland, was contending against smaller British forces. In North Africa another 215,000 Italians, ill equipped for desert warfare or indeed for anything else, gingerly crossed the Egyptian frontier in September 1940 and laboriously prepared for a further advance. Not content with this, Mussolini launched an attack from Albania into Greece on 28 October. He said to Ciano, 'Hitler always faces me with a *fait accompli.* This time I am going to pay him back in his own coin.'

Hitler was not in fact surprised or perturbed though he later made out that he had been. At the time he welcomed the Italian attack on Greece as a means of securing his Balkan Front. Mussolini was free to go ahead with an independent action for the last time. He made a poor use of his opportunity. The Greeks were more adapted than the Italians to mountain warfare and soon drove them back into Albania. More and worse trouble came to Mussolini from the British.

The British had always stationed a fleet in the Mediterranean from the time of Nelson on.

Now they maintained an army also in Egypt for the protection of the Suez Canal. With no prospect of intervention on the Continent, there seemed no other place for their forces to go to. When France fell out of the war there were shortlived doubts whether the British could hold the Mediterranean and Egypt by themselves. On 16 June 1940 Sir Dudley Pound, the First Sea Lord, suggested to Admiral Sir Andrew Cunningham, the naval Commander-in-Chief in the Mediterranean, that he should block the Suez Canal and withdraw the bulk of his fleet to Gibraltar and the rest to Aden. Cunningham disliked this as a further blow to British prestige. Pound did not insist, and the question of remaining in the eastern Mediterranean was never formally discussed by either the Chiefs of Staff or the War Cabinet.

The three British commanders in Egypt reported that they could hold it only if they were reinforced. On 16 August, at the height of the Battle of Britain, a third of the existing tank strength was ordered to Egypt. From this moment Great Britain was committed to war in the Mediterranean on an ever-increasing scale, with all that this implied in its demands on material and shipping resources. Implicitly there was also a negative decision that had great significance for the future. Though Australia and New Zealand had been told that, in case of a Japanese attack, Great Britain would cut her losses in the Mediterranean and 'sacrifice every interest, except only the defence and feeding of this island' for their defence, the British government in fact neglected the Far East and gambled that Japan would remain neutral.

More elaborate arguments for remaining in Egypt were often propounded. The Mediterranean and Suez Canal were presented as the lifeline of the empire, which no doubt they had been in peacetime. But when Italy entered the war, the Mediterranean was closed to British shipping and so remained until 1943. Far more British shipping was consumed in sending supplies to Egypt round the Cape and then in reopening the Mediterranean than was gained by reopening it, and the British came near to losing the Battle of the Atlantic largely because of their Mediterranean obsession. The British also claimed to be in Egypt in order to bar Hitler's march to the oilfields of Iraq and Persia. Hitler never harboured this project, though maybe he ought to have done. If he had any intention of marching on the oilfields, it was across the Caucasus after defeating Soviet Russia, and in that case the British forces would have had to withdraw from Egypt in order to resist the German advance.

The British were encouraged to hang on in the Mediterranean for more positive reasons. Churchill hoped to win new allies: the French at one end of the Mediterranean, Turkey at the other. The first of these hopes led to an abortive British attack on Dakar, West Africa, in September 1940, an attack that only increased French hostility and discredited de Gaulle who had largely prompted it. Hopes in regard to Turkey led to nothing at all except incessant demands for military supplies which the British were unable to provide. More ambitiously the British looked forward to the time when they would break into the continent of Europe from the south – the soft underbelly as Churchill mistakenly called it later. New Gallipolis lay temptingly on the horizon. These were rationalizations. The British were in the Mediterranean because they were there. They fought there because there was nowhere else for them to fight. This simple fact determined the main weight of British, and later of American, strategy until the last year of the Second World War.

The British position in Egypt and more generally in the Middle East was a curious legacy of imperialism. Ostensibly Egypt and Iraq were independent kingdoms, and even in Palestine the British mandate theoretically existed in order to promote there a national home for the Jews, not for the benefit of the British Empire. The two Middle Eastern kingdoms soon learned the limits of independence when they tried to operate it. In 1941 British armed forces crushed an Iraqi attempt to take over the RAF bases.

In 1942, when the King of Egypt attempted to nominate a favourite of his own as Prime Minister, his palace was surrounded by British tanks, and the British Ambassador presented him with a deed of abdication which he was ordered to sign at once unless he appointed a prime minister whom the British preferred. In Palestine the British refused to allow any Jewish immigration so as not to offend the Arabs. Nevertheless it gave the British a moral advantage, at any rate in their own eyes, that they were on the spot and could deal with any movement to throw them out as a rebellion, whereas the Germans had to commit an act of aggression when they laid hands on any strategic area such as Norway or Belgium. All the same it was a little odd that Egypt, the main British base in the Middle East throughout the war, remained theoretically neutral until 1945.

In the summer of 1940 it seemed doubtful whether the British could remain in Egypt or the Middle East despite the reinforcements that were coming in. The Italian armies in Africa outnumbered the British by five to one. The Italian navy and air force were also markedly superior on paper. Cunningham, the British naval Commander-in-Chief, was aggressively minded. He repeatedly led his fleet into dangerous waters. The Italians, obsessed with their doctrine of 'a fleet in being', always made off. Cunningham therefore followed them home. On 11 November aircraft from the carrier *Illustrious* attacked the Italian fleet in its harbour at Taranto. Three battleships were sunk. Half the Italian battlefleet was out of action; the rest withdrew to Naples on the west coast of Italy. The British thus recovered command of the eastern Mediterranean. They did not reflect that they had won it by air power and that this might soon turn against them.

Wavell, Commander-in-Chief of the army in Egypt, was a more cautious character. He was the senior serving commander and had a reputation of the highest distinction. His admirers saw in him a second Cromwell, and certainly, if any soldier had challenged Churchill in the

British troops take control of Iraq

Second World War, it would have been Wavell. However, though he had thoughts of rebellion, he kept them to his private diary. His old zest was gone. He was weighed down by his immense responsibilities which extended over the entire Middle East as well as Egypt itself. He was exasperated by the repeated 'proddings' that came from Churchill. In July 1940 he was summoned home, and Churchill, faced with his taciturnity, decided that he lacked 'the fighting spirit'. There was no obvious substitute and he returned disgruntled to Egypt.

Wavell was surprised into success. In his methodical way he intended first to deal with the Italians in Abyssinia. As a preliminary he projected a punch against the Italian army on the frontiers of Egypt so as to secure his rear. This 'raid in force', as Wavell called it, succeeded beyond all expectations. On 7 December General O'Connor, with a total force of 35,000 men and 275 tanks, passed through a gap in the Italian

lines and took the Italians in the rear. The Italians had no training in mobile warfare and collapsed in face of tanks and aircraft as the French had done in the previous May. O'Connor swept on. He took Tobruk by assault on 22 January 1941. On 9 February he reached El Agheila. The whole of Cyrenaica was in British hands. With a strength of never more than two divisions, they had destroyed ten Italian divisions and taken 130,000 prisoners; 438 British soldiers were killed, 353 of them Australians. The victory was as overwhelming on a smaller scale as that of the Germans in France had been.

Yet this moment of victory was also the moment when Great Britain ceased to be an independent power capable of waging a great war from her own resources. By the beginning of 1941 British financial resources were almost exhausted. Left to themselves the British would have had to concentrate on their export trade and would have remained only nominally in the

General O'Connor, the conqueror of Libya

war. This did not suit President Roosevelt, who wished Great Britain to act as America's sword until such time as she herself entered the war.

In March 1941 Roosevelt instituted lend-lease, perhaps the most dramatic political stroke of the war. The United States became 'the arsenal of democracy' and did not ask for payment. There was a heavy price to be paid all the same. The American authorities stripped Great Britain of her gold reserves and her overseas investments. They restricted her exports, and American businessmen moved into markets that had

hitherto been British. The British economy was geared solely to war. Keynes said truly, 'We threw good housekeeping to the winds. But we saved ourselves and helped to save the world.' Thanks to lend-lease Great Britain kept up a misleading appearance as a Great Power until almost the end of the war.

Victory in North Africa obscured the decisive change in Great Britain's position. The victory itself did not last long. O'Connor's supplies were running low. But the Italian ports in Cyrenaica were undamaged and at his service, and he was

Italians surrender and become prisoners of war

eager to complete the conquest of Italian North Africa by pressing on to Tripoli. There was nothing to stop him. However, he was abruptly ordered to halt and to return the bulk of his forces to Egypt. Hitler had decided to intervene in Greece. In this paradoxical way the Italian defeats in Greece saved them from immediate defeat in North Africa.

Great Britain had given a guarantee to Greece before the war. As long as Italy alone was involved, the Greeks did not call on this guarantee for fear of provoking Germany. The British

sent a few aircraft to Greece and took over Crete, though, with their faith in sea power, they did little to fortify it. Mussolini was at first too proud to ask for German assistance. Hitler, with his mind set on the invasion of Russia, regarded the Mediterranean with indifference. He soon had second thoughts. Anxious as ever about a second front, he feared that the British might break into the Balkans while German forces were engaged in Russia. Reluctantly he decided to get Mussolini out of his mess. In theory the Duce continued to be treated as Hitler's only equal. In practice Italy became a helplessly dependent satellite. Like France before her, she fell out of the Great Power League. Only Great Britain ostensibly maintained the reputation of the European Great Powers who had won the First World War, and even she ultimately found the going almost too much for her.

German aircraft were sent to Sicily, whence they soon shook British control of the central Mediterranean. Rommel, one of Hitler's favourite generals, was sent with a tank division, later expanded into the Afrika Korps, to Tripoli. Rommel was a dashing cavalry commander rather than a general and quite without Guderian's real understanding of tank warfare. But his dash was enough to throw out British calculations. They had judged his speed by their own and expected him to be ready for an offensive in June. Instead he attacked on 30 March. Like O'Connor before him, Rommel had intended only a raid in force. He, too, was surprised into success. The advanced British positions col-

Rommel *opposite* and the Afrika Korps arrive in Tripoli

lapsed. O'Connor himself was taken prisoner. By 11 April the British had lost all their gains in Cyrenaica with the exception of Tobruk which remained as an isolated garrison to their subsequent embarrassment.

Hitler's original intention in Greece had been simply to occupy Salonika, which he would then hand over to Bulgaria. In December 1940 he even attempted to win over Greece by offering to mediate between her and Italy. When this attempt failed he decided that all Greece would

have to be occupied. Hitler counted on assistance from Bulgaria and on the benevolent neutrality of Yugoslavia. This he secured on 25 March though in exchange for a promise not to use the Yugoslav railways. Two days later there was a patriotic *coup d'état* in Yugoslavia which overthrew the Prince Regent and placed the young King Peter on the throne. The German armies, poised to invade Greece, were turned against Yugoslavia and destroyed her armies within a week – the speediest victory even in this fast-moving war. Yugoslavia was dismembered. Macedonia went to Bulgaria; a Fascist Croatia was installed under Italian protection, and a rump Serbia under German. Germany also carried off Slovenia and the railway to Trieste. Moreover the Germans were now free to use the Yugoslav railways. Yugoslavia's heroic gesture actually made the German victory in Greece easier.

The British had been debating since January whether to aid Greece if Germany intervened. Military arguments were all against it. The British had few forces to send and in particular very few aircraft. But political arguments took over. It would be humiliating for Great Britain not to aid a country she had guaranteed. British intervention would be the prelude to a Balkan coalition of Greece, Yugoslavia and Turkey. As Smuts, the South African Prime Minister, who happened to be in Cairo, put it: 'Which course would put heart into the freedom-loving nations?'

There was a confusion of counsels. Churchill was at first all for intervention and then became reluctant to abandon the prizes of victory in North Africa. Eden, who had just moved from the War Office to the Foreign Office, and Sir John Dill, the CIGS, came out to Egypt and surveyed the situation. Eden went to Ankara, and Dill to Belgrade. In both capitals they painted a glowing picture of British intentions. Thus when cautious warnings came from Churchill and the War Cabinet, Eden and Dill resolved to be for once more bellicose than their chief. The military plans were also at sixes and sevens. The British

Left German troops in Sarajevo, starting place of the First World War

Left, below British troops in Greece

wanted merely to hold a bridgehead in southern Greece. The Greeks were reluctant to withdraw from Albania where they had been victorious. As a result the Germans broke through the Monastir gap between the Greek army in Albania and that at Salonika and advanced almost without meeting resistance.

By the time British forces landed in Greece, Yugoslavia had collapsed and the Greek armies were on the point of defeat. The British troops never made serious contact with the enemy. Some of them were already being evacuated while others were still arriving. The British sent 62,000 men to Greece; 50,000 were taken off, a figure that included some 10,000 Greeks along with the King and his government. All the heavy equipment was again lost. It was a lesser Dunkirk and all to no purpose. Heart was not put into the freedom-loving nations. Though Churchill had in fact expressed doubts about the expedition, the blame for failure fell on him. It was the old story of ambitious projects pursued with inadequate means.

There was one piece of cheering news elsewhere. The Italian forces in Abyssinia were decisively defeated. On 5 May the Emperor Haile Selassie returned to his capital – the first victim of Axis aggression and the first to be restored. He inherited from the Italians modern schools, hospitals and roads that he himself had been unable to provide. On 19 May the last Italian troops surrendered. A considerable British force was freed for action in other fields. Roosevelt declared the Red Sea no longer a war zone, and American merchant shipping could thus bring supplies all the way to Suez.

There was a more whimsical interruption. On 10 May Rudolf Hess, Hitler's deputy as Führer,

First out, first back: Haile Selassie returns to Addis Ababa

dropped from the skies on to a Scotch farm. He had come as an emissary of peace, confident that anti-Churchill forces led by the Duke of Hamilton would accept his olive branch eagerly. The Duke, now a serving officer in the RAF, did not respond. Churchill at first refused to believe the story of Hess's arrival. Then he said, 'Well, even if he is Hess, I am going to watch the Marx brothers' and departed to his private cinema. The episode was of no importance. Hess had long ceased to count in Germany or to be involved in Hitler's counsels. He had no inkling of Hitler's coming attack on Soviet Russia and merely repeated the old argument, often used by Hitler himself, that Great Britain and Germany had no cause for quarrel. He was ignored and treated as a prisoner of war. Afterwards he was condemned most unjustly as a war criminal. His real crime was to have proposed peace between Great Britain and Germany, an act, as Churchill called it, of 'lunatic benevolence'. Despite the talk of a negotiated peace, this was the only practical initiative taken by either side. It was a trivial one.

The arrival of Hess in Scotland was no more than a nine days' wonder. The British had more serious things to worry about. It seemed that the entire Middle East was on the point of being lost. On 2 May Iraqi troops attacked the British air bases in Baghdad and elsewhere. On 11 May Darlan, who was now the effective head of the Vichy government under Pétain, agreed that German aircraft should be allowed to use air bases in Syria on their way to Iraq and that Rommel should be supplied through Bizerta in Tunisia. A few days later the first German aircraft flew in. Syria, under its Vichy governor, threatened to become a German outpost.

Crete was an even more pressing danger. Allied forces there had been swelled to over 40,000 by the arrival of British and Greek troops from Greece. The Royal Navy dominated the eastern Mediterranean if sea power alone were considered. But the British were lamentably weak in the air. There were only seven fighter aircraft in Crete, and these were withdrawn on 20 May, the first day of the German attack. The few British fighters had to cover 300 miles each way from their bases in Egypt. It was as though Sir Hugh Dowding had had to conduct the Battle of Britain from across the Scottish border. The only ports of any size were on the north of the island and thus directly exposed to German attack from the air. Defences had been neglected during the six months of British occupation. Sir Bernard Freyberg, who took over at the beginning of May, was the seventh commander during these six months.

Freyberg had often shown himself a daring fighter and was now confident. On 5 May he telegraphed to Churchill: 'Cannot understand nervousness; am not in the least anxious about airborne attack.' It seemed inconceivable that the Germans could take Crete without command of the sea. But this is what they did; 715 German aircraft won the battle for Crete. The attack began on 20 May with a massive drop of paratroops. Some of them managed to seize a corner of the Maleme airfield, and the next day the Germans flew in troop carriers and gliders when the airfield was still under fire. The British reacted late and ineffectively. Two seaborne German convoys were intercepted by British destroyers. One suffered heavy loss; the other turned back unscathed. No seaborne supplies reached the Germans during the fighting. But the Germans were irresistible once their control of Maleme was secure.

Churchill might order: 'Victory in Crete essential at this turning point of the war. Keep hurling in all you can.' The order was impossible to execute. The German air force dominated the sea and made it unusable by the Royal Navy during daylight. Losses mounted. On 26 May Freyberg decided that the battle was lost. Attempts were made to evacuate the British troops from tiny ports on the south coast. Cunningham persisted for a further night. He signalled to the fleet: 'We cannot let the Army down'; and he answered the protest of his staff: 'It takes the Navy three years to build a ship. It would take three hundred to rebuild a tradition.'

German paratroops descend on Crete   *Overleaf* **The tide of German conquest, 1938–41**

He also said, 'Three squadrons of fighters would have been enough to save Crete.' But there were no fighters available, thanks to the British obsession with bombers for the strategic bombing of Germany.

Crete was lost; 18,000 British troops were evacuated, 13,000 remained behind. They and all the Greek troops in Crete became prisoners of war. The Royal Navy lost 3 cruisers and 6 destroyers. Two battleships, the only aircraft carrier, 2 cruisers and 2 destroyers were damaged beyond local repair. The British lost control of the Aegean which provided the Germans with a secure route from Salonika to Constantsa and the Black Sea for the next three years. The Germans paid a price also. True, they had conquered Yugoslavia, Greece and Crete with only 5000 killed. But the paratroops suffered heavily, and 220 aircraft had been lost. Hitler, in Liddell Hart's phrase, had sprained his

wrist. He abandoned any idea of an airborne attack on the Suez Canal or on Malta. The airborne conquest of Crete was the only one of its kind.

Nor did Hitler send more aid to Iraq and probably had never intended to do so. The British recovered control of Iraq early in June and overthrew the so-called rebel government. By then all German aircraft had withdrawn from Syria, and the Vichy government had cancelled the permission for supplies to go to Rommel through Bizerta. However, de Gaulle persuaded the British government that the French forces in Syria would respond to the call of Free France. He was wrong. Wavell, hard pressed everywhere, had to divert a considerable British force to Syria. Fighting went on until the end of June. Something like a thousand men were killed on each side. When the French finally surrendered, hardly any agreed to join de Gaulle. A Free

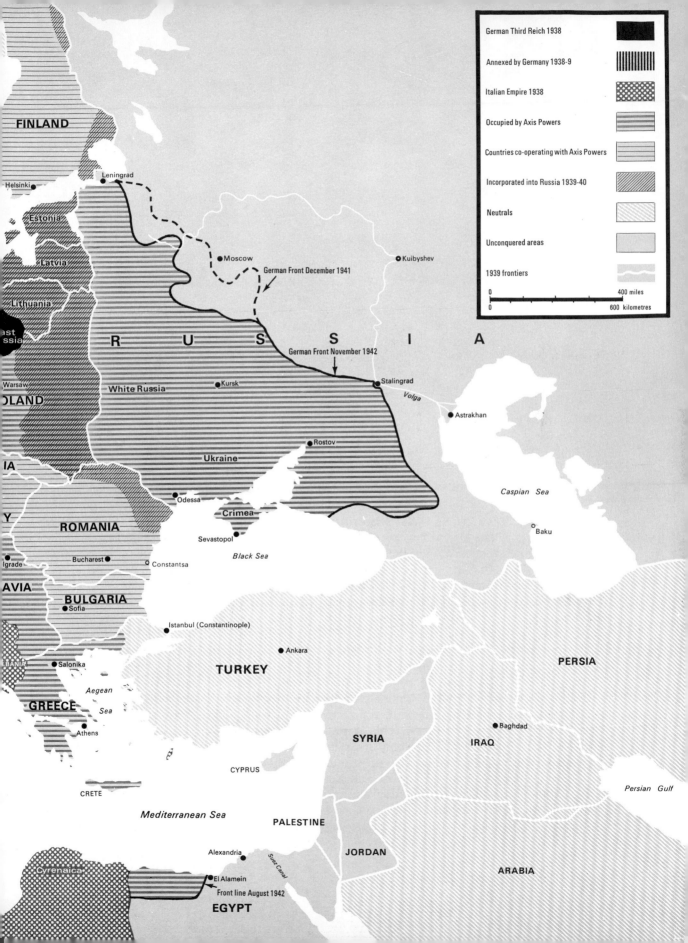

FINLAND

Helsinki

Leningrad

Estonia

Latvia

ast
ssia

Lithuania

Moscow ○Kuibyshev

German Front December 1941

R   U   S   S   I   A

Warsaw

OLAND

German Front November 1942

White Russia

Kursk

Stalingrad

Volga

Astrakhan

Ukraine

Rostov

IA

Odessa

Caspian   Sea

Crimea

Y

ROMANIA

Sevastopol

○Baku

Igrade

Bucharest ●

○ Constantsa

Black Sea

AVIA

BULGARIA

Sofia

Istanbul (Constantinople)

PERSIA

BANIA

Salonika

Ankara

Aegean

TURKEY

GREECE

Sea

Athens

SYRIA

Baghdad

IRAQ

CYPRUS

Persian   Gulf

CRETE

Mediterranean Sea

PALESTINE

Cyrenaica

Alexandria

JORDAN

Suez Canal

ARABIA

El Alamein

Front line August 1942

EGYPT

Combat between friends: French dead in Syria

French regime was set up in Syria. The British, anxious to conciliate the Arabs, insisted on a promise of independence after the war. This strengthened de Gaulle's conviction that the British planned to carry off the French Empire as their spoils of war, and Churchill was soon complaining that his cross was the Cross of Lorraine – de Gaulle's symbol.

Wavell realized that his position was in danger after this run of failure. To impress Churchill and much against his own conviction, he agreed to launch an offensive against Rommel. Battle Axe, as it was grandiosely called, began on 15 June. It was designed to relieve Tobruk and drive Rommel out of Cyrenaica. Rommel sprang a surprise which should have been no surprise at all. The German 88-mm gun, though called a flak (anti-aircraft) gun, had in fact a dual purpose and was as effective against tanks as against aircraft. The British, misled by its name, had no idea of this and imagined that Rommel's

use of the gun was a stroke of genius. The British lost 91 tanks against a German loss of 12, and British commanders clung to the quite unfounded notion that German tanks were better than British. Battle Axe was broken off after three days. This was a portent. Thanks to the anti-tank guns, defence had recovered the upper hand. Future battles would see hard fighting, not a breakthrough after a few hours.

The failure of Battle Axe brought the end for Wavell. Churchill had lost all faith in him. On 21 June he was dispatched to India as Commander-in-Chief, a remote command or so it was supposed. General Sir Claude Auchinleck, the previous Commander-in-Chief in India, took Wavell's place in the Middle East. But the Middle East no longer occupied the centre of the stage. On 22 June, the day after Auchinleck's appointment, the Germans invaded Soviet Russia. War for world power had begun in earnest.

The coming of
world war
June – December 1941

5

The German invasion of Soviet Russia was the greatest event of the Second World War – by far the greatest in scale and also greatest in its consequences. Most consequences of the war were conservative, putting things back where they were before. European frontiers were little changed except where Russia was concerned, and the same was true of most European regimes with the same exception. In a wider perspective the war merely speeded up what was already happening. The United States was already a World Power. The British Empire was already in decline. It was already becoming clear, as the rulers of Japan themselves appreciated, that China would outlast Japan and almost equally clear, as some American observers recognized, that the Communists would ultimately become the champions of Chinese independence. But Russia was, in Churchill's words, an enigma wrapped in a mystery. Was the Communist system approaching collapse? Was Soviet Russia a Great Power at all? The Great Patriotic War gave the answer. Hitler had always wanted to turn the world upside down. He succeeded, though not to his own advantage. Hitler died in the bunker. But thanks to Hitler, Soviet Russia was revealed as a World Power, and the consequences are with us to the present day.

The decision to invade Russia was the only one made by Hitler entirely on his own initiative. Previously he had reacted to events and taken advantage of them. The Czech crisis and the Polish crisis were shaped by others as well as by Hitler; Chamberlain and Daladier, Beneš and Joseph Beck all played a part. The German in-vasions of Norway and France were responses to Anglo-French belligerence, just as the invasions of Yugoslavia and Greece were responses to British strategy in the Mediterranean. Not so the invasion of Russia. For precisely twelve months from the French armistice Hitler brooded over the problem of what to do next. From whatever point of view he looked at it – ideological, geo-political, strategical – he always came up with the same answer: invasion of Russia. On 22 June 1941 he put the answer into practice.

It is possible to interpret Hitler's invasion of Russia as the working out of ideas that he had held from the beginning of his political career. It is equally possible to interpret it as the conse-quence of the immediate situation when he was at war with Great Britain and did not know how to defeat her quickly. Hitler himself gave both interpretations, often almost in the same breath. This is the nearest we can come to answering the question whether Hitler followed a long-term plan or improvised successes as occasion offered. It seems that he did both at once.

Certainly the invasion of Russia can be pre-sented, and was presented by Hitler, as the logical consequence of doctrines he had enunci-ated for twenty years or so. He had begun his political career as an anti-Bolshevik, dedicated to the destruction of Soviet Communism. Belief that Jews led and inspired Communism intensified his zeal for this crusade. He had saved Germany from Communism or so he claimed; now he would save the world. Many others had been attracted by this idea. Hitler was the only one who acted on it.

Lebensraum (living space) was a special doctrine of Hitler's own that he learned from geopoliticians in Munich shortly after the First World War. Germany must control the Heartland if she were to become a World Power, and only the conquest of Russia could achieve this. *Lebensraum* meant more than acquisition of territory, though here Hitler talked with contradictory voices. Sometimes he proposed to exterminate the inhabitants of Russia and replace them by a non-existent surplus of Germans. Sometimes he spoke, in more practical terms, of controlling Russia's resources. This accorded well with the German economic aim of autarky, which required Russia's raw materials to keep going and was already receiving them from the existing Russian population. Soviet Russia was lavishly supplying Germany with raw materials, either from her own resources or by promoting their transit from the Far East. The invasion, far from alleviating Germany's shortages, created them: no more oil from the Caucasus, no more tin or rubber from the Far East.

At this point Hitler switched from long-term arguments to immediate ones. Certainly Russia was supplying German needs now. But how long would this last? Sometimes Hitler said that Germany was secure for Stalin's lifetime. More often he asserted that Stalin was preparing to stab Germany in the back as soon as she was more deeply involved against Great Britain. Russia was making new demands on Finland and so would soon threaten Germany's supply of iron ore from Sweden. In August 1940 Russia had recovered Bessarabia and acquired northern Bukovina from Romania. Soon she could enter Romania and cut off the supply of Romanian oil as well as her own. Again, Russia had encouraged the Yugoslav resistance to Germany and had prevented Turkey from entering the war on the German side. Clearly Russia was on the march to the Balkans and the Straits. Hitler saw a more direct threat. The Russians were increasing their armed forces. Hitler soon convinced himself, and his generals also, that the invasion of Russia was a preventive war. Napoleon had used the same argument more than a century before.

Great Britain also came into the picture. The British were virtually defeated or at any rate incapable of winning. Yet they went on with the war. The only possible explanation Hitler saw, though in fact an erroneous one, was that the British were counting on Russian assistance. Once Russia was defeated, the British would give up and agree to a negotiated peace. Here again Hitler used a contradictory argument. An invasion of Russia, he said, was essential before Great Britain collapsed. Otherwise the German people would not follow him into a new great war.

Here was the most practical motive for Hitler's decision. Whatever the long-term arguments for invading Russia, it was in practice the only thing for him to do. Germany had virtually no navy. Her air force had proved incapable of battering the British into surrender. But she had a large army, and Russia was the only place where it could be used on a large scale. After talking fearsomely of Russia's strength, Hitler finally justified the invasion by announcing her weakness. The Germans had defeated the French army, reputedly the strongest in Europe, within six weeks. The conquest of Russia would be far easier. Russia, he insisted, did not possess even the strength she had possessed in the First World War. The economic system was in chaos. The Communist dictatorship was hated. Stalin had killed off most of the Russian generals and officers during the great purge.

We know the outcome and therefore regard Hitler's great decision as a catastrophic blunder. This was not how it looked beforehand. Practically all qualified judges thought that fighting would be over within a few weeks. No German general expressed doubts as some had done before the invasion of France. British Intelligence gave the Russians ten days. Cripps, the British Ambassador in Moscow, said a month. Dill, the CIGS, thought the Russians might last six weeks. In America Roosevelt's military advisers told him, 'Germany will be fully occupied in beating Russia for a minimum of one month and a possible maximum of three.' The directors of American strategy·assumed that, with Russia eliminated, Great Britain would be in imminent peril by the autumn and that the United States would have to put 300 divisions into the field if Germany were to be defeated – in the event they got by with 100.

There is even more powerful evidence. The Russians themselves were in desperate anxiety. Their preparations, though great, were entirely defensive. They were also tardy. Stalin assumed that a German attack would come only when Great Britain had been defeated. Hence he dismissed as provocations the well-founded warnings he received from the British and American governments. He accepted almost any humiliation in order to postpone a German invasion. Soviet supplies to Germany were increased without any adequate recompense. Soviet recognition was withdrawn from the governments whose countries Germany had overrun, even though, as with Yugoslavia, Russia had encouraged their resistance. When the German army actually invaded Russia, Stalin at first believed that all was lost. He said after the fall of Kiev, 'Everything that Lenin worked for has been destroyed for ever.'

In short, Hitler decided to invade Soviet Russia not because she was dangerous but because her defeat would be inordinately easy. It is true that Hitler always gambled. This time he thought he was betting on a certainty. The invasion was meant to be the last of his small wars, not the first of his great ones. The German armies that invaded Russia were little stronger than those that had invaded France. Material reserves were supplied only for one month's 'major combat expenditure', and on Hitler's order German munitions production was cut down by 40 per cent in the autumn of 1941 on the ground that no more would be needed.

Nor did Hitler seek for allies as he might have done for any really great enterprise. Romania was brought in, more as a necessary starting point for German forces than for her own

The Spanish Blue Division invades Russia

strength. Hungary joined in also, so as not to lose the competition with Romania for Transylvania. But Hitler did not reveal his plans to Mussolini and was irritated when the latter insisted on sending Italian troops to the Eastern Front. There was little attempt on Hitler's part to sound the note of an anti-Communist crusade, and the assistance he received from Fascist sympathizers, including the Spanish Blue Division, was trivial.

Hitler's dealings with Japan were the most extraordinary of all. His alliance with her had been promoted as an instrument against Russia.

But when Matsuoka, the Japanese Foreign Minister, came to Berlin in April 1941, he was told nothing of German plans and instead was urged to turn Japanese forces south against the British at Singapore. Hitler was determined not to share the spoils of Russia with Japan. Instead he wanted Japan to embarrass the British and Americans in the Far East and thus ensure Germany's position in western Europe during her invasion of Russia. Matsuoka accepted Hitler's advice. On his return journey through Moscow he signed a neutrality pact with Stalin – a pact that both parties observed until the last week of the war. Back in Tokyo Matsuoka urged an early attack on Singapore. His cabinet colleagues, still hoping for an agreement with the United States, hesitated and got rid of him when the German invasion of Russia seemed to belie his calculations. But less formally they moved in the same direction. Japan ceased to be even a remote threat to Russia, and this was in part Hitler's own doing.

German preparations for invasion were made in slapdash fashion, on the assumption that victory would be too easy to require long-term plans. The General Staff had little information about Russian forces or conditions. Russia was treated as though it were France, a country with good roads and plentiful supplies, including oil. The German tanks were tracked. Their supply vehicles were not. Hence the armoured divisions, and still more the rest of the German armies, depended on good roads that did not in fact exist. The German General Staff recognized that food would present a problem. An economic directive stated, 'There is no doubt that millions of people will be starved to death if we take from the country the things we need.' This did not trouble the German generals.

The commanders-in-chief were the same as in the French campaign; the strategic plans, however, were much less precise. The General Staff meticulously delivered three army groups to the Soviet frontiers. Leeb's group in the north pointed along the Baltic coast to Leningrad with its industries. Bock, with the strongest army

German armaments move up to the Soviet frontier

group, pointed directly to Moscow in the centre. Rundstedt's army group in the south pointed to the Ukraine and ultimately, it was hoped, to the Caucasus. No clear decision was made as to which should be the main target. Hitler held that the industrial regions and sources of raw materials should be conquered first and that Moscow be then encircled as well as directly assaulted. The generals hankered after an immediate march on Moscow, the political capital and centre of communications.

The difference seemed to be of little importance. The 'battles of the frontiers', it was supposed, would last some four weeks; the rest would be a matter of mopping up the scattered remnants of the Russian armies. In fact the German General Staff, usually so devoted to planning ahead, this time followed Napoleon's maxim – a favourite also of Lenin's: 'On s'engage et puis on voit' (get in and see what happens). Ill consequences followed from the first. In the French campaign every advance made by the

ahead on their own or merely clear the way for the main armies.

The Germans invaded Russia only with equality of forces, counting on their superior skill and the prestige of victory. Together with their allies they had 200 divisions; the Russians had 209, thinly spread along the frontiers. The Germans had 3350 tanks, only 600 more than they had had in the French campaign. The Russians had some 25,000, most of obsolescent design, though the T-34, of which there were comparatively few at the time of the German invasion, was the best tank of the war. The Germans had 3000 aircraft, the Russians twice

Soviet T-34 tanks in action

two armies of Bock and Rundstedt brought them closer together. In Russia the advance of the three army groups pulled them further apart, and the more the Germans advanced, the wider became the gaps on their front. As a final confusion, the Germans failed to resolve the dispute that had already raised its head in France: whether the armoured divisions should forge

as many, again antiquated. One enemy the German General Staff altogether ignored: space. In France the German armies initially advanced some 250 miles and then rested for a fortnight before pursuing the shattered French another 200 miles. In Russia the distances were five times as great, and there were few intermissions. In France the Germans had ten aircraft for each kilometre of front; in Russia they had one. As Keitel confessed after the war, 'Hitler talked as if the Russian campaign were a sure thing. . . . But now that I look back, I am sure it was just a desperate gamble.'

The aim of the Russian campaign was conquest, not merely victory. European Russia was to become a German colony. Hitler insisted that the Soviet political structure would collapse at the first blows. What was to take its place? The question was never resolved. Rosenberg, supposedly the Nazi expert on Russian affairs, wanted to win over the inhabitants, dissolution of the Communist party, liberation of the national minorities, and return of the collective farmlands to the peasants. In the former Baltic states this programme was applied with considerable success. Elsewhere Hitler would have none of it. For him terror and extermination were the right answer. The SS were to take over the conquered territories. All political commissars and Communist leaders were to be executed without trial, an order that the generals accepted after a feeble protest. They were also told that, as Soviet Russia was not a party to the Geneva convention, there was no need to observe the laws of war. This, too, the generals accepted. For them, as for Hitler, the Slavs were subhuman, mere beasts. Chivalry was forgotten, and German soldiers, acting on the orders of their superiors, murdered two million Russian prisoners of war and over ten million Russian civilians in the course of the war. Attila had come again.

It came to be believed later that Barbarossa, the invasion of Russia, was originally fixed for 15 May and was then delayed by the unexpected revolution in Yugoslavia, thus losing a vital month. This was a legend invented by the German generals to excuse their defeat by the Russians. It has no foundation in fact. Only 15 out of the 150 German divisions allotted to the first assault were diverted to the Balkans, hardly a serious loss. The German mobilization plans for the Eastern Front were not complete by 15 May for an entirely different reason: shortage of equipment, particularly of motor vehicles.

Hitler was trying to launch what became an all-out war on the basis of a peacetime economy. Even with the month's delay, 92 of the German divisions, *i.e.* 40 per cent, had to be supplied, wholly or in part, with French material. The delay may even have been fortunate. In mid-May the Russian soil was still heavy after the spring thaw. By mid-June it had dried out.

Barbarossa began on 22 June 1941, thus echoing Napoleon's invasion of Russia almost to the day. The attack was launched without warning. The German declaration of war was delivered when fighting had already begun. Molotov expostulated, 'What have we done to deserve this?' Everywhere the Russians were taken by surprise. Fifteen hundred of their aircraft were destroyed on the ground. The German armies rolled forward even faster than they had done in France. But the results were not the same. With 'subhuman' obstinacy the Russian soldiers refused to admit that they were beaten. When hopelessly surrounded, they continued to fight until their supplies were exhausted. Considerable Russian forces, though bypassed by the German tanks, fell back through gaps in the German lines and resumed the battle. Often they attempted desperate counter-offensives. At the end of June heavy rain found all the German wheeled vehicles bogged down for two days. Halder, safe at headquarters, remarked complacently, 'Now, for once, our troops are compelled to fight according to their combat manuals. In Poland and in the west they could take liberties, but here they cannot get away with it.' A frontline officer passed a different verdict: 'Situations were sometimes so confused that we wondered if we were outflanking the enemy or whether he had outflanked us.'

By the end of July the 'battle of the frontiers' had been duly won. The Soviet armies had been everywhere driven back. Army Group Centre was at Smolensk. The other two groups were approaching Leningrad and Kiev. But the main aim had not been achieved. The Soviet armies, far from dissolving, were growing stronger. In the first days there was indescribable chaos on

Happy days for the German invaders

the Soviet side. No clear orders came from Moscow except to fight ruthlessly. Generals who gave the order to retreat or even allowed a retreat to take place were shot in true Jacobin fashion, and sometimes whole units with them. After ten days Stalin recovered his nerve. On 3 July he addressed the Soviet people for the first time in his life. His hearers were astonished at his Georgian accent. A few weeks later Stalin, already Prime Minister, became Commander-in-Chief. From this moment he ran the war more directly and more personally than any other war

leader. Most of the best Soviet generals had been killed in the great purge. Timoshenko in the centre was undistinguished. Budyenny in the south was distinguished only by his whiskers. But things were beginning to change. Zhukov, probably the greatest general of the Second World War, was already organizing a reserve army in front of Moscow.

The Germans were now faced with the problem implicit in Barbarossa from the first – whether to place the main weight of their attack in the centre or on the wings. Hitherto they had evaded the problem by advancing on all three fronts at once. They could do so no longer. Their strength was running out. Halder recorded: 'At the beginning of the war we reckoned on 200 Russian divisions. We have already counted 360.' When Guderian asked for more tanks, Hitler replied that he had none to spare and added, 'If I had known that the figures for the Russian tanks which you gave in your book were the true ones, I would not – I believe – have started this war.' Guderian wished to race straight to Moscow with his tanks. Kluge, his immediate superior, told him, 'Your operations hang by a thread.' Hitler said, 'My generals do not understand the economic aspects of war.' For almost a month the German generals, the General Staff and Hitler debated what to do next while their armies stood still. No decision was reached until 23 August. It was this period of inaction, not the month before the campaign started, that was the really vital loss of time in the campaign.

Hitler had said, 'The world will hold its breath.' The British reaction was not slow in coming. On the evening of 22 June Churchill spoke on the BBC. He said, 'Can you doubt what our policy will be? We have but one aim and one single, irrevocable purpose. We are resolved to destroy Hitler and every vestige of the Nazi regime. . . . It follows, therefore, that we shall give whatever help we can to Russia and the Russian people.' This was no doubt welcome news to Stalin who had half-expected the British to follow his example of 1939 and compound with Hitler. Churchill's declaration was enthusiastically greeted by the factory workers. The Communists were converted overnight to support of the war, and Communist shop stewards became strike breakers where they had been wreckers. Things were different higher up. Labour leaders outdid the Conservatives in their distrust of Russia. They had no faith in either her sincerity or her strength. In the War Cabinet only Beaverbrook, with his eye on the effect in the factories, was wholeheartedly on Russia's side. Churchill was perhaps single-minded as he claimed. It did not occur to him, and still less to other ministers, that Great Britain and the United States had acquired an ally who would win the war against Germany for them.

In the United States the invasion of Russia was a great setback for those who favoured intervention. Aid to Great Britain was one thing, aid to Communist Russia quite another. Senator Truman, already influential and one day to be Roosevelt's successor as President, declared that the Western Powers should stand aside while the Russians and Germans cut each other's throats. Roosevelt had to wait on American opinion. Though Harry Hopkins, his most intimate adviser, went to Moscow and saw Stalin in July, lend-lease was not extended to Russia until November, when it was becoming clear that she would survive, and throughout the autumn Roosevelt repeatedly emphasized that the United States was not going to be drawn into the war. Yet this was the moment when Great Britain needed American aid more than ever.

The breathing space, which was all the British imagined it was, brought them increased anxieties rather than relief. It was generally expected that German forces would reach the Caucasus by the autumn and then threaten the British oil supplies from Persia and Iraq. Auchinleck broke off his preparations for a new offensive in North Africa and began precautions in the Persian Gulf. Visiting London, he said that he would resign if ordered to start a North African offensive. The British feared for the Far East even more acutely. They anticipated, just as Hitler had done, that Japan, freed from all danger in Manchuria, would turn south and attack Singapore. The British had always assumed that they would have time to send a fleet to Singapore if it were threatened. Now they might not have time and in any case had no ships to spare. They fell back on the defence of Singapore by aircraft, but again there were no aircraft to send. Yet the British were pledged to Australia and New Zealand that they would abandon the Middle East if Singapore were endangered. Hitherto they had kept their fingers crossed and hoped that the Japanese would be deterred by the bluff of an almost undefended fortress. Failing this, American naval aid to Singapore was their last expedient.

This was the purpose for which Churchill held the first of his nine meetings with President Roosevelt. In mid-August the two great men and their advisers conferred on a warship at Placentia Bay, Newfoundland. The British purpose was not achieved. The Americans refused to discuss the Far East, condemned the Middle East as 'a liability from which the British should withdraw', and dismissed the idea that Germany could be defeated by independent bombing without a great engagement on land. The moral, highly distasteful to the British, was that they could look after Singapore themselves if they shook off their strategic obsessions with bombing and the Middle East. What Roosevelt wanted was a declaration of general principles that would influence American opinion. The outcome was the Atlantic Charter – a string of pious generalities that inspired nobody and was hardly mentioned again. The charter was not even a formal document despite its high-sounding name; it was merely an unsigned press release. Yet in a way it made sense. The British, and the Americans also when they joined the war, were not fighting to remodel the world. They were simply fighting so that they and others should be left alone – no mean ideal. At the last moment the two great men remembered Stalin and sent him their greetings, together with a vague promise of future supplies. Clearly it did not cross their minds that Russia might have something to contribute to the winning of the war or to the world after it.

Stalin had sent desperate appeals for British aid from the beginning of the invasion. With a disregard of logistics that often succeeded within Russia, he wanted an immediate second front – a British landing in France or the Balkans. Failing this he suggested that twenty-five to thirty British divisions should be sent to the

First meeting of Churchill and Roosevelt at Placentia Bay

Caucasus. Churchill dismissed the proposal as a 'physical absurdity', which it no doubt was. The British in fact were no more able to aid Russia militarily than they had been to aid Poland. They could only plead that the very fact of their continued belligerence kept some forty German divisions tied down in western Europe – second-class divisions that were of no use to

Hitler. The British also claimed that their bombing of Germany was a direct contribution to the war. This claim, too, looked less impressive when the British broke off their bombing in November because it was doing more damage to themselves than to the Germans.

The British did better over supply. In September Beaverbrook went to Moscow along with Harriman, Roosevelt's roving ambassador. The Americans had little to offer. Beaverbrook, resolutely set on aiding Russia, renounced a large part of the American supplies promised to Great Britain, and in this way most of Stalin's requests were met. Back in England, Beaverbrook ran into opposition from ministers and service chiefs. As Churchill wrote, 'The Service departments felt that it was like flaying off pieces of their skin.' Though Beaverbrook temporarily got his way, delivering the supplies to Russia was a different matter – another logistical problem never fully solved.

Political agreement with Russia also had its difficulties. The British were ready for an agreement to wage war in common and not to make a separate peace. Stalin wanted more. Even at this desperate moment he insisted that the Russia which the British were accepting as an ally was Russia with her 1941 frontiers, including, that is, eastern Poland and the Baltic states. The British were embarrassed, despite their earlier recognition that eastern Poland was not ethnically Polish. Roosevelt took the highminded line that no frontier changes should be discussed until after the war. On a more practical level he thought of the Polish voters in the United States. Yet Russia's title to the Baltic states and eastern Poland was a good deal better than that of the United States to New Mexico. The British and Americans in fact applied to the Russians standards that they did not apply to themselves. Thus early in the period of alliance the later Cold War raised its head.

Whatever the prospect of British and American supplies in the future, Russia faced the crisis of war alone. On 23 August the German generals reached decision on their next offensive, or rather Hitler imposed it on them – the first time that he openly went against their advice and took over direction of the campaign. Army Group Centre was to halt. The two groups on the wings were to destroy the Soviet armies facing them. Then all three groups would unite for the final blow against Moscow. After the war many German generals claimed that this decision was wrong and that with it Hitler lost the war. Zhukov did not agree with them: 'In August the German forces were in no position to march on Moscow and capture the city, as planned by certain German generals. Hence all attempts by German generals and historians to ascribe the blame for the defeat to Hitler are unavailing.'

There was in fact no alternative. All three groups were running out of strength, worn down by Russian resistance and the ever-increasing space in which they had to operate. Army Group Centre, being much the strongest, could reinforce Army Group South if it stood on the defensive itself. Neither of the other two groups could reinforce the Centre or protect its flanks if it pushed forward towards Moscow. At any rate the decision was made. Guderian's tanks were turned round from their advance on Moscow and struck southeastwards against the exposed flanks of the Soviet armies defending Kiev.

Both Leeb in the north and Rundstedt in the south set their armies in motion. By the beginning of September Leeb reached the suburbs of Leningrad. He had been told not to involve his tanks in street fighting or to assault the city. But Leeb wanted a victory of his own. It did not occur to him that his armoured forces might be needed elsewhere. The German tanks went forward. In Leningrad Voroshilov and Zhdanov who were conducting its defence were at sixes and sevens. Stalin suspected them of planning to break away and make a negotiated peace on their own. They were superseded – Voroshilov kicked upstairs to the Defence Committee. Zhukov took over and won the first of his victories. The Germans were halted and never assaulted the city again. By November Leningrad was almost surrounded and was kept going

Soviet lorries bring supplies over frozen Lake Ladoga

only by railway tracks laid across Lake Ladoga when it froze. More than a third of its three million inhabitants died of starvation before the siege was lifted in 1944. But Leningrad survived. On a more immediate level Leeb had no armoured forces to spare for the attack on Moscow.

In the south all went well for the Germans – the greatest cauldron battle in history, as they called it. The Russian armies of over a million men were incompetently led by Budyenny and further crippled by Stalin's order that there must be no withdrawal. While Budyenny was still pumping forces into Kiev, Kleist's armour striking up from the south met Guderian driving down unexpectedly from the north a hundred miles in the Russian rear. The Russians were too weak to break out. The Germans took 665,000 prisoners according to their own account, perhaps an exaggerated figure. They captured or destroyed 718 tanks and 3718 guns. Rund-

stedt went on to occupy the Ukraine, most of the Crimea and the Donets basin. In the course of this operation the Germans took a further 400,000 prisoners and captured or destroyed 753 tanks and 2800 guns.

Here was the great prize on which Hitler had set his heart: not only victory but conquest of Russia's greatest industrial region and the main source of her food supplies and industrial raw materials. Russia had lost a third of her industrial output and half her agricultural lands. By the end of 1941 Soviet industrial output fell to less than a half of prewar production. Germany had now her *Lebensraum*. It was all an illusion. The Russians had ruthlessly followed the policy of scorched earth during their retreat. They blew up the hydroelectric dam at Dnepropetrovsk; destroyed railways and bridges; and burned the stocks of food. The Germans made matters worse by their brutal treatment of the inhabitants. The

Left: A Partisan's Mother by S. Gerasimov

Below German soldiers hang Russian partisans

Bottom Soviet citizens sent to slave labour

coveted Ukraine brought little profit to its conquerors.

For, in the midst of defeat, the Russians achieved a great victory. The machines and factories of the Ukraine, along with their workers, had softly and silently vanished away. Before the war the Soviet government had begun to create a new industrial region east of the Urals, a region that was already producing one-third of Russia's industrial supplies by 1941. Immediately after the outbreak of war, the Russians began to move their existing factories east. In the period before the Ukraine was overrun some 500 factories were moved. One plant alone needed 8000 railway wagons to move it, yet it was again in production within four months' time. By 1942 Soviet industry was producing 2000 tanks and 3000 aircraft a month. Agriculture was more of a problem. Most of the peasants had been drafted into the army, and half the agricultural land had been lost. Food supplies never reached half the prewar level, and all Russians went hungry throughout the war.

By the end of September the Germans were free to resume their advance on Moscow. In Berlin journalists were told to prepare special announcements on the fall of Moscow and the end of the war. On 2 October Hitler told the German people, 'I say this today because for the first time I am entitled to say it: the enemy is broken and will never be in a position to rise again.' Once more all seemed to go well. There was another cauldron battle at Vyazma and Bryansk. Eight Russian armies were destroyed: 673,000 prisoners were taken, 1242 tanks and 5432 guns captured or destroyed. In Moscow there was panic. Crowds besieged the railway stations and the trains leaving for the east.

A Soviet factory moves east

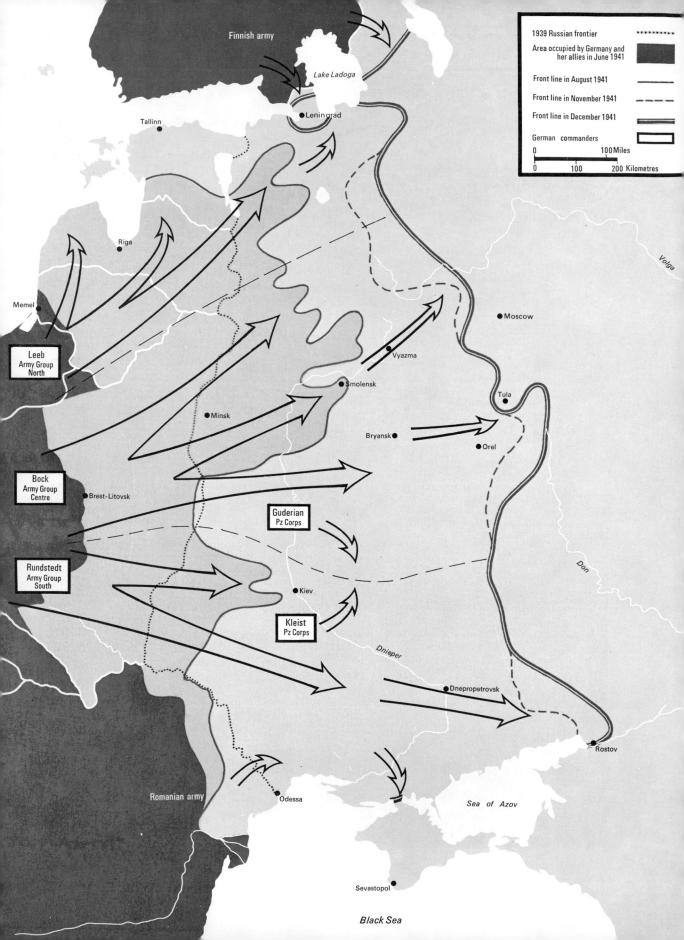

Finnish army

Lake Ladoga

● Leningrad

Tallinn ●

Riga ●

Memel ●

Leeb
Army Group
North

Minsk ●

● Smolensk

Vyazma ●

● Moscow

Tula ●

Bock
Army Group
Centre

Brest-Litovsk ●

Bryansk ●

● Orel

Guderian
Pz Corps

Rundstedt
Army Group
South

● Kiev

Kleist
Pz Corps

Dnieper

Don

● Dnepropetrovsk

● Rostov

Romanian army

● Odessa

Sea of Azov

Volga

Sevastopol ●

Black Sea

1939 Russian frontier ....

Area occupied by Germany and
her allies in June 1941

Front line in August 1941 ————

Front line in November 1941 — — —

Front line in December 1941 ══════

German commanders [   ]

0		100 Miles
0	100	200 Kilometres

Martial law was proclaimed, and the political police, the NKVD, opened fire in the streets. Gradually the evacuation became more orderly. The government and the diplomatic corps were moved to Kuibyshev; some two million of Moscow's inhabitants went further east. Stalin remained in Moscow, and Zhukov took command on the central front. On 6 November, eve of the anniversary of the Bolshevik Revolution, Stalin addressed the Moscow Soviet in the principal metro station. On 7 November, the anniversary itself, he took the salute as a military parade, somewhat diminished, marched past Lenin's mausoleum in Red Square.

The German offensive was grinding to a halt. Snow was falling. General Mud took command. German transport stuck in the mud, and the German tanks could not move forward. The German soldiers, without winter clothing, froze to death at their posts. Russian partisans sabotaged the railways. On 12 November the German generals once more debated their next step. Some of them wanted to halt and wait for the spring. How could they explain this to Hitler when they had just claimed final victory? Halder cut short the discussion: continuing the offensive was 'the Führer's wish'.

Zhukov had a fresh resource. Twenty-five Soviet divisions, the best equipped in the Soviet army, had been stationed in the Far East. Early in November Stalin authorized their transfer to the Moscow Front. Perhaps he acted on a tip from Richard Sorge, his Communist agent in Tokyo, that the Japanese were moving south and that the Manchurian Front was secure; perhaps the tip came from Lucy, the mysterious Soviet spy ring in Switzerland; perhaps Stalin merely gambled. At any rate there were no

German lorries stuck in Russian mud

more German victories. What was to have been a strategic battle degenerated into individual tactical engagements. On 27 November the German Quartermaster-General reported: 'We have come to the end of our resources in both men and material.'

On 29 November Soviet forces in the south recovered Rostov – the first German defeat in the Russian war. On 2 December German units reached the Moscow tram terminus and saw far off the towers of the Kremlin gleaming in the setting sun. Bock reported to Hitler, 'It is difficult to see what sense there is in continuing the offensive . . . particularly as the moment is now very near when the strength of the troops will be utterly exhausted.' He was grudgingly told that he could break off the attack when there was no longer any hope of success, and that moment had already arrived. German Intelligence cheerfully calculated that the Russians were not strong enough 'to carry out a large-scale offensive'. On 5 December Zhukov ordered a general offensive on the Moscow Front. The Blitzkrieg was over.

Russian troops on their way to the front

Far from the British aiding the Russians, the autumn battles in Russia brought relief to the British. With the Caucasus at any rate temporarily beyond Germany's reach, Auchinleck could at last afford the luxury of resuming the long-delayed offensive in North Africa. It was a small campaign by Russian standards – some ten divisions on each side with 710 British tanks against 174 German and 146 obsolete Italian. The superiority in tanks was no longer decisive. Rommel again made full use of his anti-tank guns, and the British tanks were again knocked

North Africa: German tanks and vehicles ablaze, December 1941

out, much to their surprise. The days when tanks could go unsupported into battle were over. The British offensive, designed to relieve Tobruk, began on 18 November. Six days later nothing had been achieved, and Cunningham, previously the liberator of Abyssinia and now in command of the Eighth Army, wanted to break off. Auchinleck, fearful of a roar from Churchill, came up from Cairo, dismissed Cunningham, and ordered the offensive to continue.

There was much confused fighting, interesting only to the expert in manœuvres. Rommel, a Prince Rupert of tank warfare rather than a strategist, raided far behind the British lines and was nearly taken prisoner in the process. When

the raid failed, Rommel, wiser than Auchinleck, decided to preserve his forces and withdrew westwards. Tobruk was duly relieved. Early in the New Year the British reached Benghazi, back where they had been after O'Connor's victory a year before. Each side had about 2500 men killed in the course of the fighting – hardly a casualty list at all by Russian standards.

This second British victory in North Africa was as barren as the first. Though Rommel had lost a third of his tanks, the British had lost two-thirds of theirs. Moreover their position in the Mediterranean was increasingly precarious. German U-boats, transferred from the Atlantic, sank the aircraft carrier *Ark Royal* and the battleship *Barham*. Italian frogmen put two more battleships in Alexandria harbour out of action. Admiral Cunningham's fleet was down to three light cruisers and an anti-aircraft cruiser. Meanwhile German air corps had arrived in Sicily and North Africa. It became impossible to pass supplies to Malta, which, far from harassing Axis communications, was itself blockaded. Worst of all the bottom fell out of the assumption on which British strategy had rested. Japan did not remain neutral. Great Britain's Far Eastern empire was in imminent danger.

Developments in the Far East followed inevitably from the Russian war and Great Britain's increasing difficulties. It was obvious to the Japanese that Roosevelt needed to turn his back on the Pacific if he were to aid Great Britain and Russia; it was equally obvious to Roosevelt himself. Both Japan and the United States wanted agreement more urgently than ever. But, as before, each wanted agreement on its own terms. The Japanese thought that Roosevelt, with his eyes turned towards Europe, would at last compromise and accept their overlordship, however disguised, of China. Roosevelt believed that the way to have done with the Japanese problem was to turn the screw still tighter. In July 1941 the Japanese extended their control of French Indo-China from the north to the south. They were thus on the borders of Siam and almost at the gates of Singapore. Roosevelt answered by freezing Japanese assets and placing an embargo on the supply of oil to Japan. The British and Dutch had no alternative but to follow suit. Three-quarters of Japan's foreign trade and nine-tenths of her oil supplies were cut off. The Japanese calculated, perhaps with some exaggeration, that their economy would collapse by the spring unless they could break the embargo. A time bomb had been placed under Japan's neutrality.

Konoye, the Japanese Prime Minister, was anxious to negotiate. He suggested a meeting between himself and Roosevelt. Roosevelt believed that the Japanese had not been softened up enough and refused. On 16 October Konoye resigned. General Tojo, the Minister of War, became Prime Minister in order to 'put the responsibility squarely on the army'. Perhaps Tojo would compromise where Konoye dared not. The Japanese offered to withdraw from Indo-China and to recognize the Open Door in China, though not to remove their troops until agreement was reached with Chiang Kai-shek. Hull, the American Secretary of State, answered by demanding that Japan must first sever her partnership with Germany. This partnership had never done Japan much good. But just at this time the Germans were pressing for closer relations. Ribbentrop, and perhaps Hitler also, had got it into their heads that Japan might compromise with the United States and thus free the American navy for Atlantic operations. They therefore gave a firm promise that they would declare war against the United States if Japan took the offensive. This was an offer that the Japanese could hardly refuse.

Time was running out. The Japanese had fixed 25 November as the date when war would become imperative for them. On 18 November the Japanese proposed a standstill agreement or, as the Americans called it, a *modus vivendi*. America would lift the oil embargo and withhold supplies from Chiang Kai-shek; Japan would withdraw her troops from Indo-China. Roosevelt was ready to agree. Hull consulted America's associates. China of course objected. The Dutch agreed eagerly. The British also agreed, but they were anxious not to be saddled with the responsibility for any American compromise and underrated Japanese readiness to go to war with the British Empire and the United States. Churchill therefore answered that Chiang Kai-shek was being put on 'a very thin diet'. At this Hull lost patience and turned down the *modus vivendi* out of hand. In this curious way the British, anxious to secure American aid against Germany and equally anxious to avoid a war in the Far East, actually gave the final push that made war in the Far East inevitable.

Singapore was indefensible. This was the nub of the British position. There were only 158 aircraft, where the minimum needed was 582. To make matters worse the British had constructed a large number of airfields for their non-existent air force – airfields that they could not defend and which were therefore so many landing grounds available to the Japanese. Army reinforcements that might have gone to Singapore had gone instead to Auchinleck. When Dill suggested that the North African offensive should be postponed, Churchill wilfully misunderstood him and accused him of proposing to evacuate the Middle East. Churchill had a weapon, or rather a bluff, of his own. He insisted that a naval force should be sent to Singapore in order to provide 'a vague menace'. On 2 December Admiral Tom Phillips arrived at Singapore with the battleship *Prince of Wales* and the battle-cruiser *Repulse*. The aircraft carrier that was scheduled to join them scraped its bottom in Jamaica and was unable to move. Before Phillips left London, Air Chief Marshal Harris said to him, 'Tom, don't get out from under your air cover. If you do, you've had it.' Phillips disregarded this warning. However, he recognized that his two ships could not withstand the entire Japanese navy and intended to withdraw from Singapore if war started. So much for the 'vague menace'.

The British were haunted by the fear that Japan might attack Singapore without going to war against the United States and that they would be left to fight alone. Desperate attempts were made to draw the Americans in. On 10 November Churchill announced that, if Japan and the United States were involved in war, a British declaration of war would follow 'within the hour'. The Americans made no similar declaration in return.

As a matter of fact, the Japanese never contemplated an isolated attack on Singapore and the British positions in the Far East. If they went to war, they meant to conquer the whole of their Greater Asia Co-Prosperity Sphere, as they called it, in a series of rapid blows. Then, secure in control of Malaya, Borneo and the Dutch East Indies, they could withstand an American counter-attack and wait for an acceptable compromise. The Japanese were confident that they could deal with the British, Dutch and American naval forces actually in the Far East. A shadow hung over their calculations. The main American fleet was at Pearl Harbor, seemingly beyond Japan's reach. The answer was provided by a single man, Admiral Yamamoto. From his earliest days Yamamoto, unlike most naval men, had believed in air power. Thanks to him, the Japanese navy was strongly equipped with aircraft carriers. Yamamoto, encouraged by the success of the British operation at Taranto in November 1940, proposed to use these carriers in order to eliminate the main American fleet by a surprise attack on Pearl Harbor. The Japanese Cabinet accepted his proposal. On 1 December the Japanese Imperial Council resolved that, while it would be wrong to go to war for the sake of the Co-Prosperity Sphere, Japan must fight if her national existence were at stake – and the Council deemed that it was. The die had been cast.

The Americans knew of the Japanese decision and should have foreseen what would follow from it. They had broken the Japanese codes and for months past had been reading all the Japanese messages. A warning that war was imminent was duly sent out on 27 November. But, as often happens in war or just before it, the Americans

had formed a picture. Obsessed with anxiety for Singapore and the Philippines, they never conceived of an attack on Pearl Harbor and neglected the many indications that pointed to it. There is an alternative explanation, still favoured by some Americans, that President Roosevelt deliberately took no precautions at Pearl Harbor in order to provoke a Japanese attack and so sweep America into war. This seems unlikely. No statesman, however unscrupulous, will wilfully begin a war with the loss of a large part of his fleet. Moreover the final neglect of precautions at Pearl Harbor turned on a series of accidents so far-fetched that no human ingenuity could have designed them.

For the Americans received clear warning about Pearl Harbor at the last moment. On 6 December the American cryptographers began to decipher a fourteen-part message, reciting Japanese grievances. When the first thirteen parts were shown to Roosevelt that evening, he said, 'This means war.' Early the next morning the Americans deciphered the final passage which instructed the Japanese Ambassador to deliver the full message at 1 p.m. But 7 December was a Sunday. Why should the Japanese wish to deliver an important message on a Sunday afternoon? The naval officers who puzzled over this hit on an answer. Pearl Harbor was the only American base in the Pacific where the sun would have risen at that time. The naval officers guessed rightly. The punctilious Japanese proposed to declare war half an hour before the attack on Pearl Harbor. Unfortunately for them the message was too long for the Japanese Ambassador to decipher in time, and he delivered it only after the attack had started.

The breaking of the codes was a naval affair. Admiral Stark recognized the significance of the Japanese message but remarked that the defence of Pearl Harbor was in the hands of the army. He therefore sent the message over to General Marshall, the army Chief of Staff. Marshall was out riding. When he returned he learned that the army signalling stations were temporarily out of action. He was too proud to use the naval

The Japanese attack on Pearl Harbor

ones and therefore sent his warning to Pearl Harbor by the commercial line. The message, relayed through San Francisco, reached Pearl Harbor at 7.33 a.m., local time. There it was handed, along with other cables, to a messenger on a motor bicycle. He chugged up the hill towards military headquarters. Bombs began to fall. The messenger hid in a ditch. Then, being himself a Japanese, he was held up by road blocks, accused of being a Japanese paratrooper, and told to go home. He held on and loyally delivered the message at 10.45 a.m. when all was over.

The Americans received an even clearer warning. Shortly after dawn two radar operators detected an unknown aircraft on their screen.

They reported this to their superior who told them to close down the station at 7 a.m. and attend church parade. They continued to operate for a little while by which time the single aircraft had become a host. They assumed that these were American aircraft flying in from a carrier. They closed the station. Pearl Harbor lay undefended, aircraft massed on the airfields, battleships lashed together in harbour, most of the anti-aircraft guns unmanned, and the ammunition under lock and key.

The Japanese attack started shortly before 8 a.m. and lasted for under two hours. The Japanese operated from six aircraft carriers, supported by two battleships and an attendant fleet. They sent in 360 aircraft, of which only 29 were lost. Four American battleships were sunk, though only one was a total loss; four more were severely damaged. Ten other warships were sunk or put out of action; 349 American aircraft were destroyed or damaged; 3581 American combatants and 103 civilians were killed or injured. When the Japanese withdrew at 10 a.m. the American Pacific fleet had almost ceased to exist. The Japanese operation at Pearl Harbor, however unscrupulous, was a stroke of military genius. In the Second World War only the German breakthrough at Sedan can be compared to it. An English historian, Guy Wint, has written:

One day the Japanese triumph at Pearl Harbor will be regarded in a different light from that in which it was inevitably seen by the opposite side at the time; the memory of treachery will fade: it will stand out as a most memorable feat of arms.

Nevertheless the Japanese victory was not as great as it might have been. All four American

American sailors fire-fighting after the attack

aircraft carriers were away from Pearl Harbor – three at sea and one under repair in California; and aircraft carriers were more important than battleships as later events were to show. Again, the Japanese made no attempt to destroy the vast American oil stocks on Hawaii, which were in fact almost equal to the entire supplies of Japan. Further, the Japanese rejected the idea of landing troops on Oahu, the island on which Pearl Harbor is situated, since the troop transports were needed elsewhere. Thus the Americans remained in possession of a first-class naval base and were only deprived, temporarily or permanently, of battleships past their prime.

Pearl Harbor gave the signal for world war. When the Japanese Ambassador called on Hull an hour and a half later than he should have done, bombs were falling at Pearl Harbor and a declaration of war was hardly necessary. Winston Churchill was at dinner at Chequers when the butler entered and said, 'Excuse me, Sir, we have just heard on the kitchen radio that the Japanese are attacking Pearl Harbor.' Churchill rose from his seat and left the room, announcing with evident relief, 'I am going to declare war.' Actually the British declaration of war did not follow until the next day – time enough, however, to be ahead of the war resolution in Congress. The other Allies followed suit. Even China at last declared war on Japan and threw in a declaration of war against Germany for good measure. Soviet Russia of course had better things to do and kept out of the Far Eastern war until 1945.

When Hitler learned the news of Pearl Harbor, he said to one of his associates, 'We are fighting the wrong people. We ought to have the Anglo-American powers as our allies. But force of circumstances has compelled us to make a world-historical error.' The mind boggles at the speculation of what would have happened if Hitler had delayed his declaration of war against the United States for even a few weeks: by then the Americans would have been involved in the Pacific and turned their backs on Europe. Hitler never considered this course seriously despite his first reactions. The very unscrupulousness of the Japanese action appealed to him. He told the Japanese Ambassador, 'You gave the right declaration of war. This method is the only proper one. One should strike as hard as possible and not waste time declaring war.'

Maybe Hitler wanted to show that he could be as loyal to Japan as Churchill had been to the United States; maybe he thought that Germany was already at war with the United States as nearly as made no difference; maybe he was excited beyond measure by the magnitude of events. This seems the most likely explanation. When the Reichstag convened on 11 December to hear the declaration of war on the United States, Hitler said:

I can only be grateful to Providence that it entrusted me with the leadership in this historic struggle which, for the next five hundred or a thousand years, will be described as decisive, not only for the history of Germany, but for the whole of Europe and indeed the whole world. A historical revision on a unique scale has been imposed on us by the Creator.

Mussolini also announced Italy's declaration of war on the United States in less ecstatic terms. The circle was complete. World war had begun.

Hitler had never wanted war against either England or America, at any rate not for many years to come. The Russian war was the only one of his own choosing. The Japanese had never wanted war against England and America or even against China. Mussolini had never wanted war against anyone stronger than Abyssinia or Greece. The Axis powers had moved cautiously forward in a series of small improvised wars until an unwelcome world war caught up with them. Italy had already practically fallen by the wayside. Germany and Japan held strong positions. Germany controlled the entire continent of Europe and the resources of European Russia. Japan was on the point of dominating Greater East Asia – Malaya, Burma, Borneo and the Dutch East Indies.

The apparent conquerors recognized their basic weakness. Neither of them could sustain a long war. A few days after the check in front of Moscow Hitler said to Jodl, his closest military adviser, 'Victory can no longer be achieved.' Yamamoto wrote to his sister after Pearl Harbor, 'Well, war has begun at last. But in spite of all the clamour that is going on, we could lose it'; and to a fellow admiral, 'The fact that we have had a small success at Pearl Harbor is nothing. People should think things over and realize how serious the situation is.' It was Churchill, not Hitler or Yamamoto, who had most reason to rejoice: 'So we had won after all.'

Roosevelt signs the declaration of war on Japan, Germany and Italy

6

Germany and Japan at their zenith 1942

In June 1941 the war had been an ineffectual duel between England and Germany. Six months later it became a world war. All the Great Powers and most of the small ones were drawn in. War was waged in the Atlantic and Pacific oceans and in every continent except America. The Japanese had a last run of easy victories in the hundred days that followed Pearl Harbor. Thereafter there were few surprises, and victory was determined by superior strength. The problem was no longer how to outwit the enemy but how to mobilize greater forces against him. Organization counted for more than quickness of wits. The world war that began in December 1941 was a slogging match as the First World War had been before it.

The coalition against Germany, Italy and Japan, the United Nations as it came to be called, was potentially far stronger than its enemies – stronger in resources, stronger in manpower, stronger also in strategical position. Though Germany and Japan had vastly extended their dominion, they had failed to break their encirclement. In theory they were still besieged. But the United Nations had a long way to go before they could turn this siege into a reality. The United States was invulnerable, despite the alarm when a Japanese submarine appeared off the coast of California. Both Russia and Great Britain had still to beat off Axis attacks – Russia on her own soil, Great Britain in the Far and Middle East and perhaps even in her home island. Russia and Great Britain were already organized for war. The United States was still on a peace footing. Millions of

men had to be mobilized and trained. Industry had to be turned to war purposes. In the end America's resources proved so great that she was able to supply the needs of war and raise the standard of living of her people at the same time.

The Russians had in the widest sense no strategic problem: their sole concern was to defeat the German armies and indeed they engaged three-quarters of the German land forces throughout the war. For the British and Americans an essential preliminary was to recover command of the seas – from the Japanese navy in the Pacific, from the German U-boats in the Atlantic. After that, their choice of action was wide open and correspondingly difficult to make. Should they strike first against Japan, as many Americans wished to do? If, as in fact they decided, they put victory in Europe first, where should they act – in North Africa and the Mediterranean or by direct assault in northern France? Perhaps even they should rely on the decisive effect of independent bombing? There was a deeper problem. In December 1941 Great Britain, Russia and the United States were linked only by a common hostility to the Axis. How could the United Nations be made more than a phrase?

These were the problems that Churchill took to Washington immediately after Pearl Harbor. Though the British were largely dependent on American supplies and were in the long run bound to become the weaker partner, they had some immediate advantages. They had been at war for over two years and had learned some-

An Anglo-American convoy in 1942

thing from the experience. The Americans often refused to profit from these lessons and suffered, for instance, heavy shipping losses on their Atlantic coast before they sulkily adopted convoy on the British model. Churchill himself was a powerful British asset. In the words of General Ismay: 'In his grasp of the broad sweep of strategy – "the overall strategic concept" as our American friends call it – he stood head and shoulders above his professional advisers.' It is a matter of some debate whether Churchill's strategic ideas were correct, but he could certainly deploy them in powerful prose. The Americans, in contrast, had little clear idea what to do except to win the war.

Agreement on one point was reached at once and virtually without discussion: the defeat of Germany was put before that of Japan. This followed from the earlier discussions before Pearl Harbor. Moreover the Pacific was bound to be principally a naval affair, and the American army wanted action of its own. With its mobilization scarcely begun, it could do this only by supporting the British, and they were committed to the European theatre. There was a remarkable consequence. The Americans, in their forthright way, aimed from the beginning at a direct attack on Germany. The British, however, were not fighting Germany on land. They were fighting Italy. Hence the Americans, by deciding not to act primarily against the less important enemy, Japan, were drawn into acting against Italy, who was less important still. This decision was not clear cut at the first Washington conference. The British held out the long-term bait of an assault on Germany to which all the rest would be preliminary. In war, however, the preliminaries have a way of turning into the real thing, as happened in this case. Unwittingly the first Washington conference determined that a land campaign against Germany – the Second Front as it came to be called – was put off for two and a half years.

This difference over strategy lay in the future. The basic achievement at Washington was to cement a partnership between Great Britain and the United States closer than had ever been previously created between allies in wartime. This was accomplished in casual and personal ways. There was no revival of the Supreme War Council that the Allies had set up towards the end of the First World War and Great Britain and France in the early months of the second. All the states at war with the Axis and/or Japan were duly recognized as the United Nations, but only Russia and, to a lesser extent, China went their own way. The rest were satellites – the British Dominions and the exiled European governments of Great Britain; the South American republics, so far as they were drawn in, of the United States – and conformed more or less willingly to the directions of their respective patrons.

Strategy was directed by the Combined Chiefs of Staff Committee – in theory the British and American Chiefs of Staff sitting together. In practice, with the committee meeting in Washington, the British were represented by a subordinate delegation, while the American Chiefs of Staff were present in person. For this and other reasons the United States gradually came to predominate. Nevertheless in December 1941 only the British were actually engaged in the war and thus staked out their claim to retain the status of a Great Power under changed circumstances.

The Chiefs of Staff Committee operated strategies laid down for them. All the important decisions were made by Churchill and Roosevelt, and the Anglo-American alliance rested simply on their personal relations. Each was supreme in his own country – Churchill theoretically restrained by the War Cabinet, Roosevelt restrained by nobody. Churchill poured out his thoughts on paper. Roosevelt rarely revealed his thoughts. Churchill easily developed an emotional attachment towards anyone with whom he was associated – towards Roosevelt and sometimes even towards Stalin. Roosevelt had no emotional ties despite his affable air. He was a politician all the time, forthcoming in appearance, almost impossible to pin down when it came to action.

There was another essential element in Anglo-American relations. It was an economic, as well as a military, partnership. Great Britain was on the receiving end of lend-lease, and the Americans recognized the obligation to keep her going, though not on too generous a scale. The American economy was still on little more than a peacetime level. The impulse to step it up came from Beaverbrook, the only Cabinet Minister who accompanied Churchill to Washington. Beaverbrook told Roosevelt, 'United States production schedules at present indicated in 1942 should be capable of at least a 50 per cent increase.' Roosevelt took Beaverbrook's advice. When he announced his production programme to Congress, he ran his pencil through the proposed list and pushed up the figures by a half – 45,000 tanks, for instance, in 1942 instead of 30,000. American war production was run with the improvised zest that Beaverbrook had shown when he turned out fighter aircraft at the Ministry of Aircraft Production, and with the same success. An American official historian has written: 'Lord Beaverbrook's intervention was the climax of the campaign for increased production which had been waged throughout 1941; and the results were indeed remarkable.'

Lend-lease was extended to Soviet Russia as well as to Great Britain and her satellites, and on more generous terms. The British had to account for every item they received. The Russians received everything the United States could spare and the British convoys deliver. Apart from this there was no common strategy and no joint action except in Persia where the British and Russians took over the railways and a little later dethroned the Shah. The Russians rarely asked for direct military aid after their alarms in the autumn of 1941, and the British and Americans had none to provide. Instead the Russians asked insistently for a second front, by which they meant an Allied landing in western Europe, and preferably in northern France.

This request was to cause a considerable stir in British politics. It had little influence on Anglo-American strategy. The Americans urged preparations for a landing in case Russia were in imminent danger of defeat, and the British seemed to acquiesce. In practice the very existence of an eastern front led to an indefinite postponement of action in the west. If the Russians continued to engage the bulk of the German army, an immediate second front was unnecessary. If the Russians were defeated, Germany would become invulnerable on the continent of Europe for a long time, and the Western Powers would need to consolidate their hold on Africa and the Mediterranean. One point the British and Americans did not consider at this time or perhaps ever: they did not take any precautions against a complete Russian victory.

There was another striking omission in the discussions on strategy at Washington. The British had prepared for 1942 a great bombing campaign against Germany, and Sir Arthur Harris, soon to become head of Bomber Command, was convinced that independent bombing could win the war if there were enough of it. The American air force commanders agreed with him. The heads of the other services, both British and American, emphatically did not. They were convinced that Germany would be defeated only by great battles on land. The dispute was not fought out at Washington or even mentioned. Hence the two strategies ran side by side for over two years. Armies were prepared and plans laid for an ultimate invasion of Europe. The American navy prepared for battles against the Japanese. At the same time the RAF, and subsequently the American air force, went their own way and conducted an independent bombing of Germany which, they insisted, would win the war all on its own.

This bombing campaign struck the popular imagination more than any other wartime experience and gave the Second World War its special character. Nearly everyone in England and Germany and most people in other parts of Europe heard the wail of the sirens and knew life in the shelters. Afterwards the devastated cities of Europe – London and Coventry, Berlin, Hamburg and Dresden – became the symbols of the Second World War. In the absence of large-scale fighting on land, the bombing campaign became for the British the triumphant demonstration that the war was being waged and on an offensive pattern. A few debated the morality of a strategy directed indiscriminately against the civilian population. Hardly anyone appreciated that the air offensive was a disastrous mistake even within its own terms of reference.

Until 1944 the British and Americans had neither the techniques nor the types of aircraft with which to conduct precision bombing – a strategy that was to prove really effective. American daytime bombing was a lamentable failure. The British could only conduct area bombing at night – a strategy originally supposed to operate against the German factories and, when this failed, against German morale. Neither objective was achieved.

Indiscriminate bombing did more harm to the Allies than to the Germans. The production of heavy bombers was a greedy affair. More than a third of British war production was devoted to it, and much of the lend-lease supplies as well. There were fewer resources to spare for the production of tanks and until 1943 virtually none for that of landing craft. Indiscriminate bombing diverted aircraft from more useful tasks as well. The Royal Navy demanded aircraft for the Atlantic patrols against the U-boats – a more urgent, though less dramatic, activity than the bombing of Germany. The RAF refused to release any. Occasionally the War Cabinet intervened, but in no time at all the RAF pulled its aircraft back again. The Atlantic patrols went short; the Far and Middle East went short; the Second Front went short. And all for a bombing strategy that failed to produce results.

Sir Arthur Harris was a skilful publicist. His thousand-bomber raid on Cologne in May 1942, for instance, was designed for its effect on British opinion rather than on the Germans. At Cologne, according to the official German report, 'within two weeks the life of the city was functioning almost normally'. The British newspapers did not know this, and Harris's critics within the government could not resist his further claims. Harris was not dismayed by demonstrations that bombing was not producing decisive results. He argued that an ineffective campaign now would train Bomber Command for a more effective one later. What really carried the day for indiscriminate bombing was the simple rule that it is better to do the wrong thing in wartime than to do nothing at all. If the British did not bomb Germany, it would almost seem that they were not at war with her. This had been Haig's argument for the Somme and Passchendaele, and Sir Arthur Harris was the Haig of the Second World War.

There were of course some compensations. Over a million Germans were diverted from the factories into air-raid precautions. The factories themselves switched from producing bombers to producing fighters and this made retaliation by the Germans increasingly difficult. Even more important, the German fighters were kept at home for the defence of German cities and almost disappeared from the battlefronts. When the Allies landed in Normandy in 1944 they had complete command of the air. Similarly the heavy flak guns, which were dangerously effective weapons against tanks, were kept in Germany. These were inestimable, though unforeseen, gains from the bomber offensive.

The discussions at Washington centred on the defeat of Germany and Japan. But for much of 1942 the two enemy Powers were still rolling forward. This was particularly true of Japan. With the destruction of the main American fleet at Pearl Harbor, her way was clear. The Japanese had never envisaged such a position, and their run of success was the greatest improvisation of the war. It was achieved with very small forces, usually smaller than those of their opponents. The bulk of the Japanese army remained in Manchuria throughout the war, and much of the rest was on the mainland of China. The Japanese won by superior speed and skill and also of course by their possession, however temporary, of sea power.

In theory the Allies had two strongholds – the Americans at Manila, the British at Singapore. Both depended on the arrival of reinforcements by sea, and the loss of sea power had not been foreseen. The Americans had assumed at one time that the Philippines would have to be abandoned in case of war. But in the summer of 1941 General Douglas MacArthur was sent out to take command. He was America's most glamorous general, his grey hair dyed black – a dye that ran in hot weather – and his glittering uniform designed by himself. He was also America's most senior general, having retired from the post of Chief of Army Staff in 1935, and even his successor Marshall was terrified of him.

MacArthur insisted that he could hold the Philippines until relief arrived, and there was no attempt to overrule him. Things went badly from the start. Most of the American aircraft were destroyed on the ground on the first day, despite a warning that Pearl Harbor had been attacked. The Americans fell back into the Bataan peninsula and then into the fortress of Corregidor. No reinforcements arrived. On 11 March 1942 MacArthur himself was ordered to leave. Before going he declared: 'I shall return.' On 6 May Wainwright, his successor, surrendered at Corregidor. The Americans and their Filipino allies lost 140,000 men. The Japanese casualties were 12,000. This was a heavy price to pay for the assertion of MacArthur's prestige.

On the British side Hong Kong told the same story. The Chiefs of Staff had always recognized that this was an advanced post, indefensible in time of war. In August 1940 they recommended withdrawal. No action was taken. Instead,

American and Filipino prisoners of war on their death march

as late as October 1941, two further battalions were sent in to provide a 'more worthy' defence. The Japanese attacked from the mainland on 8 December and completed their victory on Christmas Day. They took 12,000 prisoners of war, for whom a hard fate lay ahead. The Japanese casualties were under 3000.

Singapore was the great British hope. It could be defended only if Japanese landings in northern Malaya were prevented, and for this a British advance into Siam was necessary. The British authorities hesitated to infringe Siamese neutrality, much as they had done with that of Belgium in 1940, and anyway Siam was ready to welcome the Japanese. When the British finally resolved to act, it was too late; the Japanese had already begun to land. On this news Admiral Tom Phillips knew that he should take his great ships to safety. But he could not bring himself to leave without first doing something to help the army. On the afternoon of 8 December 1941 the *Prince of Wales* and the *Repulse* sailed north, with Phillips in command, to strike at the Japanese transports. He had no air cover. He

General Wavell inspects the defences of Singapore

failed to find any Japanese transports, turned back, and then resolved to have another go. The British force was spotted by a Japanese submarine. On 10 December it was attacked by high-level bombers and torpedo bombers. The *Repulse* was sunk soon after midday, the *Prince of Wales* an hour later. The Japanese lost three aircraft.

This stroke sealed the fate of Malaya and Singapore. The Japanese were able to land further troops without opposition; they had command of the air. Time and again the British positions were encircled or bypassed almost without fighting. At the end of January the Japanese reached Singapore. They had suffered 4500 casualties; the British had lost 25,000 men – mostly prisoners. At home Churchill still refused to believe that Singapore could fall. Fresh troops were sent, disembarking from the transports straight into captivity. The Japanese opened their assault on Singapore on 8 February. A week later the British surrendered, at the exact moment when Japanese supplies had run out. The Japanese captured Singapore with a

Below The sinking of the *Prince of Wales*

Bottom Japanese troops attacking Singapore

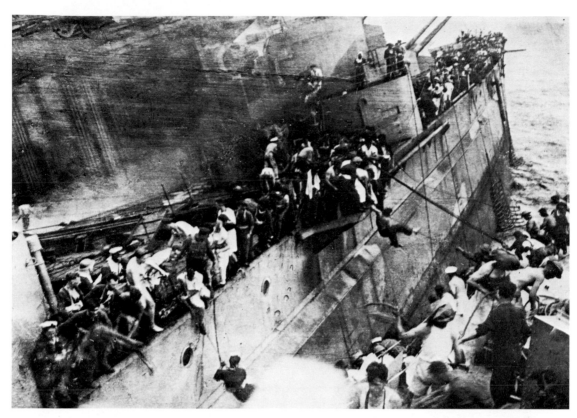

Left Singapore: arrival of Australian reinforcements

Left, below Dutch prisoners of war in Japanese hands

force of 35,000 men. The defenders numbered 80,000, all of whom became prisoners of war. It was the greatest capitulation in British history and one of the most discreditable.

The Japanese tide of conquest was not yet stayed. Late in December 1941 they had entered Burma. The British thought of defending first Rangoon and then Mandalay. In the end General Alexander who had arrived to take command decided that complete withdrawal was the only possible course. Burma was abandoned. Early in May 1942 British forces of some 60,000 reached Assam after a thousand-mile retreat. Further east the Japanese had landed in Indonesia on 6 January and thereafter made steady headway. At the end of February Admiral Doorman, commanding a mixed Dutch and British force, attempted to attack the Japanese convoys. Japanese naval forces intervened and after a three-day battle Doorman's entire fleet was destroyed. Nothing was left to set against the Japanese advance. On 8 March the

Dutch surrendered; 98,000 Dutch East Indian troops went into captivity.

The Japanese had now cut a wide swathe of conquest from the borders of India to those of Australia and running far out into the Pacific Ocean. The Greater East Asia Co-Prosperity Sphere had been achieved. It was feared that the Japanese would go further. The British feared for Ceylon, the Australians for Port Darwin. The British had somehow managed to gather a scratch naval force at Ceylon – five obsolete battleships and three small aircraft carriers. In April a far more powerful Japanese fleet sailed into the Indian Ocean. Somerville, the British admiral, was in possession of the Japanese ciphers. He therefore withdrew to his secret hiding place at Addu Atoll, 600 miles southwest of Ceylon. Hence, though the Japanese did a good deal of damage when they attacked Colombo and sank two cruisers, they did not find Somerville's fleet. The Japanese then withdrew and never returned. They had no troops to

The surrender of Singapore

spare for an invasion of Ceylon which lay far beyond the bounds they had drawn for their Co-Prosperity Sphere, and their naval raid was simply an attempt at another Pearl Harbor on a smaller scale. The British did not realize this and feared that the Japanese might seize a naval base in Madagascar or even join hands with the Germans in the Middle East. In fact there was never the slightest coordination of strategy between Germany and Japan, and the Japanese were too concerned with the Pacific to have time for the Indian Ocean. All that was left from these fears was a British occupation of Madagascar that began in May and was completed in September. The occupation did not improve relations between the British and the Free French.

Japanese advance towards Australia also soon came to a halt. Early in April they planned to occupy Port Moresby in Papua and press on towards Australia. The Americans, well briefed by the Japanese cipher messages, prepared their reply. On 8 May the two naval forces met in the Coral Sea. They were roughly equal with two carriers on each side. The Battle of the Coral Sea was a portent. For the first time in history two fleets fought at a range of over a hundred miles without sighting each other. Great battleships were outdated; carriers came into their own. The Americans lost a heavy carrier, the *Lexington*; the Japanese lost only a light carrier. But they broke off their expedition.

Admiral Yamamoto was alarmed. The Americans were recovering far sooner than he had expected. He determined to destroy the remainder of the American Pacific Fleet while it was still weak and thus force the Americans back to the coast of California. His objective was Midway Island, halfway to Pearl Harbor, and he proposed to lure the American fleet north by a preliminary attack on the Aleutian Islands. Here the American breaking of the Japanese codes came into its own. Admiral Nimitz, the American commander, had full knowledge of Yamamoto's plan and disregarded the Aleutian decoy. The Japanese, in contrast, were acting in the dark. They did not even use

Legend:
- Japan 1933
- Japanese occupied by 7 December 1941
- Japanese expansion (with dates)
- Major sea battles
- Jap. air strikes outside area of occupation
- US Pacific Task force

0 ___ 500 Miles
0 ___ 800 Kilometres

USA

S
S
R

MONGOLIA

Manchuria

Peking

Nanking

Hankow

...king

Shanghai

Yellow Sea

...nton

Hong Kong
25 Dec. 41

FORMOSA

C
H
I
N
A

SAKHALIN

KURILE
ISLANDS

HOKKAIDO

Vladivostok

Sea of Japan

KOREA

Tokyo

JAPAN

OKINAWA
(Jap.)

IWO JIMA
(Jap.)

MARIANA
ISLANDS
(Jap.)

GUAM
(US) Dec. 41

Bering Sea

Dutch Harbor
June 42

ALEUTIAN ISLANDS
(US)

ATTU

Japanese Carrier
Striking Force

7 Dec. 41

Pearl Harbor

HAWAIIAN
ISLANDS
(US)

MIDWAY
(US)

US victory
June 42

Nimitz

Furthest advance of
Japanese 7 Dec. 41

WAKE IS
(US)
Dec. 41

Furthest extent of Japanese domination by July 1942

LUZON
Manila
May 42

Philippines

May 42

...c. 41

CAROLINE ISLANDS

Japanese mandate

MARSHALL
ISLANDS
(Jap.)

GILBERT IS.
(Br.)

Pacific Ocean

South China Sea

B...rneo
Jan. 42

CELEBES
Jan. 42

DUTCH EAST INDIES

New
Guinea

Apr.
42

Papua

Rabaul

SOLOMON IS.

US victory
Mar. 42

Timor Sea

Jap. victory
Feb. 42

Timor

Darwin
Mar. 42

Port
Moresby

Coral Sea

GUADALCANAL

US victory
Mar. 42

NEW HEBRIDES
(Br.)

Halsey

SAMOA
(Br./US)

AUSTRALIA

MacArthur

NEW
CALEDONIA
(Fr.)

FIJI
IS. (Br.)

TOBAGO IS.
(Br.)

NEW ZEALAND

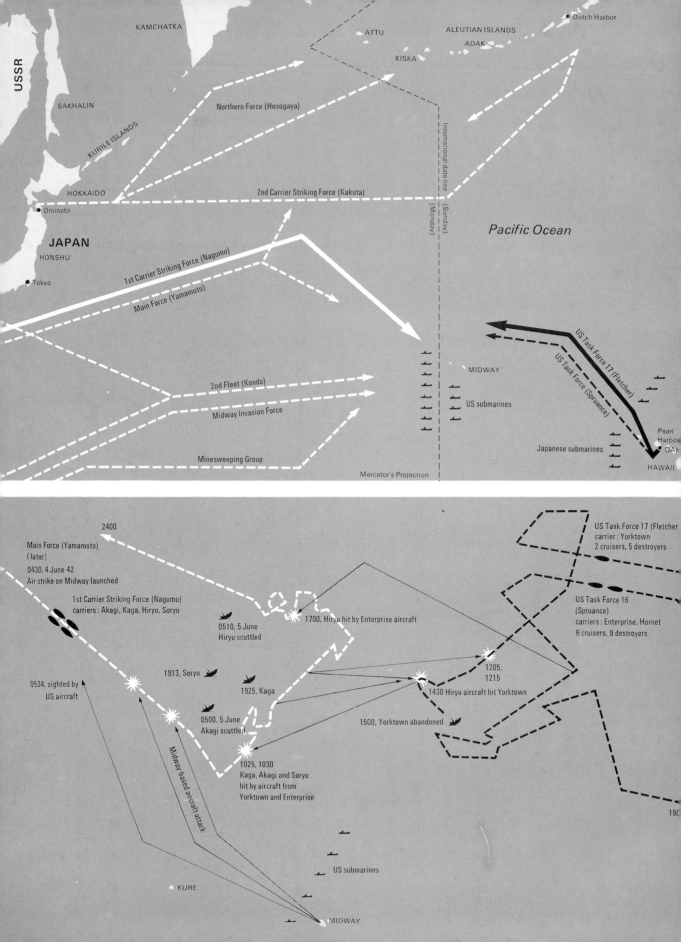

KAMCHATKA

ATTU

ALEUTIAN ISLANDS
ADAK

Dutch Harbor

KISKA

USSR

SAKHALIN

Northern Force (Hosogaya)

International date line

(Sunday)
(Monday)

Pacific Ocean

KURILE ISLANDS

HOKKAIDO

2nd Carrier Striking Force (Kakuta)

Ominato

JAPAN

HONSHU

1st Carrier Striking Force (Nagumo)

Tokyo

Main Force (Yamamoto)

US Task Force 17 (Fletcher)

US Task Force (Spruance)

2nd Fleet (Kondo)

MIDWAY

US submarines

Midway Invasion Force

Pearl
Harbor

Minesweeping Group

Japanese submarines

OAHU

HAWAII

Mercator's Projection

2400

US Task Force 17 (Fletcher
carrier : Yorktown
2 cruisers, 5 destroyers

Main Force (Yamamoto)
(later)

0430, 4 June 42
Air strike on Midway launched

1st Carrier Striking Force (Nagumo)
carriers : Akagi, Kaga, Hiryu, Soryu

1700, Hiryu hit by Enterprise aircraft

US Task Force 16
(Spruance)
carriers : Enterprise, Hornet
6 cruisers, 9 destroyers

0510, 5 June
Hiryu scuttled

0534, sighted by
US aircraft

1913, Soryu

1205,
1215

1925, Kaga

1430 Hiryu aircraft hit Yorktown

0500, 5 June
Akagi scuttled

1500, Yorktown abandoned

Midway-based aircraft attack

1025, 1030
Kaga, Akagi and Soryu
hit by aircraft from
Yorktown and Enterprise

190

US submarines

KURE

MIDWAY

radar despite the two radar sets that the Germans kindly presented to them. Even so, Japanese strength seemed overwhelming. They put to sea with 11 battleships, 8 carriers (4 of them large), 22 cruisers, 65 destroyers and 21 submarines – the greatest fleet concentration in the history of the Pacific. Against it Nimitz had no battleships, 3 carriers (with Midway as a sort of carrier in reserve), 8 cruisers and 17 destroyers.

On 4 June Japanese carrier-borne aircraft attacked Midway, confident that the American fleet was far away. When they were back on deck rearming, American aircraft flew in and sank all four of the large Japanese carriers, along with 330 aircraft, within five minutes. The Americans lost one carrier, *Yorktown*. The great battleships never saw action at all. There was no quicker or more dramatic reversal of power in all history.

At one moment the Japanese dominated the Pacific Ocean. Five minutes later they were down to equality in carriers – the essential weapon. Nine months later the Americans had 15 battleships against 9 Japanese and 19 carriers against 10. The five minutes at Midway spelled the ultimate doom of Japan.

Nevertheless Japan's achievement was in appearance tremendous: in the course of some three months she had conquered an empire at practically no loss. She had broken the American blockade. She controlled all the world's rubber, 70 per cent of its tin, and the oil of the Dutch East Indies. With the conquest of Burma, China was cut off from the outer world, and Chiang Kai-shek seemed to lie at Japan's mercy. British prestige had been shattered by the loss of Singapore. Politically the Japanese made little use of their success. Far from leading the

A Japanese heavy cruiser wrecked by US naval aircraft at Midway

yellow races against the white, they exploited the territories they had conquered and soon made themselves more hated than ever the British and Dutch had been. The Co-Prosperity Sphere proved an empty phrase.

Moreover the Japanese had already a vulnerable point. The three million tons of oil they secured from the Dutch East Indies were enough for their peacetime needs. But they were now conducting a war along long sea lanes and fighting a sea war with large naval forces. Soon American submarines were sinking their supply ships. Hence the Japanese merely waited on events. Their victories had been won against an America virtually at peace. Now they had to face an America mobilizing for war, and they knew they were no match. Their hopes were pinned on Germany. If Germany used up American strength, still better if Germany won, the Americans might be ready after all for a compromise peace.

For much of 1942 and even afterwards it still seemed that Germany might come up to Japan's expectations and win the war. The Germans came near to disrupting Allied communications across the Atlantic; they reached the gates of Alexandria; recovering from their defeat in front of Moscow, they gave every appearance of being on the point of defeating Russia. In the autumn of 1941 the British seemed to have mastered the U-boats in the Atlantic. Soon, however, sinkings went up again. In June 1942 they reached the ominous total of 700,000 tons. Admiral Doenitz had more U-boats than ever before, enough to operate his new tactic of hunting in packs. In the course of 1942 the Allies lost nearly eight million tons of shipping and built only seven million. The RAF steadfastly refused to be diverted from its bombing of Germany. When finally compelled to cooperate, it dropped 20,000 tons of bombs on U-boat bases without putting a single U-boat out of action.

March 1943 was the worst month of the war for the Allies in the Atlantic. The British Admiralty recorded: 'The Germans never came so near to disrupting communications between the New World and the Old as in the first twenty days of March 1943.' Dramatic change was at hand. The British perfected two new devices: huff-duff (high-frequency direction finding) which located U-boats, and centrimetric radar, which enabled small radar sets to be produced for aircraft and small warships. Admiral Max Horton, in command of the Western Approaches, put these instruments to good use. Instead of hunting the U-boats across the ocean, he organized support groups that struck back at them when they attempted to attack a convoy.

On 4 May two British support groups fought a battle with a U-boat pack in which 7 U-boats were sunk and only 12 merchantmen lost. A little later 5 U-boats were sunk without sinking a single merchantman. Doenitz could not afford such losses. He broke off the U-boat campaign and reported to Hitler, 'We are facing the greatest crisis in submarine warfare, since the enemy, by means of new location devices, makes fighting impossible.' The U-boat campaign was never effectively renewed. Horton's support groups, sustained by huff-duff, centrimetric radar and aircraft patrols, had won the Battle of the Atlantic.

The Atlantic was not the only drain on British maritime resources in the course of 1942. Convoy to Russia was almost as damaging. Supply was the only way in which the British and Americans could aid Russia, and it was pressed as a demonstration as much as for any practical effect. The Russians in their first desperation asked for anything that could be sent. It gradually emerged during 1942 that the Russians could themselves turn out all the tanks and aircraft they needed, and most of the supplies sent from the West at such cost remained unpacked on the quays of Archangel. Not until 1943 did the Americans send what the Russians really required: food, medical supplies and above all troop-carrying vehicles. Meanwhile the convoys struggled through the icy northern waters. The first twelve convoys got through without loss.

Danger sprang up by a side wind. Hitler became convinced that the Allies were preparing to land in Norway. He ordered the two battlecruisers *Scharnhorst* and *Gneisenau* back from Brest to Trondheim – where incidentally their passage through the Channel outraged British opinion – and sent *Tirpitz*, the most powerful ship afloat in European waters, to join them. The Norwegian landing never came off, despite occasional advocacy of it by Churchill. But henceforth there hung over every convoy the menace of a major naval battle, at a time when the Admiralty could not afford to lose any escort vessels.

Disaster struck in July 1942. On Churchill's insistence convoy PQ 17 sailed for Archangel despite the long light nights. Admiralty Intelligence mistakenly reported that *Tirpitz* had put to sea. Dudley Pound, the First Sea Lord, overruled the local commander and ordered the escort to withdraw and the convoy to scatter. The merchantmen were left at the mercy of the German U-boats and aircraft. Twenty-four out of 35 merchantmen were sunk on what later proved to be a false alarm. Only two further convoys, both escorted by an aircraft carrier, sailed in the remainder of 1942 and none in the light months of 1943. In all 40 convoys sailed and 100 ships were lost. Ironically, little was achieved by this high sacrifice. Three-quarters of the Allied aid to Russia went through Persia, a safer though less dramatic route.

The grim situation in the Atlantic and the disasters of the convoys to Russia made the first nine months of 1942 the gloomiest time of the war for the British people. Rations had to be cut. Coal was running short. Ordinary people, though not perhaps the governing classes, were exasperated by the failure to aid Russia. The loss of Singapore, coming on top of the sinking of *Prince of Wales* and *Repulse*, shattered the British sense of empire, and imperial unity was threatened in a more practical way when the Australians complained that Great Britain had failed to protect them.

For the first time the storm blew against Churchill himself. After all, the catastrophes in the Far East were largely his doing. He had underrated the danger from Japan, relied on 'the vague menace' of two great ships not defended by aircraft, and disregarded the warnings of his advisers. It was the culmination of many occasions when Churchill had insisted on useless sacrifices for the sake of prestige – a characteristic that in fact waits on victory. There was talk of

**Supply routes to Russia: convoy PQ 17
left and American trucks in Persia**

creating an independent Minister of Defence. Perhaps Wavell should be the new Cromwell. Churchill beat off these attacks by his oratory, but he reconstructed his government for the only time in the war. Beaverbrook, the only minister who advocated the Second Front, left office. Sir Stafford Cripps, who enjoyed totally undeserved credit for bringing Russia into the war, became Leader of the House of Commons and figurehead of the government. Churchill paid the further price of allowing Cripps to proceed to India where he fruitlessly entertained the Indian leaders with the prospect of Dominion status after the war. Gandhi dismissed this as 'a postdated cheque'. A by-stander added, 'and drawn on a crashing bank'.

Churchill's oratory could win votes in the House of Commons. It could not win victories. Churchill had sacrificed the Far East for the sake of North Africa and now needed a repetition there of the victories of December 1940. Times had changed. The British fleet had lost command of the Mediterranean. Malta, instead of harassing the Axis convoys, was under attack by German aircraft and U-boats and hard pressed to survive. In January 1942 Rommel, essaying a tank foray, to his surprise pushed the British back to the lines of Gazala, thus robbing them of two-thirds of their territorial gains. Thereafter Malta occupied the centre of the picture. Churchill and the Chiefs of Staff wanted a new offensive so that aircraft from North Africa could go to Malta's assistance – the exact opposite of the position in December 1940 when Malta had made the first British offensive in North Africa possible. Auchinleck refused to be hurried, and Cripps on his way to India reported that an immediate offensive would be 'an unwarrantable risk'. The War Cabinet debated whether to dismiss Auchinleck. Instead, on 10 May, it sent him a peremptory order that he must fight a major battle in order to distract the enemy from Malta.

At the same time the Axis leaders were debating whether to launch a full-scale attack on Malta. Raeder was strongly for it as he had always been. In his view, if Malta fell, the Axis forces would take Egypt and conquer the Middle East. Hitler remembered the heavy paratroop losses in Crete and was anxious to conserve the Luftwaffe for his forthcoming offensive in Russia. Rommel insisted that he could reach Alexandria unaided and moved towards an offensive without waiting for authority to do so. Hitler and Mussolini accepted his initiative, and Mussolini crossed to Libya with a white horse in order to lead the entry into Cairo.

Rommel struck first on 26 May. The British had a 3 to 1 superiority in tanks and a 3 to 2 superiority in guns. According to Liddell Hart who was well qualified to judge correctly, 'the British had a qualitative advantage as well as a very large superiority in numbers'. But they were badly led. Apart from Auchinleck, who had to control the entire Middle East and worry about his northern flank on the Caucasus as well as to direct the battle, no one was up to the level of his task. The British broke up their tank forces; Rommel kept his together. In Rommel's words, 'the British threw their armour into the battle piecemeal and thus gave us the chance of engaging them on each separate occasion with just enough of our own tanks'. The outstanding

Western Desert: Free French soldier after Bir Hacheim

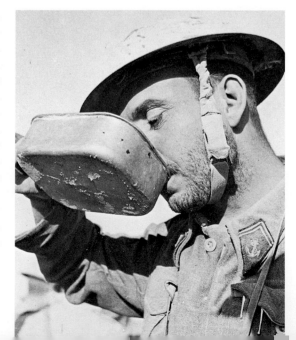

feature of the battle was the defence of Bir Hacheim by Free French forces – the beginning of France's military renaissance.

By mid-June the British had lost control of the battle. They began to fall back. It had never been envisaged that Tobruk should be held as an isolated outpost as it had been the previous year. Its defences had been neglected, and its supply by sea was now too great a burden for the fleet to carry. Churchill did not understand the situation and telegraphed from London: 'Presume there is no question in any case of giving up Tobruk.' Ritchie, the commander of the Eighth Army, therefore left a considerable

force in Tobruk and fell back to the frontier, meaning to link up again with Tobruk within a few days. Rommel was too quick for him. He carried Tobruk in a single day, taking 35,000 prisoners – more than his own entire force.

On 25 June Auchinleck went up to the frontier and took over command of the Eighth Army. He rejected any idea of standing on the present position where the wide spaces of the desert meant that Rommel could encircle the British from the south. He decided to fall back to El Alamein only sixty miles from Alexandria. Here a sea of soft sand prevented any encircling move. The lines of El Alamein could be carried only by direct assault. Rommel was now living solely on captured British supplies; his tanks were down to sixty. The Italian general, theoretically his Supreme Commander, ordered him to halt. Rommel cheerfully replied that he would not 'accept the *advice*', and invited his superior to dine with him in Cairo.

The British only just won the race to El Alamein. On 1 July when they were beginning to take up a defensive position there, Rommel caught up with them. He had only forty tanks and his improvised attack miscarried. In Alexandria there was panic. The British fleet passed

Left General Ritchie is puzzled

Below British prisoners of war are taken at Tobruk

through the Suez Canal into the Red Sea. The British Embassy began to burn its files, and the British Ambassador ordered a special train, waiting with steam up to carry him and his staff to the comparative security of Palestine. All unknown, the worst was now over. On 4 July Rommel wrote home: 'Our strength is exhausted.' It was now the turn of the Germans to depend on supply lines across a thousand miles of desert. The Germans had run out of resources. The British, though in fact better equipped, had lost confidence in all their leaders except Auchinleck himself. There were three more weeks of sporadic fighting which petered out at the end of July. The Germans were still only sixty miles from Alexandria. But they would get no further. First El Alamein, as this confused engagement with disorganized forces came to be called, was decisive. The Axis advance in North Africa was stayed for good.

In England the surrender of Tobruk and the rumoured preparations for the abandonment of Alexandria had an impact almost as shattering as the fall of Singapore. Churchill himself lost heart for the only time in the war. Once more he was criticized in the House of Commons. Once more the cry was raised for an independent Minister of Defence with the additional proposal that the Duke of Gloucester should be made Commander-in-Chief – not a happy idea. There was a formal motion of no confidence – an indignity that Lloyd George never suffered during the First World War. Churchill beat off the motion by 476 votes to 25 with some 40 deliberate abstentions. But once more it was victories, not votes, he needed. Against everyone's expectation they were not slow in coming.

North Africa was a small-scale affair except in the eyes of the British public – a few hundred tanks on either side and victory often won by a few dozen. Events on the Eastern Front would determine the fate of Germany and the outcome of the war. After the setback in front of Moscow the German command was in disarray. Rundstedt wished to withdraw to a shorter defensive

line and resigned when his advice was not accepted. Bock and Leeb soon followed him. Brauchitsch, the Commander-in-Chief, broke down and resigned also. He had no successor. Hitler himself became Commander-in-Chief on the Eastern Front, directing operations down to the smallest detail. At the same time he was Supreme Commander of all the German forces, Nazi leader and dictator of Germany. These four tasks were beyond the capacity of any single man, yet nothing could be done without Hitler's authority.

Hitler's first command on the Eastern Front was 'No Withdrawal'. He remembered the retreats of the First World War and claimed that they had always shaken morale. The Germans established a chain of defended positions round which the attacking Russians surged in vain. For a few weeks in December 1941 the Russians believed that they had already won the war. Stalin told Eden that, though Russia could do nothing against Japan at the moment, 'in the spring we shall be ready and will then help'. These high hopes were disappointed. The Russians recovered much territory and established a number of salients, but they failed to take any of the German strongholds. It was the turn of the Russians to be exhausted when their offensive petered out in February 1942. As Alan Clark rightly says, this was Hitler's finest hour. The confidence of the German army had been restored. But there was a heavy price to pay. The Luftwaffe was worn down by the transport flights it had had to make during the winter. Divisions, though up in number, were reduced in strength. Nearly a million half-trained recruits were drawn in. The German army was no longer the great fighting force it had been in June 1941.

The German generals wanted only a limited offensive or perhaps none at all. Hitler saw, as they did not, that 1942 was Germany's last chance to win the war. With the failure of the Russian counter-offensive, his hopes rose once more: this time he would destroy Russia's military and economic power once and for all. He had always favoured attacks on the flank as

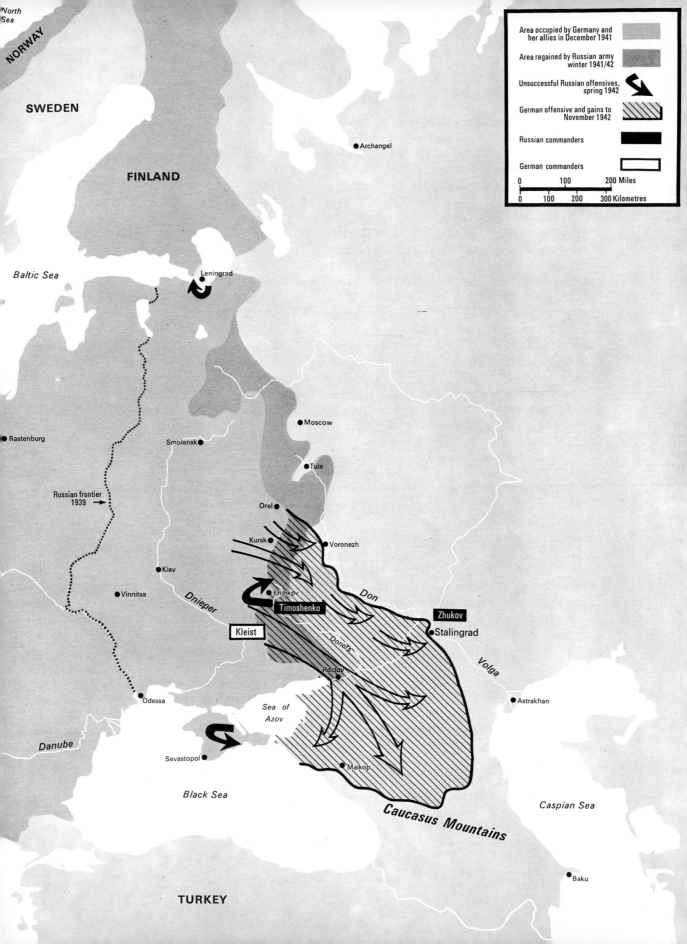

North
Sea

NORWAY

SWEDEN

FINLAND

Baltic Sea

● Archangel

Leningrad

● Rastenburg

Smolensk ●

● Moscow

● Tula

Russian frontier
1939 →

Orel ●

Kursk ●

Kiev ●

● Vinnitsa

Dnieper

Voronezh ●

Kharkov ●

Timoshenko

Don

Zhukov

Stalingrad ●

Kleist

Donets

Volga

Rostov ●

● Astrakhan

Odessa ●

Sea of
Azov

Danube

Sevastopol ●

Maikop ●

Black Sea

Caspian Sea

Caucasus Mountains

● Baku

TURKEY

Area occupied by Germany and
her allies in December 1941

Area regained by Russian army
winter 1941/42

Unsuccessful Russian offensives,
spring 1942

German offensive and gains to
November 1942

Russian commanders

German commanders

0   100   200 Miles

0   100   200   300 Kilometres

against a direct offensive, and now the generals were in no position to impose their oldfashioned strategy. There was to be no new attack on Moscow. In the north a diversionary attack on Leningrad would draw off Russian forces. But the great objective was to be Stalingrad far away to the southeast. The General Staff agreed, after some grumbles, that this was a practicable objective. Perhaps the Red Army would be destroyed on the way. In any case, the capture of Stalingrad would cut communications between central Russia and the oilfields of the Caucasus.

There was again equivocation between Hitler and his generals as there had been over Barbarossa. For the generals, Stalingrad was the final objective of the year's campaign. For Hitler it was only a beginning. Once it was taken he would either wheel north and encircle Moscow – the flanking strategy he had followed in France in 1940 and had wanted to follow in Russia in 1941. Or if the Russian army were still too strong for this, he would wheel south and secure the Caucasian oilfields. As a further equivocation Kleist, commander of the most southerly army, was secretly told by Hitler not to bother about Stalingrad and to go for the Caucasus straight away.

The Russians made the German task comparatively easy by a grossly misconceived strategy. Misled by their successes during the winter, they believed that they could take the offensive despite having only an equality of strength. There were three such offensives, widely dispersed, all conducted in the old bullheaded way and with Stalin always insisting that they must be pressed at all costs. All three were complete failures. In the Crimea the Russians lost 100,000 prisoners and 200 tanks. Outside Leningrad they lost an entire army, and Vlasov, its commander, deliberately surrendered to the Germans in the hope of leading an anti-Stalinist army of liberation. The worst disaster was the attempt to take Kharkov. Timoshenko, with 600 tanks, advanced into a pocket just when the Germans were moving to eliminate it.

The Russian flanks began to close behind them. Timoshenko appealed for a halt. He was ordered to press on and did so until his armies crumbled away. The Russians lost 240,000 prisoners and some 1000 tanks. When the German offensive began, the Russians had only 200 tanks on their entire Southern Front.

The German advance began on 28 June. Three armies broke the Russian front on either side of Kursk and went rolling forward. All southern Russia seemed wide open before them. On 20 July Hitler rang up Halder and said, 'The Russian is finished.' Halder replied, 'I must admit, it looks like it.' On the left wing of the offensive the Germans established a bridgehead over the river Don at Voronezh. The generals would have liked to go beyond the Don in order to secure their flank. Hitler answered that this would carry them away from their true objective of Stalingrad and that, as the Russians were incapable of an offensive, the Don itself would provide full cover for the flank. The German armies therefore would be quite safe in pressing forward into the wide corridor between the Don and the Donets.

More than this, in the excitement of victory, Hitler divided his forces. Kleist was released from any further concern with Stalingrad and told to go for the great prize of the oil beyond the Caucasus. His forces at first encountered little opposition. On 8 August the Germans sighted the first oil derricks at Maikop. The advance slowed down as the Germans reached mountainous country. When snow fell early in October, Kleist could go no further. The Germans never reached the main oilfields of the Caucasus on which Hitler had set his heart.

Kleist's advance did not mean that the aim of taking Stalingrad was abandoned. On the contrary Hitler believed that he had strength enough for both operations at once. The capture of Stalingrad would sever Russia's oil supplies. Besides, as the city of Stalin its capture would symbolize Stalin's defeat. Paulus, commanding the advance in the centre, was therefore ordered to press on. He had a rougher time than Kleist.

German troops on the Don

It took a month of hard fighting before the German forces reached the outskirts of Stalingrad. This was fighting of a new kind. The Russians had learned how to retreat. They no longer held their ground and fought on to the last man. Instead they fell back as soon as their flanks were threatened. There were no fresh encirclements. There was no German breakthrough. The Russian armies survived, though weakened. All the time, reinforcements were coming down by train from Moscow. On 23 August Paulus reached the Volga. Hitler moved his headquarters from Rastenburg to Vinnitsa in the Ukraine. The vital thing, he ordered, was 'to capture as quickly as possible the whole of Stalingrad itself and the banks of the Volga'. There was no need to worry about the Don flank; the Romanian and Hungarian armies would look after that. At the same time the Russians, too, made their preparations. Generals, later to be famous in history, made their appearance. Chuikov was placed in command at Stalingrad; Zhukov, the one Soviet general who had never been defeated, took supreme control of the Southern Front.

On 24 August, though no one knew it, the Nazi Empire also had reached its term.

This was an empire even greater than the Japanese and one also attained after stupendous victories. There was no longer any talk of a New Order or of uniting all Europe under German leadership. There was a unity only of exploitation. Slave labour sustained German industry. Europe's resources fed the German war machine and provided the Germans with a high standard of life. In the early months of 1942 a decision was taken which gave the Nazi Empire its unique quality of evil. This was the decision to liquidate the Jews or, as Himmler, chief of the SS, called it, 'the final solution'. This ghastly decision had a long background. Anti-semitism was the strongest element in Hitler's mind, and the elimination of the Jews from German life an aim which he pursued from the moment he came to power. Jews were removed from the professions and from business. They were encouraged to emigrate, as many of them did to the great intellectual impoverishment of Germany. Before the war they were not murdered systematically. Germany's conquests swelled the number of potential German victims from half a million to eight or ten millions. In 1940, after the fall of France, Hitler planned to remove all the European Jews to Madagascar. Many of them were rounded up in concentration camps in preparation for their removal. The Madagascar plan came to nothing.

This was the situation at the beginning of 1942. The SS had already murdered thousands of Jews in Poland and Russia in an unsystematic way. The decision taken by Himmler and other SS leaders was to make these murders scientific. Hitler warmly approved. On 15 August 1942, inspecting an extermination camp with Himmler and SS-Gruppenführer Globocnik, he complained that the killings were proceeding too slowly: 'The whole operation must be speeded up, considerably speeded up.' Globocnik suggested that they should bury bronze plaques recording that it was they who 'had the courage to complete this gigantic task'. Hitler replied, 'Yes, my good Globocnik. I think you're perfectly right.'

The Final Solution was not a matter of massacre and wild destruction as other great crimes in history have been. It was the application of advanced modern science to evil ends. Anti-semitism and all the talk about race were supposed to be scientific. Hence science was to be applied to racial ends and to produce a 'pure' people. Chemists devised the most scientific forms of extermination. Doctors tortured the Jews for allegedly medical ends and ransacked the bodies. Skilled technicians built the death camps and perfected the incinerators. Even those who originally hesitated soon felt, as Oppenheimer said about the hydrogen bomb, that the problems of the Final Solution were beautifully sweet. Perhaps consciences were less tender in the general holocaust of war. At any

Concentration camps: the survivors and the dead

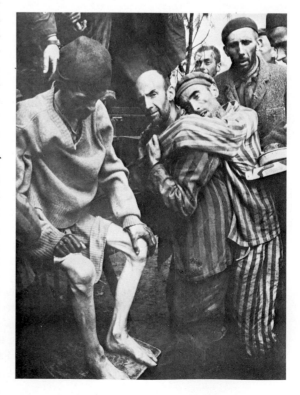

rate no one in high places protested. German resources were diverted from war to the murder of innocent people. How many will never be known, perhaps four million, perhaps six. Far away in Russia a lone German sergeant called Anton Schmid systematically helped Jews to escape, until he was detected and shot. He was the good German of the Second World War.

The record of other peoples was not much better. The French police fully cooperated with the Germans in loading the murder trains. The Hungarians handed over all foreign Jews though making some attempt to preserve their own. The Pope remained silent. In Denmark, however, when the alarm was raised, the entire population joined in concealing the Danish Jews until they could be ferried to safety in Sweden. The Dutch would have done the same if it had been within their power. The racial madness went further. Anti-semitism had a long history, but no one until the Nazis had thought of eliminating the Gypsies. Now they, too, were rounded up and sent to the gas chambers. The French historian, Henri Michel, writes of the murder of the Jews:

This was the most atrocious crime in all the history of mankind. Its unfortunate victims did not, by their death, aid in any way the success of the German armies. They were killed in application of a morality based on the will to power and on racism, in the service of which one of the most advanced peoples in the world placed their qualities of organization and scientific knowledge, because their sense of discipline and their patriotism had gone totally astray.

The memory of Oświęcim and the other murder camps will remain when all the other achievements of the Nazi Empire are forgotten.

7

The turning point 1942

While the Russians were fighting desperately for survival, their great allies in the West seemed to be merely talking. This appearance was misleading. Great Britain and the United States were maritime powers and could not wage war as they wished until they had recovered command of the seas. This meant not only the ceaseless battle with the U-boats. It also demanded an economic battle in America for the production of ships to replace those that had been lost. This battle was conducted so effectively that the British and Americans were able to launch a seaborne invasion of North Africa in November 1942 even though the U-boats had not yet been mastered.

The inevitable delay was incomprehensible to the Russians, and they were not mollified by the running of the convoys to Archangel. In May Molotov, the Soviet Foreign Minister, visited the West for the first time. In London he showed himself surprisingly amenable. He dropped the demand on which he had hitherto insisted for recognition of Russia's 1941 frontiers and agreed to a straightforward military alliance with Great Britain that was supposed to last for twenty years. In return he wanted the immediate opening of a second front. Churchill explained the difficulties and, while ready to do what he could, refused to make any binding promise. In Washington Roosevelt was more forthcoming or perhaps more careless and authorized a statement that 'full understanding was reached with regard to the urgent task of creating a second front in 1942'.

The difference was not merely that of temperament between the two men, Roosevelt expansive and generous in conversation, Churchill quick to resist when someone else tried to push him. There was also a basic difference of outlook. At the Washington conference in December 1941 there had been agreement to defeat Germany first. The Americans, thinking in terms of a 'mass-production' war, proposed to go against the enemy at his strongest point as soon as they were ready to do so. The British husbanded their limited resources and contemplated a direct assault against Germany only when she had been worn down by encirclement and campaigns elsewhere. The American and British Chiefs of Staff held prolonged discussions that lasted from April until June. The Americans were gradually persuaded that a large-scale landing in northern France was impossible for 1942. American forces would be far from ready for a major campaign. The U-boats caused an increasing shortage of shipping, and the American navy, cheerfully going its own way, refused to divert landing craft from the Pacific.

The Americans pleaded for at least the establishment of a bridgehead at Cherbourg. The British convinced them that this, too, was impracticable except as a desperate expedient if Russia were in danger of defeat. On 21 June, when Churchill was again in Washington, the Combined Chiefs of Staff ruled out any landing in France before 1943. Were the two Great Powers then to do nothing for another twelve months? A landing in French North Africa seemed the only alternative. This had come in originally by a side wind. Roosevelt, intensely disliking de Gaulle, believed that he could cajole the French government at Vichy and that American, though not British, forces might well land in French North Africa by invitation. Vichy did not respond. It became clear that any landing in North Africa would have to be a military operation. The Combined Chiefs of Staff reported that any action in French North Africa would be a diversion from the main field of battle and therefore undesirable.

This did not suit the two political chiefs. Churchill wanted action somewhere to break the long run of setbacks in the Middle East. Also he feared that, unless there were some action in the European sphere, the Americans would turn their attention to the Pacific. Roosevelt needed some dramatic stroke in order to influence the elections to Congress in the autumn. French North Africa was the only place that filled the bill. Roosevelt told his advisers that if northern France were ruled out, then they 'must take the second best – and that is not the Pacific'.

The British loss of Tobruk and subsequent retreat to El Alamein gave the final push. Some diversionary action seemed urgently necessary. American forces alone would not be enough if it came to an opposed landing. The British would have to take part also, whatever the effect on the Vichy government. The Chiefs of Staff added their rueful warning that a full-scale campaign in North Africa would preclude a landing in northern France not only for 1942 but for 1943. Neither Churchill nor Roosevelt heeded this warning. Events were to prove the Chiefs of Staff right.

Strategical arguments could be paraded for the decision. Mastery of the Mediterranean would save shipping, though of course the shipping was being mainly consumed because of the African campaigns. Conquest of French North Africa would give the British and Americans something to hang on to if Hitler defeated Russia and so remained in control of Europe. The Germans would have to go to the aid of their Italian ally, and their resources would be diverted from Russia and France to North Africa. The landing would thus be both an effective substitute for the Second Front and a preparation for it. These arguments were really irrelevant. The decision was made for political rather than for strategical reasons. Even so it was a strange outcome that the first Anglo-American action was taken against a former ally who, it was still hoped, would become a friend.

The prospect of combined action brought a change in the way campaigns were commanded. Hitherto the British had got by with independent command of the three services. In Egypt, for instance, Auchinleck ran the war on land and Cunningham the war at sea, while Tedder, the air commander, assisted one or other at his discretion. The Americans hankered after a supreme commander on the analogy of the President himself. A first shot at this had been made early in 1942 when Wavell became Supreme Commander from India to Indonesia. This command soon dissolved under the impact of Japanese successes. Thereafter, with a predominantly naval war in the Pacific, it would have made sense for Admiral Nimitz to become Supreme Commander. But the great General MacArthur could not be overlooked. Hence two supreme commands were appointed – MacArthur in Australia and the southwest Pacific, Nimitz in the central Pacific and whenever operations were entirely naval. As might be expected they conducted two independent and in time contradictory campaigns – MacArthur set on returning to the Philippines, Nimitz aiming directly at Japan. Since their forces were almost entirely American, with some Australians thrown in, their position provided no real precedent for combined command. General Eisenhower, appointed to command the landings in French North Africa, was the first true Allied Supreme Commander of the Second World War.

Someone had to break the news to Stalin that there would be no Second Front in 1942, and Churchill agreed to do it. On his way he passed through Cairo. He found the British army be-

Unwelcome news for the British Ambassador – 'There will be no withdrawal, no withdrawal, no withdrawal'

wildered by retreat, Auchinleck looking apprehensively over his shoulder for the arrival of a German army in the Caucasus, and the Ambassador's special train still waiting. Churchill assembled the Ambassador and his staff on the embassy lawn, rated them for their alarm during what was known at the front as the Great Flap, and said fiercely, 'There will be no withdrawal, no withdrawal, no withdrawal.' The special train was disbanded, and that evening the Ambassador appeared, seemingly unruffled, at the Gezira Club.

Auchinleck refused to contemplate a renewed offensive. Churchill determined to find more aggressive leaders. Maybe, too, he hoped to find more amenable ones. Alexander was summoned from the borders of Burma to replace Auchinleck, Montgomery from England to command the Eighth Army. Alexander was a born Supreme Commander: gentle, conciliatory,

and not perturbed by the enemy, politicians, or his own generals. Montgomery was the best British field-commander since Wellington: abrasive and self-confident, he came at the right moment when methodical planning was taking the place of expedients and improvisations. Churchill's choices were justified in the long run. His immediate reward, however, was to encounter two generals even more set on delay than Auchinleck had been.

In Moscow Churchill got on better than he had expected. For the first time Stalin met a statesman of the first rank – a sign that Soviet Russia had fully returned to the ranks of the Great Powers. Responding to his new eminence, Stalin laid aside his old tunic and appeared henceforth in the glittering uniform of a field-marshal. This was a strange encounter: Churchill had promoted the War of Intervention against the Bolsheviks; Stalin personified Bol-

Dieppe: the landing that failed

shevism in the eyes of the world. Now both men were singleminded in their determination to defeat Hitler. Stalin growled at the postponement of the Second Front. He warmed to the landings in North Africa and said, 'May God prosper this enterprise' – the old seminarist no doubt coming out in him. Churchill virtually promised the Second Front for 1943: 'A deadly attack upon Hitler next year.' Evidently he had not absorbed the warnings of the Chiefs of Staff.

While the British stood on the lines of El Alamein and the Russians gathered at Stalingrad, there was a splutter of the Second Front after all. On 19 August British and Canadian troops landed at Dieppe. This enterprise had a confused background. It began as a first exercise in combined operations. Montgomery, then in command in England, insisted that there must be full air and naval support. The RAF answered that they had no aircraft to spare; the navy

would not risk any of its big ships. The preparations went on of their own momentum – combined operations with nothing to combine. Montgomery departed to Egypt, fortunately for his reputation. Some 6000 men landed at Dieppe with inadequate air cover and few destroyers in support. They failed to capture any of the German strongpoints and suffered heavy casualties. Of the Canadians, five thousand went forth and three thousand did not return. Some valuable lessons were said to have been learned, though it is hard to say what they were. The real lesson was a warning against improvisation, whether at Gallipoli, in Norway and Greece, or now at Dieppe. This lesson was learned, and eighteen months of detailed planning preceded the successful landings in France on 6 June 1944.

There was now a long period of waiting or, as Churchill called it, one of 'stress and strain': no

British offensive in Egypt until the end of October, no landing in French North Africa until 8 November, unrest and political discontent at home, mounting losses in the Atlantic. There was no pause at Stalingrad. The city straggled for some twenty miles along the right bank of the Volga. Hence it could not be encircled and regularly besieged. It could only be taken by direct assaults, even more deadly than the trench fighting of the First World War. Early in September the Germans were still much the stronger – three to one in men and over six to one in tanks. But their supplies had to come from thousands of miles away. The Russians were now so far east that they drew theirs direct from the new factories beyond the Urals. With their backs to the Volga, they ferried in fresh men and supplies every night. There was another sinister development for the Germans: as they moved more and more of their own forces to the Stalingrad Front, the long exposed flank along the

Don had to be handed over to the Romanians and the Hungarians, troops whose fighting quality was doubtful.

The assault on Stalingrad was a senseless struggle like Verdun before it. The Germans had cut the Russian traffic on the Volga once they reached the river banks north and south of Stalingrad and had nothing to gain by taking the city itself. They went on for the sake of prestige. Hitler was bewitched by the prospect of capturing the city of Stalin. In September Halder was driven to resign and with him went the last scrap of the army's independence. Hitler ran ahead of events as he had done in the previous year. On 8 November he addressed the traditional Nazi gathering in the beer cellar at Munich and said of Stalingrad: 'Do you know what? We're modest; we've got it. And you can be quite certain that no one will ever be able to get us out now.' Goebbels announced that 'the greatest battle of attrition that the world has ever seen' was taking place. The attrition was operating against the Germans. The Russians kept Stalingrad going as a bait luring them to destruction. The Russians contested every house and every factory. The German tanks were reduced in the endless street fighting. Meanwhile Zhukov kept Chuikov and his Sixty-second Army on a thin diet. Only 5 Russian infantry divisions crossed the Volga between 1 September and 1 November. At the same time 27 new infantry divisions and 19 armoured brigades were created beyond the Don. The German generals began to send warnings. Hitler rejected them. The attack must go on: 'The last battalion will decide the issue.' Withdrawal would be a confession of defeat, 'unthinkable in the cosmic orientation of world political forces'. In any case the warnings were not very urgent. None of the German generals believed that the Russians could mount a general offensive.

The first successful Allied offensive of the autumn came in Egypt. Montgomery patiently built up his strength. Rommel, desperately short of fuel,

The assault on Stalingrad

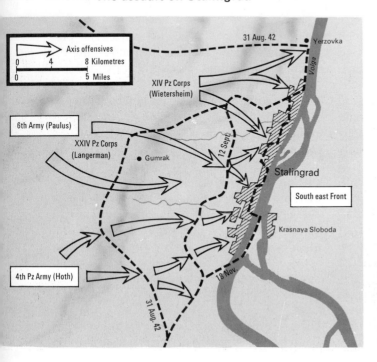

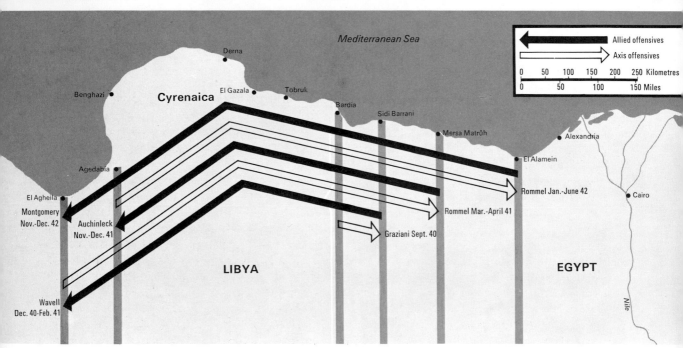

Mediterranean Sea

Derna

Benghazi

Cyrenaica

El Gazala

Tobruk

Bardia

Sidi Barrani

Mersa Matrûh

Alexandria

Agedabia

El Alamein

El Agheila

Rommel Jan.-June 42

Cairo

Montgomery
Nov.-Dec. 42

Auchinleck
Nov.-Dec. 41

Rommel Mar.-April 41

Graziani Sept. 40

LIBYA

EGYPT

Wavell
Dec. 40-Feb. 41

Nile

Allied offensives
Axis offensives

0   50   100   150   200   250 Kilometres
0   50   100   150 Miles

decided to disrupt the British preparations before it was too late. On 30 August he launched the Battle of Alam el Halfa, breaking into the enemy positions in the fashion that had so often brought him victory before. Montgomery refused to be hustled. The British tanks fought a purely defensive battle, receiving the Germans hull down. With only one day's fuel supply left, Rommel broke off the battle. Montgomery let him go. Not for him the improvised counter-strokes of earlier campaigns. Rommel, a sick man, left for Germany. Churchill prodded Montgomery and received the answer: 'If the attack begins in September, it will fail; if we wait until October, I guarantee a great success and the destruction of Rommel's army; must I, despite this, attack in September?' Churchill prodded no more.

The delay was turned to good purpose. During September only two-thirds of the Italian shipping across the Mediterranean reached its destination, during October only one-half and not a single tanker. The Axis tanks were down to three issues of fuel in hand when they expected to have thirty. Meanwhile men and American supplies flowed in unimpeded through the Suez Canal. When the battle started the British had 230,000 men to the Axis 80,000 and 1440 tanks against the 260 German and 280 obsolete Italian. Montgomery meant to put this superiority to good use. There were to be no daring forays of the old kind; instead, a slogging match, a battle of attrition. Montgomery applied the principle laid down by Sir William Robertson when he was CIGS in the First World War – that victory goes to the general with the longer purse – this time with the difference that he possessed it.

The second and more famous Battle of El Alamein started on 23 October. The British tanks assaulted the Axis line at its strongest point. They failed to break through the mine-fields into open country. Montgomery, who liked to claim that everything was going according to plan, had to pull back and try again. Rommel, who had hurried back from Germany, stopped him once more. But the Afrika Korps

El Alamein: British infantry go into action

was now down to 90 tanks; Montgomery still had nearly 800. In London Churchill raged against the slow progress of the offensive, and even Brooke, the CIGS, began to wonder whether he 'was wrong and Monty was beat'.

On 2 November the British lost 200 tanks, and Rommel was down to 30. He resolved to withdraw. The next day a peremptory order from Hitler made him turn round and try to hold the lines of El Alamein at all costs. In the confusion the British tanks at last broke through on 4 November. There seemed a splendid chance to cut off the Axis forces. But the British moved too slowly. Their attempts at encirclement were always too narrow, too cautious and too late. Rommel got away. The British took 10,000 German prisoners and 20,000 Italians; they also collected on their way 450 abandoned tanks and

The Battle of El Alamein

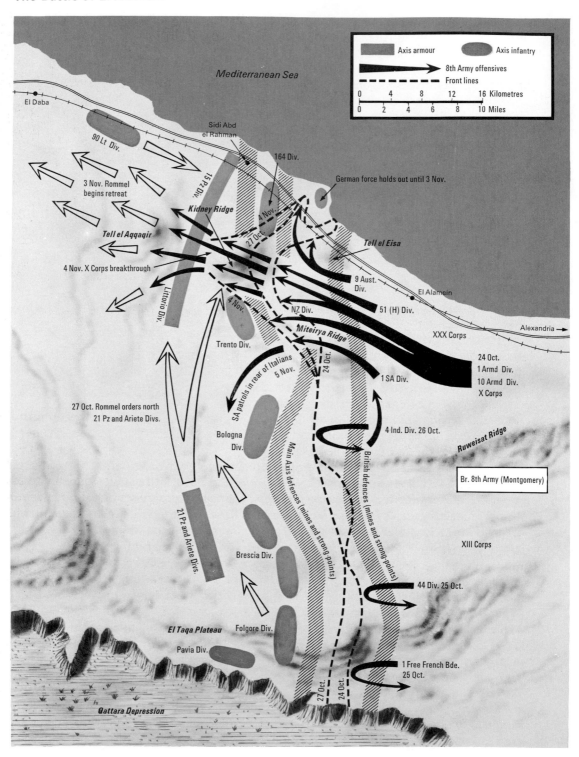

Mediterranean Sea

El Daba

90 Lt. Div.

Sidi Abd
el Rahman

164 Div.

German force holds out until 3 Nov.

15 Pz. Div.

3 Nov. Rommel
begins retreat

Kidney Ridge

4 Nov.

27 Oct.

Tell el Aqqaqir

Tell el Eisa

4 Nov. X Corps breakthrough

9 Aust.
Div.

El Alamein

Littorio Div.

4 Nov.

NZ Div.

51 (H) Div.

Miteirya Ridge

Alexandria

Trento Div.

XXX Corps

SA patrols in rear of Italians
5 Nov.

24 Oct.

24 Oct.

1 SA Div.

24 Oct.
1 Armd Div.
10 Armd Div.
X Corps

27 Oct. Rommel orders north
21 Pz and Ariete Divs.

Bologna
Div.

4 Ind. Div. 26 Oct.

Ruweisat Ridge

Br. 8th Army (Montgomery)

21 Pz and Ariete Divs.

Brescia Div.

XIII Corps

Main Axis defences (mines and strong points)

British defences (mines and strong points)

44 Div. 25 Oct.

El Taqa Plateau

Folgore Div.

Pavia Div.

1 Free French Bde.
25 Oct.

27 Oct.

24 Oct.

Qattara Depression

Legend:

Axis armour

Axis infantry

8th Army offensives

Front lines

| 0 | 4 | 8 | 12 | 16 Kilometres |
| 0 | 2 | 4 | 6 | 8 | 10 Miles |

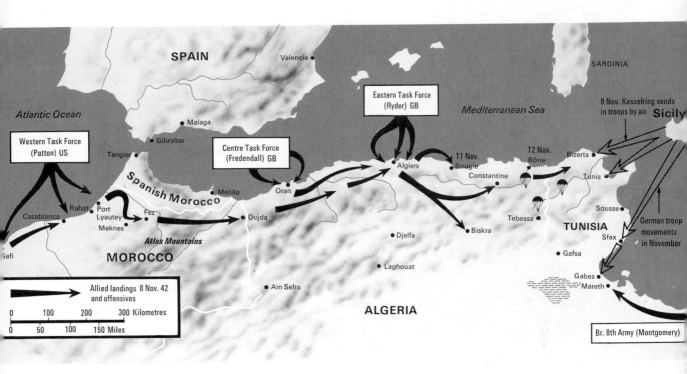

Allied landings in North Africa, 8 November 1942

over 1000 guns. Their own casualties were 13,500. Montgomery went methodically forward. Rommel at first intended to stand 500 miles west of Benghazi, and Hitler ordered him to do so. Then Rommel played Mussolini against Hitler. Mussolini gave permission for a withdrawal to the frontier of Tunisia, and there Rommel prepared his final stand for the spring of 1943.

It was not only defeat at El Alamein that sent Rommel all the way back to Tunisia. It was also the news that British and American forces had landed in French North Africa on 8 November. Ironically this enterprise, which had sprung partly from the desire to relieve the hard-pressed British forces in Egypt, actually followed the decisive British victory. It also took place a week after the Congressional elections which it had been designed to influence. The landings began in muddle and confusion as might be expected from a first essay in combined operations. The

Americans wanted only to establish a foothold on the Atlantic coast; the British hoped to clear the Mediterranean and wanted to land right up to the frontier of Tunisia. Each side got a little of its way. The Americans landed at Casablanca, a pointless exercise; the British were allowed to go as far as Algiers, which proved to be not far enough.

There was also political confusion. The Americans still hoped to play along with the Vichy authorities in North Africa, if not with Vichy itself. The British who had no such hope were overruled. De Gaulle was allowed no share in the enterprise, indeed was not even informed of it. When Vichy proved unresponsive, the Americans picked on Giraud, an elderly French general who had escaped from a German prison. He was brought out from France by submarine. He proved tiresome. He demanded a landing in France itself and that he should be made Allied Supreme Commander. He therefore had to be locked up in Gibraltar until all was over. In any case the French officials in North Africa refused to acknowledge him. There were 120,000 French troops in North Africa, a formidable opposition when the Allies could only put ashore 10,000. At the last moment Darlan, Pétain's righthand man, turned up in Algiers. This seemed a stroke of luck. It is now known, however, that he was not there by chance: the Americans had been negotiating with him as well as with Giraud. Darlan's intention was to go with the winning side. After prolonged hesitations he agreed to collaborate with the Allies as he had previously done with the Germans. He was helped to this decision by the news that German forces had entered unoccupied France and that the Vichy government had lost its somewhat questionable independence. One prize escaped the Germans: on 27 November, when they reached Toulon, the French admiral there, disregarding Darlan's order to join the Allies, scuttled his fleet.

In North Africa Darlan's order to cease resistance was obeyed. Eisenhower recognized him as High Commissioner. There was an outcry in Great Britain and to a lesser extent in the United States. On 15 November the church bells had been rung throughout England in honour of the victory at El Alamein, a victory for freedom as well as for British arms. Now the Allies had put in power Admiral Darlan, a persistent and virulent collaborator with the Nazis. Was this the outcome of the anti-Fascist crusade that the Allied peoples had been promised? Roosevelt pleaded that the deal with Darlan was 'only a temporary expedient, justified only by the stress of battle'. The immediate problem was solved on Christmas Eve when Darlan was assassinated by a young French Royalist, who was himself immediately tried by a French court-martial and executed. Giraud was put in as the least objectionable substitute. The deeper problem remained: the British and American governments wanted no change in Europe except that Hitler should disappear.

The delays in Algiers and the failure to land further east threw away the greatest gain that the landings should have brought. By the time Allied forces began to advance, German and Italian troops were pouring into Tunis, where the French Governor-General collaborated with them. The Allied operations were conducted badly. The troops were inexperienced, and the commanders equally so. In Eisenhower's words:

the best way to describe our operations to date is that they have violated every recognized principle of war, are in conflict with all operational and logistic methods laid down in textbooks, and will be condemned in their entirety by all Leavenworth and War College classes for the next twenty-five years.

By the middle of December the Axis had some 25,000 troops in Tunisia, the Allies nearly 40,000. The rain fell in torrents. On Christmas Eve Eisenhower abandoned the offensive. This setback finally ruled out any chance of a landing in northern France during 1943: the Allied forces were clearly stuck in North Africa for a long time. In other ways the halt proved, in Liddell Hart's words, a blessing in disguise. Hitler and Mussolini had time to move into Tunis a quarter of a million men – all their remaining fighting troops in the Mediterranean area. They were a hostage to fortune.

The Russian victory came third in the series and was on a greater scale. On 19 November six Russian armies broke through the Romanian and German lines north and south of Stalingrad. On 23 November the two attacking forces met near Kalach. Paulus and the Sixth Army were cut off. Paulus hesitated to withdraw. His prestige, as well as Germany's, was at stake, and he imagined that he could hold his hedgehog position as the Germans had done outside Moscow in the previous year. Hitler of course took the same line and grew even firmer when Goering assured him, quite untruly, that the Luftwaffe could keep the Sixth Army going with airborne supplies.

On 20 November Manstein, reputedly the most brilliant German general, arrived to take command of the armies of the Don. He, too,

Nederland zal herrijzen

UW LEUZE

HUN DAAD

Hinter den Feindmächten:

der Jude

NO surrender!

HOLLAND
THE HOME OF A FREE PEOPLE

ILS DONNENT LEUR SANG

DONNEZ VOTRE TRAVAIL
pour sauver l'Europe du Bolchevisme

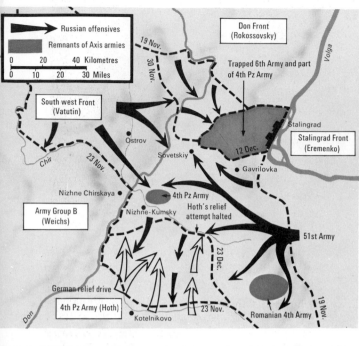

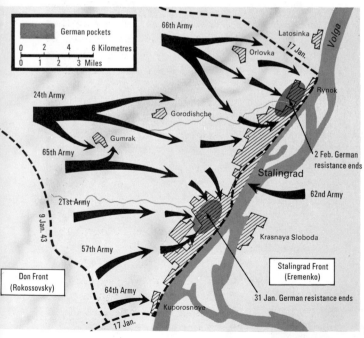

Stalingrad: the Russian counter-attack and recapture of the city

hesitated. If Paulus withdrew, the Russian armies would be freed to destroy the entire German forces scattered from the Don to the Caucasus. In any case the Russian lines were hardening. Paulus could no longer break through even if he nerved himself to do it. He would have to be rescued. An armoured force under Hoth began a laborious advance towards Stalingrad. By the middle of December it was only thirty miles away and could go no further. Paulus must move on his side. On 19 December Manstein's chief Intelligence officer flew into Stalingrad. He argued that withdrawal was still possible. Paulus's Chief of Staff answered that withdrawal would be 'an acknowledgment of disaster. Sixth Army will still be in position at Easter. All you people have to do is to supply it better.'

In any case there was confusion of counsels. What Manstein wanted was 'Winterstorm': Paulus should link up with Hoth and thus open a corridor through which the Sixth Army could be supplied. Paulus answered that he could not launch an armoured force towards Hoth without denuding the perimeter of his Stalingrad pocket. Hence the only possible operation was 'Thunderclap' – complete withdrawal. Paulus asked: would Manstein give the order for Thunderclap? Manstein never replied. It was not only that Hitler forbade it. It was essential for Manstein that the Sixth Army should remain where it was. For the Russians had again broken through higher up the Don, and the Sixth Army must continue to pin down the encircling Russian force of half a million troops and a third of the Russian artillery. This decision doomed the Sixth Army. On 31 January 1943 Paulus, who had just been made a field-marshal, surrendered, and the last German troops followed suit on 2 February. Of the 91,000 Germans who went into captivity, only 6000 ever returned. Hitler observed bitterly, 'Paulus has not known how to cross the threshold of immortality; he should have shot himself.' Goebbels proclaimed three days of national mourning, and the coming of 'total war'.

Top The Red Flag flies again over Stalingrad

Above Field Marshal Paulus surrenders

The sacrifice of the Sixth Army was not in vain. Kleist's army was able to withdraw from the Caucasus. Manstein had time to fall back and regroup. For once Hitler modified his rigid stand. He agreed with Manstein to trade space for time: 'we have here a battlefield that has room for strategical operations'. The Russians continued to advance. In the north a Russian offensive broke the encirclement of Leningrad. On 15 February the Russians took Kharkov. It was now their turn to outrun their supplies. The Germans struck back. Though they failed to encircle the Russian forces and took only 9000 prisoners, they recaptured Kharkov on 13 March. Then the fighting petered out in the slush of the spring thaw.

Stalingrad was not perhaps, as it is often claimed to be, the decisive battle of the Second World War. The armies of the satellites – Romanian, Hungarian and Italian – were broken and never recovered. But in March 1943 the Germans still stood on the line from which they had started their offensive of 1942. They had recovered their fighting spirit and showed at Kharkov that they were again masters of the field. It was they, not the Russians, who took the offensive when the fighting season of 1943 opened. Nevertheless the Russian victory at Stalingrad, far more than the defence of Moscow in the previous year, shattered the myth of German invincibility. Hitler himself said to

Jodl, 'The God of War has gone over to the other side.'

During these great events on the Volga and in North Africa, the Pacific was by no means neglected. The American Chiefs of Staff ignored the Allied decision to put the defeat of Germany first, and in the first half of 1942 twice as many American supplies went to the Pacific as to the European theatre. Thereafter the growing demands of the Pacific campaign did more than those of the Mediterranean to postpone the landings in northern France until 1944. The two Supreme Commanders, Nimitz and MacArthur, differed fundamentally in strategy, and MacArthur complained: 'Of all the faulty decisions of the war, perhaps the most inexpressible one was the failure to unify the command in the Pacific.'

Nimitz proposed to meet the Japanese head on at the extreme point of their advance. The result was a prolonged struggle for Guadalcanal in the Solomon Islands. It lasted from August 1942 until February 1943. There was a ding-dong battle with the original 6000 on either side swelling to 50,000. There were six heavy naval engagements, with roughly equal losses, a balance that the Japanese could less easily afford. On 7 February they gave up and withdrew. They had lost 25,000 men, the Americans a good deal less. But it was a gloomy prospect if the Americans were to proceed at this rate from the Solomon Islands to Tokyo.

MacArthur intended to move faster. When he first took command, he found that the Australians were preparing to abandon Sydney and hold only the southern part of the continent. Within three months he converted them to an offensive. The field of combat was New Guinea, which became uniquely Australia's war. For almost two years ill-equipped Australian troops fought a jungle war against the Japanese which ended in complete victory. Essentially it was not to MacArthur's taste. As an artist in war, he envisaged a leap-frogging strategy – bypassing the Japanese strongholds and leaving them 'to wither on the vine'. Once he received a grudging supply of ships and aircraft, he began to operate this way, and throughout 1943 the Japanese positions were falling one after another without direct assault. It was a high irony of war that General MacArthur should follow a flexible maritime strategy, while Admiral Nimitz continued to think in conventional military terms.

One offensive did not take place in 1942 and only ineffectually in the early months of 1943. The Americans constantly pressed the British to move against the Japanese in Burma and thus reopen the Burma road to Chungking. Here was a curious reversal of the roles in Europe. There the British had faith in de Gaulle, and the Americans had none. In the Far East, the Americans believed that Chiang Kai-shek had a great army eager to fight the Japanese and capable of doing so. The British did not share this belief. In both cases the British were right. All Chiang and his associates wanted was to line their pockets with American dollars. The British had troubles enough in India after the breakdown of the talks with Congress. Gandhi once more proclaimed civil disobedience and was again imprisoned. The British were unable to recover control of the Indian Ocean. The mountains and jungles that had saved them after their retreat from Burma now protected the Japanese. After much American prodding the British began a land offensive towards Burma in December 1942. It was a total failure, and the British forces withdrew in May 1943. For them, though not for the Americans, the Far East would have to wait.

So the campaigning season of 1942 ended: the last year of Axis victories, the first of Allied ones. The Allied victories were in a sense defensive. The Axis advance had been stopped at El Alamein and Stalingrad, and the Japanese in New Guinea and Guadalcanal. But the Germans were still far into Russia; the Axis forces were still in Tunis; Japan still held her Co-Prosperity Sphere. The defeat of Japan and the Axis had yet to come.

Allied offensives at last 1943

8

In 1943 the great Allies were at last on the move: the Russians rolling back the Germans, the British and Americans not so clear what they were up to. The year began with a dramatic meeting between Roosevelt and Churchill at Casablanca – the first time a President had left American soil or nearby waters since Woodrow Wilson attended the peace conference at Paris in 1919. Roosevelt was eager to exercise his personal charms on Stalin, and Churchill was determined to keep in the ranks of the Great Powers. But, with the fighting at Stalingrad and beyond the Don in full swing, Stalin could not leave Moscow, which was too far for Roosevelt. He and Churchill, with their respective staffs, therefore met alone at Casablanca from 13 to 24 January. Churchill telegraphed to Attlee on arrival: 'Conditions most agreeable. I wish I could say the same of the problems.'

The British knew what they wanted: to clear North Africa and then somehow knock out Italy, continue the bombing of Germany, and sit tight in the Far East. Only Churchill had qualms: 'This is not what I promised M. Stalin last August.' The American view was not so clear cut. They had accepted action in the Mediterranean as a stopgap and were now anxious to have done with it. Then, if there were to be no Second Front in 1943, they would divert most of their forces to the Far East.

As often happened, events rather than the wranglings between the Chiefs of Staff imposed the decisions. With the Axis forces still in Tunis, the campaign in North Africa would have to be reinforced and carried to a conclusion. By that time it would be too late to accumulate forces during 1943 for a landing in northern France, and those in North Africa should go to Sicily for want of anything better to do. After that the Chiefs of Staff would think again. The Americans regarded the conquest of Sicily as merely completing the opening of the Mediterranean to Allied shipping; the British saw it as a first step towards finishing with Italy. Roosevelt did not mind what happened as long as there was action somewhere, and the American Chiefs of Staff had difficulty in holding back in the Mediterranean when an American, General Eisenhower, was in supreme command. Shortage of shipping, a problem that was not overcome until the middle of the year, made it impossible for the British to mount any offensive towards Burma, though the Americans meant to push on in the Pacific, whatever their commitments elsewhere. Both parties happily agreed on the bombing of Germany, the Americans in the conviction that their Flying Fortresses could operate in the daytime. This conviction proved to be mistaken.

There were also political acts at Casablanca. De Gaulle was summoned from England and ungraciously shook hands with Giraud. The Americans thought they had tied de Gaulle down. This, too, proved mistaken. De Gaulle was a skilful political operator despite his lack of material resources; Giraud was politically all at sea. Within a few months Giraud was manœuvred out of office and disappeared from the scene. A consultative assembly, composed of deputies and others who had escaped from France, was set up in Algiers and gave de Gaulle a cloak of

'There's a war on, you know.' Roosevelt and Churchill at Casablanca

On the last day of the Casablanca meeting Roosevelt announced without warning that 'unconditional surrender' by the Axis Powers was the Allied aim and the only terms on which they would end the war. The main thought in his mind was to avoid the troubles President Wilson had run into by agreeing to peace with Germany on the basis of the Fourteen Points. Maybe he also wanted to give Stalin some guarantee that the Western Powers would not make a compromise peace. Churchill tried to exclude Italy from the demand. As he wrote later, 'Even when the issue of war became certain, Mussolini would have been welcomed by the Allies' – a remark that was true only of himself. The British War Cabinet did not back him up, and he did not insist. Henceforth 'unconditional surrender' was the official Allied policy.

Later on there was a great fuss over this and complaints that it had prolonged the war by preventing a negotiated peace. The complaints were without substance. As early as August 1940 Churchill had defined the British war aim as the destruction of National Socialism and the total undoing of Hitler's conquests. The other two great Allies took the same view. Nothing less would have secured peace and freedom or satisfied the Allied peoples. In any case, with whom were the Allied governments supposed to negotiate? Certainly not with the Nazi and Fascist leaders, and even Germans opposed to Hitler – the so-called German Resistance – wished to keep some or all of his conquests, an unacceptable condition. 'Unconditional surrender' was not so much a policy as a recognition of facts. The Axis Powers would not yield until they had been totally defeated, and their unconditional surrender was the only means of securing this.

The Allies were a long way from achieving their aim in the winter of 1942–3. The Anglo-American forces in North Africa did not recover from their setback of Christmas 1942 until February 1943, and Montgomery arrived at the borders of Tunisia only at the same time. Rommel had a last chance of striking against the

constitutional respectability. In practice he reigned supreme, commanding the allegiance of the French Resistance from Communists to rightwing Nationalists. This was not at all what the Americans had intended when they landed in North Africa. But, as they needed French troops to take part in the fighting, they had to put up with it.

two armies before they joined up, and his campaign echoed that of Napoleon's in 1814. In the middle of February he struck against the Anglo-American forces in the north and drove them back to the Kasserine Pass. The Allied forces, though much superior in strength, fell into considerable disarray and, as the American official history remarks, 'the enemy was amazed at the quantity and quality of the American equipment captured more or less intact'. Rommel was now free to turn against Montgomery. He was too late. By the time Rommel attacked at Médenine on 6 March, Montgomery had superior forces and conducted a firm defensive battle as he had done at Alam el Halfa six months before.

Rommel broke off the attack the same evening and three days later left Africa for ever. Back in Germany he warned Hitler that it was 'plain

suicide' for the Axis forces to stay in Africa. Hitler told him that he had lost his nerve and should get fitter in order 'to take command of operations against Casablanca' – a project of fantasy. Montgomery methodically prepared an attack on the Mareth line which he launched on 20 March. His frontal attack was a failure, and on 26 March he switched to the inland flank of the enemy. This was a complete success. The Axis line was turned, not broken. As at El Alamein Montgomery was slow to exploit his victory and the shattered enemy got away. Altogether it was a characteristic operation: the failure of the initial attack, the improvised

Below Tunis: the end of the North African campaigns

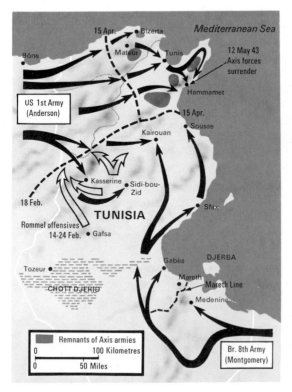

Above Far from home, Ghurka troops in Tunisia join the action with *khukris* waving

switch to the flank, Montgomery's subsequent assertion – quite contrary to the facts – that everything had gone 'according to plan', and finally the failure to exploit the victory.

The Allies now had 300,000 men and 1400 tanks in the field against 60,000 Axis combat troops and under 100 tanks. Even so they were alarmed by their previous setbacks and moved slowly. Montgomery proposed to go straight through, but was told by Alexander, who had arrived from Cairo to command the land forces, that the main offensive must take place in the north for political reasons – in fact, so that the Americans could obliterate their previous defeats. In the end the Axis forces were choked by the Allied blockade rather than beaten in the field. The Axis aircraft had lost command of the air, and when Doenitz arrived in Rome to organize convoys, he found that the Italian navy had almost ceased to exist as a fighting force.

By the beginning of May the Axis forces had run out of oil and practically out of food. Their resistance faded away. On 8 May a French corps made the formal entry into Tunis, and on 13 May the remaining Axis forces surrendered. Only a few hundred Axis troops got away. The Allies took some 130,000 prisoners who swelled in postwar accounts to a quarter of a million. Alexander sent to Churchill the grandiloquent message: 'Sir, it is my duty to report that the Tunisian campaign is over. All enemy resistance has ceased. We are masters of the North African shore.' The Mediterranean was reopened to Allied shipping, and on 26 May the first convoy from Gibraltar reached Alexandria. Italian military strength was virtually at an end. It had taken the combined might of the United States and the British Empire five months to overcome a German force that was usually only two and never more than four divisions strong.

There was renewed debate on what to do next, with Churchill and the British Chiefs of Staff again in Washington from 12 to 25 May. The British once more advocated an invasion first of Sicily and then of the Italian mainland. Marshall once more lamented the 'suction-pump' effect of the North African campaign. But there was no escape from it. It was too late to move ships and troops back to England in time for a landing in northern France in 1943, and the forces in North Africa must meanwhile do something. It was a classic example of the great factor that so often determined the course of war: the Allies in North Africa and then in

Italy were there because they were there. Churchill was almost alone in believing, as he had done in the First World War, that the Mediterranean opened a back door into Europe. There was a sneaking feeling, disproved by the event, that Italy was a vital element in the Axis and that her defeat would bring a decisive change in the balance of power. In fact her defeat alleviated Hitler's problems just as that of France had alleviated those of the British in 1940.

The invasion of Sicily took some time to prepare. The Allies had no experience of an opposed landing – their almost unopposed landing in North Africa had been difficult enough. Eisenhower at one time reported that the operation would be unlikely to succeed if opposed by more than two German divisions. Churchill stormed back: 'What Stalin would think of this, when he has 185 German divisions on his front,

British troops land in Sicily in July 1943

I cannot imagine.' Montgomery added to the troubles by insisting that there must be a single powerful landing under his command with the Americans performing only the humble function of protecting his left flank. Montgomery got his way. On the enemy side, Hitler was also hesitant what to do. He may have been misled by 'the man who never was' – a corpse dressed as a British officer who was floated ashore on the coast of Spain, complete with plans for invasions of Greece and Sardinia. More seriously, he feared betrayal by the Italians. Rommel, when asked which Italian officers could be trusted, replied, 'There is no such person.' In the end some German forces were grudgingly sent to Sicily with orders to disregard the Italians and think only of their own security.

The invasion of Sicily began on 10 July. The landings were on a larger scale even than those in Normandy eleven months later: 150,000 troops landed on the first day from over 3000 landing craft and protected by over 1000 aircraft, and half a million men were put ashore before the campaign was over. Montgomery's forces landed almost unopposed but after a few days could make no headway. Patton, the American fire-eater, broke loose from his subordinate role, and Alexander, complacent as usual, allowed him to do so. The original plan was turned upside down. Instead of Montgomery's advancing on Messina, he remained stuck on the slopes of Etna, while Patton made a prolonged pilgrimage along the west and then the north coast of Sicily. This march, though ultimately successful, had unfortunate consequences. If Montgomery had reached Messina first, most of the Axis forces in the island would have been cut off. As it was, Patton actually

'Forward!' – the only order he knew. General Patton in Sicily

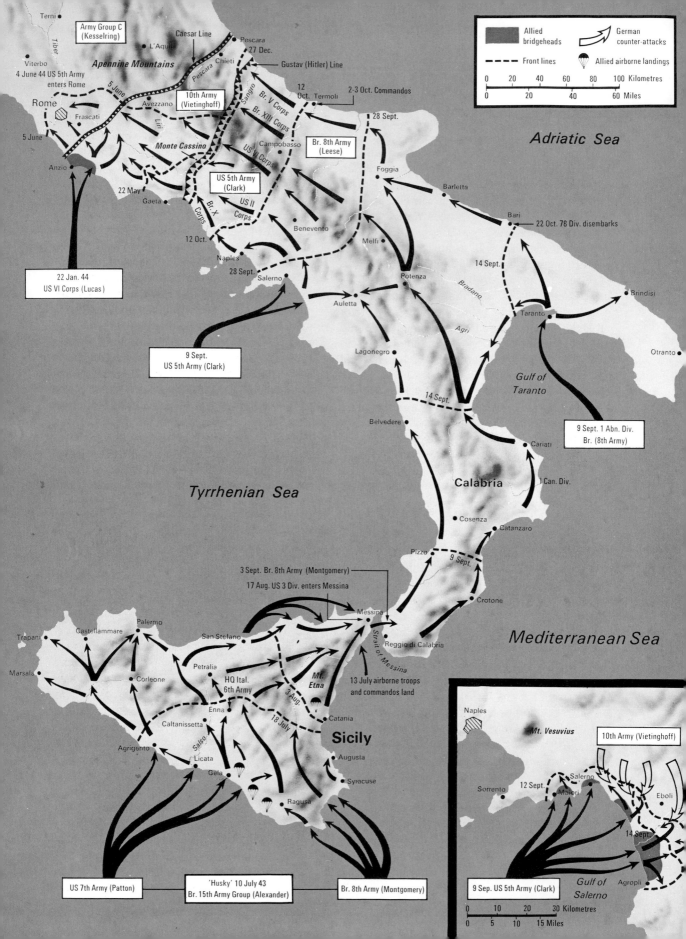

Terni
Tiber
Viterbo
4 June 44 US 5th Army enters Rome
Rome
5 June
Anzio

Army Group C (Kesselring)
Caesar Line
L'Aquila
Apennine Mountains
5 June
Frascati
Avezzano
Monte Cassino
22 May
Gaeta
Br. X Corps
12 Oct.
Naples
28 Sept.
Salerno

Pescara
27 Dec.
Pescara
Chieti
Gustav (Hitler) Line
Sangro
Br. V Corps
12 Oct.
Termoli
2-3 Oct. Commandos
Br. XIII Corps
28 Sept.
10th Army (Vietinghoff)
Campobasso
Br. 8th Army (Leese)
US VI Corps
US 5th Army (Clark)
Liri
US II Corps
Benevento
Melfi
Auletta
Potenza

Adriatic Sea
Foggia
Barletta
Bari
22 Oct. 78 Div. disembarks
14 Sept.
Brindisi
Bradano
Taranto
Agri
Otranto

22 Jan. 44
US VI Corps (Lucas)

9 Sept.
US 5th Army (Clark)

Lagonegro
14 Sept.
Belvedere

Gulf of Taranto

9 Sept. 1 Abn. Div.
Br. (8th Army)

Cariati
1 Can. Div.

Calabria
Cosenza
Catanzaro
Pizzo
9 Sept.
Crotone

Tyrrhenian Sea

Mediterranean Sea

3 Sept. Br. 8th Army (Montgomery)
17 Aug. US 3 Div. enters Messina
Messina
Reggio di Calabria
Strait of Messina
13 July airborne troops and commandos land

Trapani
Marsala
Palermo
Castellammare
San Stefano
Petralia
Corleone
HQ Ital. 6th Army
3 Aug.
Mt. Etna
Enna
18 July
Catania
Caltanissetta
Salso
Sicily
Agrigento
Licata
Gela
Ragusa
Augusta
Syracuse

US 7th Army (Patton)
'Husky' 10 July 43
Br. 15th Army Group (Alexander)
Br. 8th Army (Montgomery)

Naples
Mt. Vesuvius
10th Army (Vietinghoff)
Sorrento
12 Sept.
Maiori
Salerno
Eboli
14 Sept.
9 Sep. US 5th Army (Clark)
Agropli
Gulf of Salerno

shepherded them to safety. He took Palermo on 22 July and reached Messina on 16 August. When British troops also arrived there on the following day, they were greeted by the Americans with cries of, 'Where've you tourists been?' Most of the Axis troops got safely across the Strait of Messina without harassment, the Germans taking all their equipment with them.

Though no great military victory, the invasion of Sicily completed the ruin of Fascism. The Italian economy was approaching collapse. There were great strikes in the industrial cities of the north, Turin and Milan. Mussolini, himself a physical wreck, recognized that Italy must leave the war. The only way out, he thought, was that Hitler should make peace with Russia and move his armies to the Italian front. But when the two dictators met, Mussolini never dared to speak his mind. They met in full glory for the last time at Feltre on 19 July – the old glittering uniforms, the old Fascist and Nazi salutes. Hitler ranted about the need for iron willpower. Mussolini did not speak except to read a message that Rome had been bombed by the Allies.

In Rome various small groups speculated vaguely how Mussolini might be overthrown. Elderly politicians talked of restoring constitutional rule; some of the generals looked to Badoglio, the former Chief of Staff; some prominent Fascists hoped to save their own skins. Victor Emanuel III listened more to the generals than to the politicians, and agreed to call on Badoglio one of these days. After the Feltre meeting he almost decided to act. The discontented Fascists struck first. On 24 July Grandi, a Fascist who had always been more pro-British than pro-Axis, demanded a meeting of the Fascist Grand Council. There he proposed that Mussolini should return his powers to the King. The discussion dragged on into the night. At half past two in the morning the vote was taken: 19 voted for Grandi's motion, 8 against, 1 abstained. Mussolini said, 'You have provoked the crisis of the regime' and, refusing the traditional Salute to the Duce, stalked from the room. The next afternoon Mussolini went to the

King, still confident of his support. Victor Emanuel received him in military uniform, dismissed him from office, and informed him that General Badoglio would be his successor. As Mussolini left, he was stopped by carabinieri, smuggled away by a side door, and taken to the island of Lipari, ostensibly for his own security. Nenni, Mussolini's old Socialist comrade of prewar days, was already interned there and refused to speak to him. Throughout Italy Fascism vanished overnight. Its leaders fled, some to Portugal, some – unwisely – to Germany. The Fascist militia disintegrated without any attempt at resistance. In death as in life Fascism was a sham without substance.

Badoglio hoped to accomplish the miracle of getting Italy out of the war without either offending the Germans or making concessions to the Allies. Hitler was told that Italy would continue to fight. At the same time a succession of rival emissaries approached Allied representatives. Hitler was not deceived for a moment. Immediately after the fall of Mussolini Rommel took command of eight German divisions and secured the Alpine passes. On 28 July the Germans picked up and deciphered a scrambled telephone conversation between Roosevelt and Churchill in which they discussed the terms for Italy's surrender. When the Allies failed to make an immediate landing Hitler grew more resolute and sent reinforcements to Kesselring in southern Italy.

The Allies, in their usual fashion, dragged on their discussions for a month, this time with Churchill and Roosevelt meeting at Quebec. The Americans insisted that practical steps must now be taken for a landing in France in 1944. Men and landing craft began to move back to England, thus limiting the fighting strength of the forces allotted to Italy. But the temptation to take advantage of Mussolini's fall was irresistible. The Allies even had a vision that, with Badoglio's assistance, they might occupy Italy without fighting. In this paradoxical way, the overthrow of Fascism, which had been designed to spare Italy the horrors of war on her own soil, actually brought these horrors upon her.

In a flush of optimism, the Allies disputed how to make peace rather than war. The British Foreign Office and the American State Department, in true bureaucratic fashion, wished to impose hard terms on Italy, spelling out every detail of unconditional surrender. The soldiers at Allied Headquarters were ready for any terms that would take Italy out of the war. In the end there was a somewhat underhand compromise: the Italians would be asked to sign relatively gentle 'short' terms, and harsher 'long' terms would be imposed upon them later. (Though this tactic was operated, the 'hard' terms were never fully applied, for the Italian government cooperated with the Allies to the best of its feeble abilities.)

All this took time. On 3 September Badoglio agreed to a secret signing of the short terms and promised to cooperate with the Allies on condition there was an airborne landing in Rome. Eisenhower first agreed and then learned that the Germans were already present in Rome in strength. The airborne landing was cancelled at the last moment. On 3 September Montgomery and his Eighth Army landed at the toe of Italy directly opposite Messina, evidently doomed to inch or nibble all the way up. On 8 September Badoglio's representative at Allied headquarters was abruptly told that the armistice would be publicly announced that evening. In Rome all was chaos. The Italian troops received no orders. The Germans disarmed them and took over the city. Badoglio and the King fled to Bari. In Greece and Yugoslavia the Italian troops were also disarmed by the Germans. On Churchill's prompting small British forces landed in the Aegean Islands and were soon overcome – hardly an encouragement to the Turks to enter the war. Only the Italian fleet managed to make its escape. Admiral Cunningham triumphantly reported, 'The Italian battle fleet now lies at anchor under the guns of the fortress of Malta.'

The main Allied landing took place at Salerno on 9 September in the belief that it would be unopposed. Instead Kesselring had time to bring up six divisions. There was fierce fighting and at one moment Mark Clark, the American general in command, proposed to re-embark. He was deterred only by the protests of the British admiral. After further alarms, the Eighth Army arrived from Calabria on 16 September and the Germans fell back. But it took the Allies another three weeks to reach Naples. Elsewhere a great opportunity had been lost. Taranto, the greatest port in southern Italy, was supposed to be beyond the range of air cover. Admiral Cunningham was ready to take the risk, and a small expedition, appropriately named Slapstick, took Taranto without difficulty on 8 September. The east coast of Italy lay wide open to the invader. But there were no forces available for an advance, and once more the Germans had time to prepare their defence. North of Naples fighting dragged on unsuccessfully. By the end of the year the Allies had advanced only seventy miles beyond Salerno – mostly in the first few weeks – and were still eighty miles short of Rome. Churchill raged impotently: 'The stagnation of the whole campaign on the Italian front is becoming scandalous.' As Liddell Hart remarks, the Allies had erred by following the cautious banker's principle of 'no advance without security'.

The invasion of Italy brought with it political problems, far graver than those in North Africa. Despite the warning of the Darlan affair, the Allies operated without any clear political principles. In Sicily, for example, the Americans rearmed the Mafia, which Fascism had crushed, and its dominance endures there to the present day. Churchill, Roosevelt and the military commanders casually assumed that they could simply work through Badoglio's government, which actually declared war against Germany on 13 October. But Badoglio had no authority. In the south the revived political parties openly agitated against him. In Rome the Resistance set up a secret committee of national liberation, as much directed against the King as against the Germans. In the north there was an armed

British 8th Army on the march in Italy

Resistance, campaigning in the name of national renewal. For the Allies, liberation meant simply the removal of German and Fascist rule; for the Resistance it meant something far more profound.

The Allied rulers were exasperated at this Italian ingratitude; they were fighting to defeat Germany, not to provoke a revolution. They had a further embarrassment. The Soviet government put in its claim to a say in Italian affairs. Once again it had never occurred to the British and the Americans that they might have to treat the Russians as equals. The Russians were refused a place on the Anglo-American Control Commission that in practice ruled Italy, and were fobbed off with a seat on the Advisory Council, safely remote in Algiers. The Russians acquiesced and prepared to follow the Anglo-American model when it was their turn to liberate countries occupied by the Germans. The Anglo-Americans kept their monopoly of Italy and, in doing so, forfeited all effective say in Romania, Hungary, Bulgaria and even Poland.

There was a further confusion. On 12 September German airborne troops rescued Mussolini from the Gran Sasso, the mountain area to which he had been removed. He was flown to Munich, had a lachrymose meeting with Hitler, and was ostensibly restored to power. Establishing himself at Salo on Lake Garda, he proclaimed the Fascist Social Republic. On Hitler's insistence the Fascist leaders who had voted against Mussolini on 25 July were put on trial and all of them, including Mussolini's son-in-law Ciano, were shot. Otherwise, revived Fascism had no reality. It had to work through German advisers, was not allowed to control its own armed forces, and witnessed helplessly German tyranny over northern Italy. German agents with an Austrian background took over south Tirol and Trieste. The dismemberment of Italy seemed to have begun. Mussolini, staring out at the ceaseless rain, reiterated: 'We are all dead.'

The Americans had believed that from bases in southern Italy they would be able to bomb the oilfields at Ploeşti in Romania. These air raids followed the usual pattern: many bombs dropped and many aircraft lost without decisive effect. When the Russians occupied Ploeşti in the following year, they found nearly half the oil wells in full production.

The Allied presence in Italy had, however, a profound effect on their Balkan policy in another way. Ever since the German conquest of Yugoslavia in 1941 there had been attempts at resistance. Mihailović, a regular army officer, appealed to old-style Serb nationalism and co-operated with the exiled royal government. In his anxiety to avoid casualties, he often made local pacts with the Italian, and occasionally even with the German, occupying forces. Tito, the Yugoslav Communist leader, built up a movement of a different character. His aim was to promote a united Communist Yugoslavia, and he believed that casualties, however great, brought increasing support for his partisans. Mihailović's Fabian tactics were exactly those laid down by SOE, the British Special Operations Executive which directed subversive activities in Europe. The Resistance in France and elsewhere was told to recruit and organize supporters, act as intelligence centres, and wait for the approach of Allied armies before coming into the open. Mihailović followed this line. To his misfortune

Marshal Tito in August 1942

the storm of the world, in his own words, carried him away.

For when Italy went out of the war, Tito's partisans disarmed the Italian troops and carried off their equipment. The partisans were now an army of a quarter of a million men and were tying down eight German divisions. Churchill was eager to promote action in the Balkans, though there were no Allied troops to spare. Tito seemed to provide the answer. British agents, including Churchill's own son Randolph, reported that Tito's partisans were fighting the Germans and Mihailović's men were not. Both were put to the test. British supplies were dropped to them, and they were told to use them. Tito responded; Mihailović did not. By the end of the year all the available supplies were going to Tito, and soon afterwards recognition was withdrawn from Mihailović. When Fitzroy Maclean, the British representative with Tito, warned Churchill that he was a Communist, Churchill replied: 'Are you going to live in Yugoslavia after the war? No? Neither am I.' The build-up of Tito was a purely British venture, and present-day Yugoslavia is a British creation, though of course much more a creation of the partisans themselves. The Americans disapproved of Tito and went on supporting Mihailović until his inaction was too much even for them. Still more surprisingly, Stalin backed Mihailović and was furious when he discovered that Tito existed. Perhaps Stalin wished to please the Americans; maybe he foresaw the troubles that an independent Communist country would cause him. At any rate it was a curious situation.

With military attention concentrated on North Africa and Italy, the two Western Powers seemed almost to have forgotten Germany. But this is to overlook the air offensive: 1943 was the heyday of area or indiscriminate bombing. At Bomber Command Sir Arthur Harris continued his night attacks on an ever-increasing scale. The Americans confidently began daylight bombing with their Flying Fortresses. The Ruhr was attacked from March to June; Hamburg from July to November; Berlin from November 1943 to March 1944. Berlin alone received 50,000 tons of bombs. The German cities were devastated, and Harris wrote, 'We can wreck Berlin from end to end if the American air force will come in on it. It will cost us 400–500 aircraft. It will cost Germany the war.'

These expectations were not fulfilled. Many thousands of Germans were killed, and tens of thousands were made homeless. German production was little affected. In fact it reached its

A Flying Fortress in action

all-time high exactly at the height of Allied bombing – in March 1944. The figures tell their own story. In 1942 the British dropped 48,000 tons of bombs, and the Germans produced 36,804 weapons of war (heavy guns, tanks and aircraft). In 1943 the British and Americans dropped 207,600 tons of bombs; the Germans produced 71,693 weapons of war. In 1944 the British and Americans dropped 915,000 tons; the Germans produced 105,258 weapons of war. Certainly the German standard of life was re-

duced for the first time, though it never fell to the British level. But morale was unaffected. On the contrary, the indiscriminate bombing delivered the Germans into the hands of Goebbels and his propaganda of total war.

By March 1944 Harris confessed that the British rate of loss had become insupportable. With the Americans things were even worse. The Flying Fortresses proved unable to defend themselves in daytime from the German fighters. The two allies drew different conclusions from this setback. Harris could only propose that area bombing should be renewed, despite the losses, when Bomber Command had again built up its strength. The Americans, however, perfected a long-range fighter, the Mustang, which could accompany the bombers over Germany, and with this the air offensive took a new form.

The greatest battle of 1943 was not fought in the air or in the Mediterranean sphere. It was fought in and around Kursk from 5 to 12 July and proved to be the decisive battle of the war. When fighting died down on the Eastern Front in March 1943, the Russians had established a salient in front of Kursk. There was a temptation for the Russians to push it further, and for the Germans to cut it off. The Russians resisted the temptation; the Germans did not. Stalin remembered the unsuccessful Russian offensive at Kharkov that had ushered in the disasters of 1942. With his inexhaustible patience, he decided to wait for the German offensive and destroy it. Hitler told Guderian that 'his stomach turned over at the thought of the offensive' and yet regarded it as inevitable. He was anxious to deal the Russians a crushing blow so that he could divert forces to the aid of Mussolini, and comforted himself with the thought that the Germans had always won in the summer, even though General Winter had been too much for them.

Times had changed. The Russians had recovered from their earlier catastrophes. They had now far more guns than the Germans, more men and better tanks. With the American trucks and canned food that were now coming in, they had greater mobility. Their young generals had learned more flexible tactics from the earlier failures. As the German tank divisions moved towards the Kursk salient, the Russians strengthened their minefields and sent in more and more guns. By the beginning of July there were four Russian defence lines, stretching over a depth of fifty miles. There was no weak spot as there had been in previous German offensives. Like Montgomery at El Alamein, the Germans had to attack at the strongest points, with this difference: Mongomery had far greater resources than his enemy, the Germans were already inferior.

The German attack began on 5 July on the two flanks of the salient. The southern pincer advanced about twenty miles; the northern pincer hardly moved at all. With tanks fighting tanks there was no room for the infantry, and the German guns could not fire. Instead of a breakthrough there was a slogging match. On 12 July the Russians began a counter-offensive. There were 1500 tanks engaged on each side – the greatest tank battle in history, at any rate until the Middle East war of 1973. That evening Hitler broke off the offensive. For the first time the great army of National Socialist Germany had been beaten in the field. From this moment delay, not victory, was Hitler's purpose and his only hope.

The Germans had calculated that the Russians would be too crippled to resume the offensive. Again they were wrong. Russian reserves had hardly been drawn on during the Battle of Kursk, and at the beginning of August the Russians began an offensive that rarely relaxed until they reached Berlin. This was not an offensive of the German type with a single powerful force thrusting forward and encircling the enemy. The Russians followed much the same strategy as had brought victory to Foch and the Allies in the last months of the First World War. They attacked at a weak point and broke off whenever they encountered strong resistance, only to renew their advance elsewhere. Thanks to the American trucks, the Russians could switch quickly from one area to another, whereas the Germans were tied down to the speed at which men and horses walked.

The Soviet army was of a kind never before seen in modern warfare. At the head came the élite forces, often honoured with the name of Guards divisions: tanks, artillery, rockets, men of high professional competence and technique. Once a breakthrough had been achieved, the inexhaustible mass of infantry followed like a barbarian horde on the march: ill-trained, often undisciplined, and living off the country. Crusts of bread and raw vegetables were their only food. They could advance for as much as three weeks without receiving supplies, and when the Germans tried to cut their lines of communication, they found that there were none to cut. These Russians slaughtered the German infantry, pillaged the towns and villages through which they passed, and raped the women. They were true cannon fodder. (When after the war Eisenhower was describing to Zhukov the elaborate devices employed by the Americans to clear the minefields – flails, sweeps and so on – Zhukov remarked that the most effective way of clearing a minefield was to march the infantry over it.) After the infantry came another élite corps: the military police, who restored order, shot the worst offenders out of hand, and drove the infantry forward to fresh assaults.

Between August and December 1943 the Russians advanced on a broad front. They reached the Dnieper and crossed it. Further north they cleared the approaches to Moscow and retook Smolensk. Despite an over-all Russian superiority of 6 to 1, the German front was never broken. Only 98,000 Germans were taken prisoner in the four months of campaigning, and in November Manstein actually tried a counter-offensive – the last of its kind. Attrition, not strategic penetration, was the Russian method, and it was succeeding. Hitler said to Manteuffel who had conducted the counter-offensive under Manstein: 'As a Christmas present, I'll give you fifty tanks.' This was

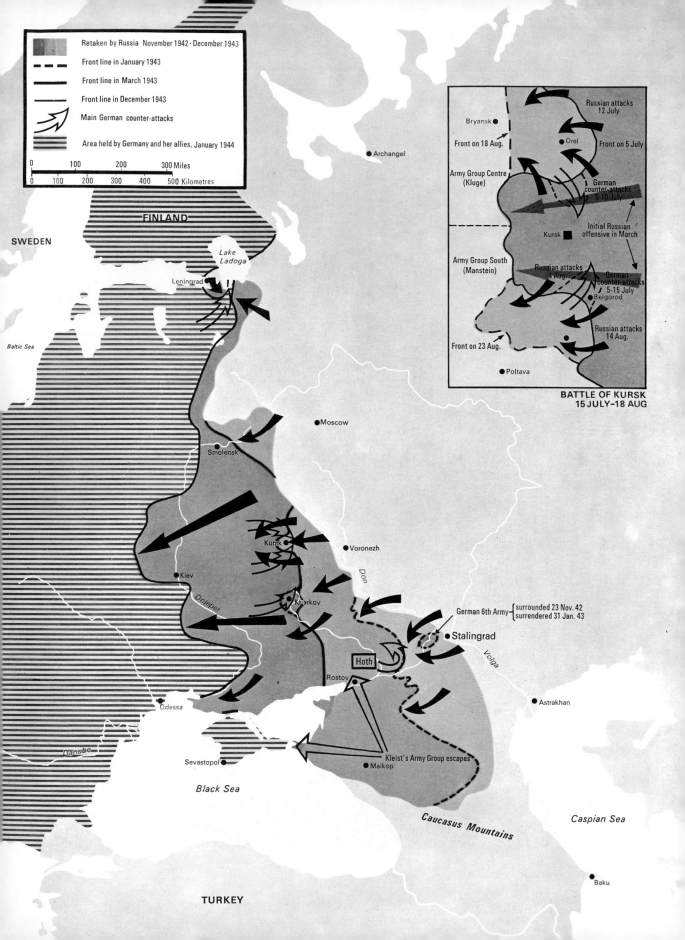

Legend:

Retaken by Russia November 1942 – December 1943

Front line in January 1943

Front line in March 1943

Front line in December 1943

Main German counter-attacks

Area held by Germany and her allies, January 1944

| 0 | 100 | 200 | 300 Miles |
| 0 | 100 | 200 | 300 | 400 | 500 Kilometres |

SWEDEN

FINLAND

Baltic Sea

Lake Ladoga

Leningrad

Archangel

Moscow

Smolensk

Kursk

Voronezh

Don

Kiev

Dnieper

Kharkov

German 6th Army { surrounded 23 Nov. 42 / surrendered 31 Jan. 43

Stalingrad

Volga

Hoth

Rostov

Astrakhan

Odessa

Danube

Sevastopol

Maikop

Kleist's Army Group escapes

Black Sea

Caucasus Mountains

Caspian Sea

Baku

TURKEY

Battle of Kursk inset:

Russian attacks 12 July

Bryansk

Front on 18 Aug.

Orel

Front on 5 July

Army Group Centre (Kluge)

German counter-attacks 5–10 July

Kursk

Initial Russian offensive in March

Army Group South (Manstein)

Russian attacks 4 Aug.

German counter-attacks 5–15 July

Belgorod

Russian attacks 14 Aug.

Front on 23 Aug.

Poltava

BATTLE OF KURSK
15 JULY–18 AUG

the best he could offer. What else remained? Only the prospect on which Hitler always counted: that the Grand Alliance would fall apart.

While the situation in Russia and the Mediterranean was changing so rapidly, the Far East seemed to have become 'the forgotten war'. Nothing stirred in Burma after the unsuccessful British campaign there ended in May. MacArthur and Nimitz competed in the southwest and central Pacific – a two-pronged advance when there were hardly supplies for one. Even so the Japanese decided in September that to hold all their gains was beyond their strength and drew up 'an absolute national defence sphere' which they fortified against the coming American offensives of 1944. The most signal American achievement was a personal one. In April 1943 their interception services learned that Admiral Yamamoto was flying to the Pacific on a tour of inspection. His aircraft was shot down, and he was killed. Chivalrous and a strategic genius, Yamamoto was the Hector of the Second World War, an irreparable loss to Japan. The American admiral who designed his death could only find this epitaph for him: 'I had hoped to lead that

scoundrel up Pennsylvania Avenue in chains with the rest of you kicking him where it would do most good.'

In November the European and Far Eastern wars overlapped, though only in a casual way. Stalin at last agreed to meet Roosevelt and Churchill at Teheran. Churchill proposed a preliminary meeting between himself and Roosevelt at Cairo. When he arrived there, he discovered that Roosevelt had outwitted him by inviting Chiang Kai-shek also. No 'ganging-up' against Stalin was possible. Instead Chiang demanded a British naval action in the Bay of Bengal before he would move against the Japanese, and Churchill was hustled into agreeing, although it meant a further diversion of vital resources from the Mediterranean.

Churchill and Roosevelt thus arrived in Teheran without having coordinated their plans, which was exactly what Roosevelt had wanted. He was now set on agreement with Stalin, even if this meant the exclusion of Churchill. It was later made a high accusation against Roosevelt that he relied solely on personal relations and failed to grasp that Stalin aimed at the establishment of world Communism. Roosevelt, not his critics, was right. Though the abolition of the

A crashed Japanese aircraft, the tomb of Yamamoto

Comintern in May 1943 meant little in itself, Stalin never moved from his policy of 'Socialism in a single country'. He used foreign Communists as his agents against the Nazis. He never wanted their success and often hampered it, as he showed in his dealings with the two independent Communist leaders, Tito and Mao Tse-tung. Stalin was set on the defeat of Germany to the exclusion of all else, and when one considers the twenty million Russian dead this is not surprising. Roosevelt might think of establishing a Free Trade Capitalist world, and Churchill of restoring the British Empire. Stalin thought only of defeating Germany.

The great question was answered almost at once. Churchill had hoped that Stalin might be tempted by action in the eastern Mediterranean and the reopening of the Straits. Instead Roosevelt, who was in the chair, asked Stalin, the expert in defeating the Germans, how it should be done. Stalin answered without hesitation: Overlord, an Allied landing in northern France. Roosevelt seconded him; Churchill acquiesced. The great decision was made: the shape of the rest of the war was determined. The Allies would land in northern France, and the Mediterranean would take second place. The two really great Powers had imposed strategy on their theoretically equal partner.

Here was another prolific source of legend for the future. Stalin is supposed to have unscrupulously diverted his two allies to the west, while he scooped up the Balkans, allegedly the centre of European strength. In fact the Balkans were almost valueless. The Romanian oilfields were nearly exhausted. Yugoslavia and Bulgaria were pure burdens. Czechoslovakia had some industrial strength, though less than that of Belgium; Hungary about as much as Luxembourg. On the other hand western Germany, to which Stalin directed the Western Allies, was the greatest prize in Europe, and any Western statesman who accepted the Balkans while the Russians took the Ruhr would have been out of his mind.

Other topics were discussed at Teheran, always with a determination to reach agreement. The most prominent of these was Poland. The exiled Polish government in London still dreamed that the miracle of 1918 might be repeated and that Germany might be defeated without Russia's winning. This was not on offer. Roosevelt did not care what happened to Poland so long as it did not upset the Polish voters in America. Churchill recognized British obligations to Poland whose independence against Germany Great Britain had guaranteed. He also recognized the justice of Russia's claims to the borderlands that Poland had seized in 1921 – lands inhabited by non-Poles of White Russian and Ukrainian stock. Agreement on this territorial question was easy and, by ethnic principles, fair. Poland would lose her borderlands to Russia and be compensated by great stretches of eastern Germany. After all, Germany was the enemy and the aggressor, and someone had to pay the bill. When the three great men were also discussing the dismemberment of Germany and the shooting of 50,000 – or as Roosevelt suggested 49,000 – German officers, the loss of East Prussia or Silesia seemed of trivial importance.

There was also a political problem involved in Poland, round which the Teheran conference skated with embarrassment. Churchill and Roosevelt hoped that, after the territorial question had been sorted out, a democratic Polish government would settle down with Soviet Russia in easy friendship; they even assumed that the exiled government in London would fit the bill. This was no longer possible. In April 1943 the Germans had announced the discovery of the bodies of 4000 murdered Polish officers at Katyn. When the Polish government appealed for an inquiry by the Red Cross, Soviet Russia broke off relations with it. Who committed the crime at Katyn may never be firmly ascertained. Even if, as seems probable, it was the Russians, four thousand dead did not weigh heavily against the six million Poles murdered by the Germans. Whatever the truth, the breach between Soviet Russia and the Poles was there.

The Big Three at Teheran

It deepened later in the same year when the exiled Polish government refused to contemplate the surrender of any prewar Polish territory, and Churchill also broke off relations with them.

Who should take their place? In western Europe, as events proved, there were democratic parties ready to take over when the Germans moved out – parties too much to the Left for American taste, but democratic all the same. In Poland, and for that matter in other east European countries, there were no such parties: only nationalistic reactionary politicians, violently anti-Russian, or Communists who were Russian agents. It is not surprising that the statesmen at Teheran averted their eyes from this troublesome prospect.

There was one other surprising development. Stalin spontaneously promised Roosevelt that Soviet Russia would enter the war against Japan when Germany had been defeated. This was an enormous relief: the Russians, not the Americans, would take on the bulk of the Japanese army. Stalin's stock boomed even higher in Roosevelt's estimation. The Russian promise also let Churchill off the hook as far as the Far East was concerned. When Roosevelt returned to Cairo, he told Chiang Kai-shek that British action in the Bay of Bengal was off. As Chiang had never intended to move in any case, the news did not distress him.

The conference at Teheran, whatever its faults, was a milestone in world affairs. The two World Powers, who had failed so signally before the Second World War, had now come together. Mutual suspicions were dimmed if not removed. The three Great Powers were pledged to hold together until the defeat of Germany – a pledge that all three honoured. It had always been clear that Hitler was doomed if the Great Powers united against him. Now they had done so, and Germany's defeat was certain.

Year of liberation 1944

9

At the beginning of 1944 the German and Japanese empires were still largely intact, though somewhat clipped at the edges. Great buffers of conquered territory still warded off the Allied assaults. By the end of the year nearly all the conquests had been lost, and the homelands of the conquerors were themselves threatened. Though 1944 did not see final Allied victory, it was for many, especially in western Europe, the year of liberation.

In theory Hitler proposed to trade space for time. In practice he would never surrender any space without a struggle. He told Manstein in March, 'All that counts is to cling stubbornly to what we hold.' This stubbornness strained German military resources. Ironically the Balkans and Scandinavia, areas into which the Allies did not penetrate until almost the end of the war, absorbed more German divisions than Italy where they did: 44 divisions against 22. There were some 50 German divisions in France and the Low Countries – 35 of them north of the Loire. These were mainly second-grade occupation troops, composed of middle-aged men and war casualties. They exploited the lands they occupied and made few demands on German resources. The fighting strength of the German army was and always remained on the Eastern Front. Here the Russians faced 180 German divisions and 60 satellite divisions of doubtful quality.

The German victories had been won with pre-war weapons, and for a long time Hitler grudged any diversion of resources to new ones. By 1944 this had changed. German inventors were developing weapons which Hitler believed would reverse the run of defeats if he hung on long enough. The navy developed the schnorkel which enabled a submarine to recharge its batteries without coming to the surface and so promised to outwit the methods with which the Allies had defeated previous U-boat campaigns. The Luftwaffe developed jet aircraft, faster than anything the Allies possessed. German scientists developed long-range rockets which promised to make London and southeast England uninhabitable. Until these were ready, the Germans relied on pilotless aircraft, operated by remote control. These developments, if they had come earlier, might well have changed the course of the war.

The Allies in comparison lagged behind. Early in the war British and refugee scientists discovered how to split the atom in a controlled way, and Churchill passed on this discovery to the Americans with an understanding, not in fact honoured, that Great Britain should share in further advances. American scientists were approaching the manufacture of atomic bombs, but it was generally believed that these would not be ready before Germany was defeated. The Allies also possessed prototypes of jet aircraft, but they shrank from going over to this new aircraft which would make their vast stock of pre-jets, and the factories that produced them, obsolete. Thus the Allies gambled on scraping through to victory with their existing equipment.

German ingenuity was, however, thwarted by a single, though rather belated, American initiative. This was the long-range Mustang

An American attack on the oil refineries at Hamburg

Facing defeat in Russia, a German grenadier shoulders his machine gun

fighter, designed to the specifications of the British Purchasing Commission as far back as 1940. Thanks to Beaverbrook, when Minister of Aircraft Production, it was later equipped with the superb Rolls-Royce Merlin engine. When Henry Ford refused to manufacture these engines for a belligerent, Beaverbrook financed production by Packard – in the words of the Rolls-Royce agent: 'The biggest, the best and most profitable job ever undertaken by the British Government.' When fitted with drop-tanks – again not a new idea, having already been used in the Spanish Civil War – the Mustang had a range of nearly a thousand miles.

For a long time, the bomber chiefs went on believing that some permutation of bomber formations would provide a pattern of irresistible machine-gun defence. Finally the Americans, though not Sir Arthur Harris, confessed their mistake. In April 1944 American bombers, escorted by Mustangs, began daylight attacks on the German synthetic-oil plants. The effect was devastating. By September the Luftwaffe, which needed a monthly minimum of 160,000 tons of octane fuel, was down to 10,000 tons. The German jet aircraft and schnorkel submarines, though produced in considerable numbers, were never able to operate effectively. This

was the one triumph of strategic bombing. It came just in time and proved decisive.

For much of 1944 war was fought in the old way. The Russian offensives did not slacken during the winter months. In the north Leningrad was at last relieved after a siege that had lasted for more than two years. Over a million of its inhabitants had died from starvation, and the survivors fully deserved that Leningrad should be known as the Hero City. As the Germans fell back they were able for once to shorten their front, and the Russians did not reach the Baltic coast until the summer. Further south there was no such alleviation. On 5 January the Russians crossed their prewar frontier with Poland – the beginning of their advance into Europe. They cleared the Ukraine between the Dnieper and the Dniester. In March they reached Romania and the line of the Carpathians. Their last stroke, achieved in May, was to liberate the Crimea. When the offensive died down, the Russians had recovered practically the whole of prewar Soviet territory. Now their way was open into the Balkans, and with this the German line, instead of becoming shorter, extended more widely and thinly than before. Implicitly, too, a great decision had been taken. The Russians

Top **Liberation comes to Riga**

Above **Soviet soldiers on the Third Ukrainian Front**

would not halt at their own borders, as Kutuzov had wished to do in 1812 and as some Western observers feared that they might do now; they would go on until they took Berlin.

The Western Allies had little to set against this record of success during the early months of 1944. Their armies in Italy were firmly arrested by the Gustav line which the Germans had established in the mountains south of Rome. As well, forces were being steadily withdrawn on American insistence for the landing in northern France. Churchill, resourceful as ever, saw a way out. Anvil, a preliminary landing in southern France, was also projected in order to draw the Germans away from the north. It could not be launched until May. Surely therefore the landing craft allotted to Anvil could be used first for a landing in Italy behind the Gustav line. Such was the origin of the landing at Anzio: a manœuvre against the Second Front rather than against the Germans.

Allied forces landed at Anzio on 22 January. They were almost unopposed, and the road to Rome lay open before them. But the old story of Gallipoli was repeated. General Lucas, the American commander, had no faith in the operation and was concerned to consolidate, not to advance. Alexander, just like Ian Hamilton at Gallipoli, was too polite to give him a shove. For over a week he made no attempt to move forward and when he did so, the Germans had become too strong for him. The Allied bridgehead was now itself endangered. Far from the landing assisting the main Allied forces facing the Gustav line, these forces had to take the offensive in order to relieve the landing.

The central point of the Gustav line was the monastery of Monte Cassino. Alexander and his generals were hypnotized by it. They were convinced that the Germans had fortified the monastery and were using it as an observation post. In reality no German soldiers had ever used it. But here was an opportunity to demonstrate that the Allies would shrink from nothing in their determination to defeat Germany. Monte Cassino, one of the great historic monuments of Europe, was systematically destroyed by Allied bombing. The Allies then discovered that the rubble was a more formidable obstacle than the monastery had been. In the end the Gustav line was turned by French troops penetrating through the mountains from behind.

The Germans began to fall back. There was an opportunity for the army in Anzio to break out and cut off the German retreat. But General Mark Clark, now in overall command of the beachhead, was determined to be the first to enter Rome. Disregarding Alexander's instructions, he left the German line of retreat open and went straight for Rome, which he entered on 4 June. Meanwhile the Germans had got away and consolidated a new line further north. The march on Rome had cost the Allies over 40,000 casualties against 20,000 German and had occupied twice as many Allied as German troops. It had not prevented the Germans from reinforcing northwest Europe, though it is possible that the reinforcements would have been greater without it. Further, the need to

Below Unloading at Anzio

Bottom German troops in the ruins of Monte Cassino monastery

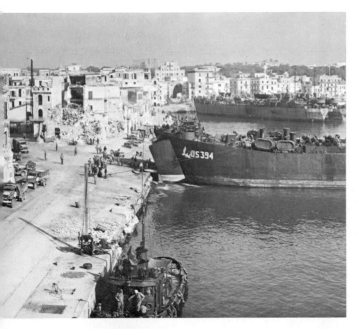

Italian partisans welcome Allied forces

the break into Europe from the south, which he had advocated from the time of Gallipoli, would at last be achieved after thirty years. The British Chiefs of Staff were more sceptical. But they wanted to keep the Italian campaign going if only because it was the one sphere where the British still predominated. The Americans insisted that nothing must be done to weaken Anvil, even though it had now been postponed until August – too late to assist the Allied landings in northern France. After a wrangle between Roosevelt and Churchill, the Americans got their way. Seven of Alexander's divisions and most of his air support were spirited away, just when Kesselring received eight fresh divisions.

The Allied armies in Italy, now hardly equal to the Germans, continued an obstinate and largely ineffective offensive. The Germans had room to manœuvre in the mountainous country that lay between Rome and the Po and withdrew cautiously, only to consolidate a new line before the Allies could overrun it. By December the Allies had reached Ravenna and had failed to take Bologna. The valley of the Po was still fifty miles away.

The approach of the Allied armies roused the partisans of north Italy, a potentially revolutionary force dedicated to a new Risorgimento. In the summer of 1944 they were pinning down 8 out of the 26 German divisions in Italy. Nearly 50,000 of them lost their lives. These partisan activities were an embarrassment to the Allies. When Alexander ended his campaign for the winter, he publicly ordered the partisans to demobilize. This was an invitation to the Germans to move against the partisans, secure from Allied interference, and they took advantage of it. Thus the Germans became implicitly the allies of the British and Americans, who now feared revolution in Italy more than they feared the enemy.

In June 1944 Italian affairs were eclipsed by the Allied landings in northern France. The Second Front had been demanded for more than two years and always put at the bottom of the list.

supply the Anzio beachhead made Anvil impossible until August, long after the landings in northern France had taken place. Altogether the Italian campaign was a poor advertisement for Italy as the soft underbelly of the Axis.

Obsessed with the significance of capital cities – Paris and later Berlin – the Allies had set Rome as their target, convinced that something tremendous would happen when they reached it. Nothing did. Victor Emanuel III handed over his powers to his son Umberto. Badoglio resigned, and an elderly politician, Bonomi, headed a coalition of anti-Fascists, extending from Communists to clericals. North of Rome the Germans were consolidating a new line of defence. Alexander pleaded that, if reinforced, his armies could reach the valley of the Po by August and drive through the so-called Ljubljana gap – another misleading geographical phrase – into Austria. Churchill was equally enthusiastic:

Now, on American insistence, it was belatedly accomplished. Perhaps the delay was justified. The landings were for once meticulously prepared instead of being laid on at a rush as other similar operations had been. The French beaches had been surveyed. Vast forces had been accumulated: 1200 fighting ships against 15 German destroyers, 10,000 aircraft against 500 German, 4126 landing craft, and 864 transport ships. There were tanks with flails to clear minefields, amphibian tanks, tanks to destroy concrete, tanks that laid their own carpets, tanks for bridging dikes. There were two artificial harbours, called Mulberries, to be towed across the Channel. Eisenhower remarked with rare wit: 'Only the great number of barrage balloons floating constantly in British skies kept the islands from sinking under the waves.'

Eisenhower had been appointed Supreme Commander, ostensibly to balance the British Supreme Command in the Mediterranean, more because of American suspicions that the British were not enthusiastic for the enterprise. His staff, composed equally of British and Americans with pedantic accuracy, numbered 4914 in July 1944 and swelled to over 30,000 before the end of the war. Eisenhower's deputy, Tedder, was British, as were the air and naval commanders. Montgomery had been brought from Italy to command the initial landings. Once the build-up made the Americans preponderant, Montgomery would revert to command of the British army group and Eisenhower himself would become army Commander-in-Chief. This imperfect arrangement had a simple explanation. Montgomery did not conceal his opinion of American deficiencies, and the American generals would not tolerate his command except in the initial stages.

The air command was a muddle. Harris and Spaatz, the two bomber chiefs, would not surrender their independence. Harris still hankered after area bombing, Spaatz after the bombing of synthetic-oil plants. As a compromise Tedder was empowered to give orders to them during the period immediately before and during the landings. These operations were on a staggering scale. Nearly all the bridges over the Seine and most of those over the Loire were destroyed. The French railway system was crippled. The German army in France needed 100 trains a day for its supply. By April it was down to 60 and by May to 32.

This Transportation Plan, as it was called, was not achieved without difficulty. Churchill feared a legacy of bitterness if many French lives were lost during the bombardment. He was supported by the War Cabinet, only to be overruled by Roosevelt who was less regardful of French feelings. Yet there was at hand a simpler and more effective way of achieving the same results. The French Resistance pleaded that they could cause more systematic damage with far less risk of lives. Their pleas were ignored. Orthodox generals had no faith in guerrilla warfare. Roosevelt was determined not to cooperate with de Gaulle, whom he distrusted far more than he did the Russians. The French Resistance was largely ignored, and de Gaulle with it. He was not told the date of the landing, even though a French army under his authority was actually cooperating with the Allies in Italy. Plans were laid for an Allied military government of France as though it were a conquered country. De Gaulle retaliated by describing as counterfeit money the 'occupation francs' that the Allies had prepared. The American objection to de Gaulle was not ideological. His offence, like that of the Russians later, was simply to be independent. Churchill, being dependent on American supplies, had to take a more subservient line; de Gaulle, having no supplies at all, could go his own way.

Should the Allies land east or west of the Seine? The coast east of the Seine, though nearer, was more heavily fortified and offered no great port as a prize. That west of the Seine had more open beaches. It was less fortified, and victory there would bring control of Cherbourg. Its superior attractions carried the day. Elaborate plans were operated to deceive the Germans. A non-existent army was established in Kent, and the

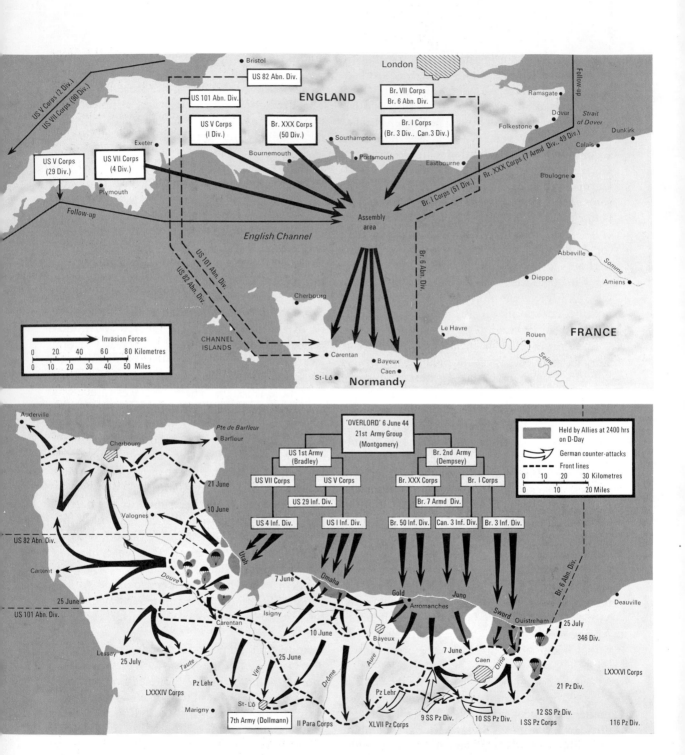

Top and above Normandy: the invasion and the campaign

" .... strictly between these four walls ! "

CARELESS TALK COSTS LIVES

Security at top level

wireless messages to Montgomery's headquarters passed through it. More bombs were dropped on the Pas de Calais than in Normandy. German reconnaissance aircraft were allowed to operate over Kent, but not further west. The Germans supposed that they had many agents in England. All had been in fact 'turned round' and sent only messages dictated by their Allied employers.

The Germans appreciated that an invasion was coming and had no means of knowing where. Rundstedt, who had been recalled to become Commander-in-Chief West, took the orthodox view that the Allies would land in the Pas de Calais. Rommel, now also a field-marshal, had a virtually independent command with direct access to Hitler. He believed that the Allies would land in Normandy, and Hitler agreed with him. For once, Hitler hesitated to back his hunch; he refused to decide between the two field-marshals, kept the armoured divisions under his own hand, and distributed the German forces equally west and east of the Seine.

There was a further confusion on the German side. Rundstedt wished to build up a strategic reserve and launch a counter-attack after the Allies had landed. Rommel wished to meet them on the beaches. Again Hitler refused to decide, and no preparations were made for either operation. The Germans were also misled by the storm that blew for three days before the landings. Rommel, convinced that nothing would happen, went to see Hitler in Germany. The commander in Normandy was conducting manœuvres in Brittany. His deputy was spending the night with a girl.

The storm almost disrupted Allied plans. D-day had been fixed for 5 June. Two days before, the meteorologist Group-Captain Stagg foretold stormy weather. Eisenhower postponed the operation. The next day Stagg promised that the worst of the storm had passed, and Eisenhower, knowing that if he did not act now he would miss the tide for a month, gave the signal to go ahead. In Paris Stagg's German counterpart failed to notice the approaching improvement in the weather. On such small chances hang the fate of nations.

The invasion of France began just before dawn on 6 June. Nearly 200,000 men were engaged that day in naval operations – two-thirds of them British; 14,000 air sorties were flown. In 1940 the Germans invading France had 19 aircraft for each assault division; in 1941, invading Russia, they had 26. On 6 June 1944 the Allies had 260 aircraft per division. Neither the German air force nor the U-boats were able to interfere. By the evening 156,000 men were ashore.

The strategic plan was much to Montgomery's taste. British and Canadian forces were to land on the eastern sector of the beaches and take Caen. They would engage the bulk of the German forces, especially the armour, in a slogging match Alamein-fashion and wear them down. Meanwhile the Americans were to land at the base of the Cotentin peninsula, secure Cherbourg and build up resources for a breakout.

Below D-Day: the landing

Right: Dawn of D-Day off the Coast of France by Mitchell Jamieson

Overleaf, left: The Storm from the Seabee Hill (top) and **Outskirts of Brest** by Mitchell Jamieson
Overleaf, right A detail from **Rocket-Firing Typhoons at the Falaise Gap, Normandy, 1944** by Frank Wootton

Things did not go altogether 'according to plan' despite Montgomery's usual claim that they did. The Americans landed successfully at one beach. At the other they disembarked too far out and failed to secure a firm foothold for two days. Further east the British dallied on the beaches as they had done long ago at Gallipoli. They did not advance towards Caen until the afternoon, and by then a German armoured division had come into action. It arrested the British advance and broke through to the beaches, though without lasting effect. Caen did not fall for a month instead of being taken on the first day. After three days the separate beach-heads were linked up. Bayeux was occupied without fighting and thus survived intact as almost solitary witness to Normandy's ancient glories. Ten days later all Allied movements were halted by a storm, the worst for forty years, that raged from 19 to 22 June. One of the artificial harbours was destroyed; air sorties became impossible; the flow of supplies almost broke down. Nevertheless the Americans cut off Cherbourg and took it on 1 July along with 30,000 prisoners. The Germans had wrecked the port installations and obstructed the harbour, so that the gain was not as great as had been hoped. The Americans had to wait three weeks before they were strong enough to break out.

The British check before Caen was not a serious setback from Montgomery's point of view so long as Hitler swallowed the bait and concentrated his forces there. Hitler did so. He was convinced that the decisive breakthrough would be attempted here and directed most of the German armour – seven divisions out of the available ten – against the British. He was also convinced that a second landing would be made in the Pas de Calais and refused to release the German forces there. As the Allied bombers had now destroyed all the bridges over the Seine and the Loire, the Germans could probably not have moved in any case. The British took Caen on 9 July after a month of heavy fighting. A high price was paid by the town which, except for its two abbeys, was levelled to the ground.

Rundstedt recognized that the war was lost. When Jodl asked him: 'What shall we do?', he answered: 'End the war. What else can we do?' He was at once dismissed and was succeeded by Kluge, a tough fighter from the Eastern Front, who arrived with high hopes, soon to be disillusioned. Rommel also disappeared from the scene. On 17 July he was badly injured when his car was attacked by Allied aircraft. He went home to convalesce. Some time later an emissary from Hitler faced him with the choice between suicide, which would be presented as a hero's death, or trial before the People's Court. For Rommel had been associated with the plans against Hitler, and these had at last exploded – unsuccessfully. Rommel chose suicide.

German generals and conservative politicians had long talked of overthrowing Hitler, who they believed was leading Germany to defeat. Many generals said they would welcome Hitler's overthrow though they would not take part in it. Others hoped that, with Hitler gone, Germany would be allowed to retain some or all of his conquests. The conspirators talked; they did not act. They waited for power to be thrust into their hands. The action came from a single man, Colonel von Stauffenberg, who had been badly wounded during the war. On 20 July, after a number of unsuccessful attempts, he managed to place a bomb in Hitler's headquarters. When the bomb exploded, he telephoned his associates that Hitler was dead. They gathered at the War Ministry in Berlin, ready to form a non-Nazi administration. In Paris army officers arrested the leaders of the SS.

Everything went wrong. Hitler's usual meeting place, a concrete bunker, was under repair, and the bomb had to be planted in a wooden shed which lessened the force of the blast. Hitler himself was protected by a heavy table. He was injured, not killed. He was even able to receive Mussolini who arrived on a visit that afternoon and could for once patronize Hitler instead of the other way round. The telephone wires from Hitler's headquarters to Berlin had not been cut. Goebbels took charge. Nazi officers loyal to

Mussolini congratulates Hitler on his escape from assassination

Hitler arrested the conspirators who themselves had no support. Some, including von Stauffenberg, were killed at once. The others were hanged under brutal circumstances after a pretended trial before the People's Court. It is satisfactory to record that the judge who conducted the trials was himself killed by an Allied bomb while performing his loathsome duties. In Paris the SS officers were released and drank champagne with their erstwhile jailers. The bomb of 20 July had no effect on the course of the war except perhaps to intensify Hitler's determination to fight on. If action be the test of resistance, von Stauffenberg was the only resister. The others waited supinely for followers, and none responded. The German generals were isolated from the soldiers and the German people.

Hitler placed great hope in his secret weapons. These came into action shortly after D-day and certainly diminished the inspiration which the landings had given to the British people. Otherwise they did not change the march of events. The pilotless aircraft, or V-1s, destroyed 25,000 houses and killed 6184 people, nearly all in London. British fighter aircraft and guns, firing shells with the proximity fuse, soon took their measure. By August 80 per cent of them were being destroyed before they could do any damage. The rockets or V-2s which started in September were more alarming. They fell without warning, and no defence was found against them. Plans were laid to evacuate London. The rockets were expensive to produce – each cost twenty times as much as a V-1 – and the Allies overran most of their launching sites before the danger became catastrophic; 1115 rockets killed 2754 people – a costly procedure but hard enough on the people of London.

Meanwhile in the Cotentin peninsula the Americans made slow progress and lost more men than in the initial landings. Montgomery determined on a further diversion. On 18 July he began an offensive south of Caen. He announced that this would shatter the German lines and carry his forces to the Seine. This may well have been a cover for his real intention of engaging the German armour while the Americans broke out from the Cotentin peninsula. If so, Montgomery succeeded in deceiving his own side rather than the enemy. When the British offensive failed to make progress, Tedder and the American generals urged Eisenhower to dismiss Montgomery. Eisenhower held his hand. The complaints were stilled on 25 July when the Americans began to advance from Saint-Lô. On 1 August their tanks reached Avranches. All France lay open before them. All the same there was a price to pay. A British victory south of Caen, which Montgomery now claimed he had never intended, would have cut off all the German forces in Normandy. The American breakthrough further west shepherded them to safety.

Patton, the American general who led the storm into France, now showed himself the equal of Rommel. He had tanks, open roads and

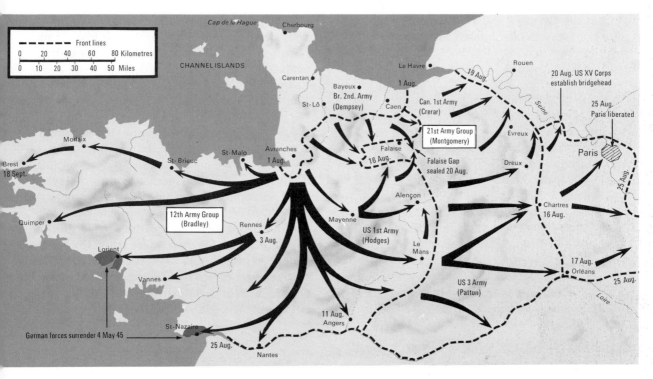

Normandy: the breakout

virtually no opposition. His instructions were to clear Brittany and take the Breton ports before turning east. These instructions sprang from a political blunder of the first magnitude. Where the Russians systematically employed nearly half a million partisans behind the German lines, the Western Allies ignored the French Resistance. Even though Eisenhower admitted that its actions against the Germans after D-day had been worth fifteen divisions, the Allied Command refused to believe that the French could liberate any part of their country unaided. The Resistance was given no guidance and few arms. Yet Patton discovered to his astonishment that his incursion into Brittany was unnecessary. The French Resistance had already taken over the province. They failed only at the ports, as Patton did also. Brest was taken after a month of fighting. Lorient, Saint-Nazaire and La Rochelle remained in German hands until the end of the war.

The Germans had lost the Battle of Normandy. Kluge wished to fall back to the Seine. Hitler in his usual manner refused. Instead he ordered a counter-offensive that would cut the American lines of communication at Avranches – an admirable operation if the Germans had had more than 145 tanks to set against over 2000. The German advance reached Mortain and then stuck. The Allies had a second chance to destroy the entire German army in Normandy. Once more they were too slow. Montgomery's forces moved south towards Falaise. Patton swung round through France and came north. The gap between the two armies remained open. Patton raged, 'Let me go on to Falaise and we'll drive the British into the sea for another Dunkirk' – hardly an appropriate remark from one who in 1940 had the Atlantic between himself and the Germans. When the net finally closed, 50,000 Germans were taken prisoner. But most of the Germans and all their remaining armour got away. Kluge himself was a casualty of the defeat. On 15 August he went up to the front and lost touch with headquarters for some hours. Hitler believed that he had gone forward to negotiate surrender and ordered him to return to Germany. On the way there Kluge committed suicide.

There was now no halting place for the Germans in France. Their shattered forces streamed back towards the German frontier. The Allied advance seemed to have become a victory march. On 15 August Operation Anvil at last took place. Some 50,000 American troops landed in the south of France. They encountered little resistance and advanced almost unimpeded up the valley of the Rhône. Militarily the landing in the south of France had little significance. The German forces there would have had to with-

draw in any case once the north was lost. Anvil had become a manœuvre against British plans for a further advance in Italy rather than against the Germans. Hitler drew the same conclusion. On the news of the landing in southern France, he moved three divisions from Italy to the Rhine.

As the Allies moved forward to the Seine and across it, they encountered the problem of Paris. Eisenhower's original intention was to bypass it, leaving it under German control. Maybe some subservient government would emerge – a modified Vichy ministry or some old hack from the Third Republic, anything in fact except de Gaulle. These projects were defeated by the people of Paris. On 15 August the metro workers went on strike. They were joined by the police. The ill-armed Resistance went into action. Hitler had ordered the total destruction of Paris.

Paris, 25 August 1944: de Gaulle, Leclerc and Juin at Montparnasse station

Von Choltitz, its governor, disobeyed him. Even so the forces of the Resistance were in danger of being crushed.

De Gaulle urged that a French armoured division under Leclerc should be sent to the capital. Eisenhower reluctantly consented – after all, better de Gaulle than the Communists. Leclerc entered Paris on 25 August, and de Gaulle followed the same day. Von Choltitz surrendered the city to him. De Gaulle's first visit was to the Ministry of War: 'I wished to show that the state . . . was returning, first of all, quite simply, to where it belonged.' At the Hôtel de Ville he refused to proclaim the restoration of the Republic, saying that it had never died and that he was its president. The Communist danger turned out to be a false alarm. Quite the contrary, the Communists were de Gaulle's most assiduous supporters. Thorez, their leader, gave the excuse that 'with the Americans in France the revolution would have been annihilated'. The real explanation lay elsewhere. Stalin was determined to prevent any Communist success outside his own sphere of power, and it was he rather than the Americans who preserved western Europe for capitalist democracy. There was a period of disorder during which the armed Resistance executed some 10,000 collaborators and also a number of Communists who had supported the war while the Nazi-Soviet Pact was in force. Within a couple of months de Gaulle reasserted the authority of the French state. Resistance leaders replaced the prefects appointed by Vichy. The Resistance forces were either disarmed or drafted into the regular army. France re-emerged if not as a Great Power at any rate as an independent country. Charles de Gaulle had deserved well of the Republic.

During the rest of August the Allied armies rolled forward, liberating most of France and Belgium. They took things easy. As one historian has written, 'A "war is won" attitude of mind prevailed in all ranks.' There were now over two million Allied troops in France – three-fifths of them American. On 1 September

Eisenhower took over command of the combined land forces from Montgomery. This was a significant moment in British history. Great Britain, hitherto an equal of the United States, dwindled into a satellite: by the end of the war there were three times as many American as British soldiers in Europe.

The change in command was followed by a sharp dispute between Eisenhower and Montgomery. Montgomery wanted a single thrust into Germany, of course under his command. Eisenhower favoured a broad advance on all fronts. Beneath the strategical arguments lay a political difference. Eisenhower could not starve Patton, an American general, for the sake of Montgomery, a British general. In any case it did not seem to matter. Eisenhower remarked on 15 September: 'We shall soon have captured the Ruhr and the Saar and the Frankfurt area.'

In fact the Allied advance stuck during the first week of September. This had little to do with the allocation of supplies between Montgomery and Patton. The Allied supply lines were now very long, the German lines very short. The Russians had exactly the same experience after every great victory. Their advances, too, petered out as they went forward and the Germans had time to regroup. Montgomery added to his difficulties by failing to clear the approaches to Antwerp after taking the port itself. He then came up with a daring expedient, far removed from his usual careful preparations. He proposed to seize three bridges over the Rhine and thus outflank the Siegfried line.

The enterprise was an airborne repetition of Anzio or Gallipoli – a brilliant idea laid on at a rush and carried out too cautiously. Paratroops captured two of the bridges. At Arnhem in Holland, their most northerly target they failed. The paratroop commander was concerned about a 'neat drop' rather than about taking the Germans by surprise, and many of the paratroops landed eight miles from the bridge. As an additional stroke of bad luck, two German armoured divisions were regrouping in the immediate neighbourhood, and Model, who had succeeded Kluge as Commander-in-Chief West, was himself with them. The British land forces could not break through. Some of the paratroops managed to withdraw; the rest were taken prisoner. By the end of September the German defences in the west were stabilized. Antwerp was cleared, though not until 28 November. The Americans took Aachen – the only scrap of German territory in Allied hands. Further south the Americans took Metz and Leclerc took Strasbourg. All France was now liberated except for a pocket at Colmar. The Allies settled down to what they expected to be a quiet winter.

The German empire in the east was also falling to pieces. The Russians opened their summer offensive on 23 June. They had 160 divisions, 30,000 guns and 5000 tanks. For once they struck against the strongest German point: Army Group Centre in White Russia. As usual Hitler forbade any withdrawal. The battle, though not on as great a scale as that at Kursk in the previous year, brought even greater results. Within a week the Russians destroyed 28 German divisions and took 350,000 prisoners – a German loss twice as great as that at Stalingrad. The German centre was blown wide open. Throughout July the Russian armies advanced across the plains of Poland. They took Lvov. On 1 August they reached the outskirts of Warsaw.

The Russians had now come some 450 miles. They had outrun their supplies, particularly as all the railways had to be changed to the broad gauge. On 29 July three fresh German divisions checked the Russian advance. This halt was not surprising. Great cities were formidable obstacles and often proved the grave of armoured divisions. The Germans learned this at Leningrad and Stalingrad, the British at Caen, and the Russians were to learn it at Budapest and Berlin. The inevitable halt at Warsaw had a tragic sequel. The London Poles had long planned to liberate Warsaw before the Russians arrived exactly as de Gaulle had forestalled the Americans at Paris. Bor-Komorowski, commander of the secret Home Army, hoped that they could 'come out in their full part as host to receive the entering Soviet armies'. Now the moment seemed to have come. The Home Army rose in revolt on 1 August. The Russians gave little aid and almost certainly were incapable of doing so. The fighting in Warsaw lasted for just over two months; 55,000 Poles were killed and 350,000 deported to Germany. The city was in ruins after the fighting, and the Germans systematically destroyed what was left of it.

The Warsaw rising and its terrible consequences captured the imagination of the world. The RAF and the American air force offered to fly in supplies to the Poles in Warsaw. The Russians refused to provide landing facilities until the rising was almost over. It appeared that Stalin had cynically abandoned the citizens of Warsaw and had allowed them to be slaughtered.

Paratroopers in action at Arnhem

The accusation was untrue. With or without a rising the Russians would have halted before Warsaw, and airborne supplies from the West would not have changed the situation. But no doubt Stalin did not regret what had happened. The rising was more anti-Russian than anti-German. The Russians had defeated the Germans, and the Poles hostile to Russia tried to take advantage of it. It was a gamble with people's lives, and the gamble failed.

Even if the rising had succeeded, nothing would have changed. The Russians could have mastered the Polish Resistance just as the British and Americans eliminated the Resistance in Italy and would have done in France if de Gaulle had pressed his independence too far. A Poland independent of both Germany and Russia perished for ever in September 1939. There remained only a choice of masters, and the Rus-

sians were on the way to victory with the Poles or without. All the same, what happened in Warsaw helped to lay the foundations of the Cold War.

The Russians did not move against Warsaw even when the rising was crushed. Instead they cleared their two flanks in the Baltic and the Balkans. Finland made peace on 2 September – a peace of remarkable moderation which has preserved a free democratic Finland to the present day. Russian forces pushed down the Baltic coast and reached East Prussia in October, their first foothold on German soil. In the south a *coup d'état* in Romania against the pro-German government on 23 August was followed by an armistice on 12 September. Romania, as the first German satellite to surrender, reaped her reward and recovered the area of Transylvania that she had lost to Hungary in 1940.

Polish Home Army soldiers with a German prisoner

Legend:
- 1939 frontiers
- Russian held territory December 1943
- Front line in May 1944
- Front line in December 1944
- Areas held by Germans at the end of 1944

0 100 200 Miles
0 100 200 300 Kilometres

SWEDEN

Leningrad

Estonia

Pskov

Moscow

Riga • Latvia

Lithuania

East Prussia
Rastenburg •

White Russia

Berlin •

Warsaw •

P O L A N D

Kiev •

GERMANY

Vinnitsa •

Dnieper

Prague •

CZECHOSLOVAKIA

Carpathian Mountains

Ukraine

Vienna •

Transylvania

Budapest
AUSTRIA

Prut

HUNGARY

ROMANIA

Dniester

Odessa •

Crimea
liberated
May 44

Sevastopol

Trieste •

Yugoslav
partisans

Belgrade
19 Oct.

Bucharest •

Black Sea

Allied advance
in Italy

YUGOSLAVIA

German withdrawal

Danube

ITALY

Adriatic Sea

Sofia •

BULGARIA

Rome •

Istanbul •

Albanian
partisans

Salonika •

Allied advance through Greece

TURKEY

Bulgaria, never having been at war with Russia, was easily disposed of. The Russians declared war and followed this up by an armistice eight days later. On 19 October the Russians entered Belgrade and joined hands with the Yugoslav partisans. Tito set up his independent government in Belgrade. As he remarked later, he was the only Communist leader who remained in his own country throughout the war and did not liberate it afterwards by returning in a Russian aircraft smoking his pipe.

The Russian advance in the Balkans was not without setbacks. Operating over such vast areas and with relatively small forces the Russians were unable to impede the German withdrawals from Greece and Yugoslavia. Moreover they stuck in the centre. There was a Communist rising in Slovakia – in this case a move against Czech centralization, not against the Russians. The Russians were unable to reach it – surely this time not an act of malicious delay – and it was crushed by the Germans. In Hungary Admiral Horthy planned to change sides. He moved too slowly. The Germans set up a Fascist government and carried Horthy into captivity. The Russians penetrated into Hungary, only to be held up outside Budapest.

By the end of the year what remained of the Nazi Empire looked like a somewhat diminished Habsburg Monarchy: Croatia and Slovenia, most of Czechoslovakia and Hungary, and northern Italy. There was another significant withdrawal. In November Hitler left his headquarters at Rastenburg for Berlin. His career as a conqueror was over, as he himself recognized not long before he committed suicide. He told Jodl, 'I should already have made this decision, the most important in my life, in November 1944, and should never have left the headquarters in East Prussia.'

In the Far East the Japanese Empire also neared its end. Hitherto the American advance had been a matter of 'island hopping', made possible by their control of the seas. Now they foresaw great land engagements against the Japanese armies in China, an anticipation which the Japanese shared. A principal American concern was that the British should reopen the Burma road to China. The Japanese were equally anxious to keep it closed and thus became the architects of their own ruin. For, while the British were puzzling how to break into Burma, the Japanese obliged them by striking first. Japanese forces encircled the British forward position at Imphal and pushed on towards Kohima. Among these forces was the Indian National Army of

Hitler on a rare visit to a bombed German town

some 7000 men, drawn from prisoners of war – an army of little account in the war, though politically embarrassing after it. For the first time an encircled position was successfully supplied from the air. The Japanese offensive was worn down. They lost 50,000 out of 84,000 men against a British loss of under 17,000. This was the first great achievement of General Slim, the ablest British leader of the Second World War. When the monsoon interrupted operations the way was clear for a British advance into Burma.

Even greater decisions were reached in the Pacific. On MacArthur's insistence the offensive was aimed towards the Philippines. From here the Americans could join hands with the Chinese – or so MacArthur supposed. The Japanese on their side believed that they could inflict on the Americans a new Pearl Harbor, and the advance of the American land forces became a bait that

lured the Japanese into action. In mid-June when the Americans were landing at Saipan in the Marianas, the Japanese began the Battle of the Philippine Sea. Though stronger in battleships, they were routed in the air. On 19 June in what the Americans called 'The Great Marianas Turkey Shoot' the Japanese lost 218 aircraft against 29 American. By the end of the battle their total loss was 1 battleship, 3 aircraft carriers and 480 aircraft. The Americans lost 130 aircraft and no ships. Japan's naval air force never recovered from this defeat.

The way was now clear for a landing in the Philippines. MacArthur, reckless for once, pushed ahead of his air cover and landed at Leyte on 20 October. The Japanese thought that their chance had come and that they could destroy MacArthur's transports before the main American fleet arrived. The resulting Battle of

American ships in action at the Battle of Leyte Gulf

Leyte Gulf was the greatest naval engagement of all time with 282 warships involved as against 250 at the Battle of Jutland. The four-day battle saw every type of action from the classic line of battle and 'crossing the T' to the sinking of battleships by aircraft from remote carriers. At one moment, when the main American fleet had been decoyed north on a false scent, a Japanese force of 4 battleships and 6 heavy cruisers was heading down on the defenceless American transports with nothing to impede them except 6 escort carriers and a small destroyer escort. The carriers were converted merchant ships, designed only for escorting convoys. Yet these slow little ships did the trick. They sank 2 heavy cruisers. Commander Evans of the destroyer *Johnston* gave the order, 'Prepare to attack major portion of Japanese Fleet', and sank a third heavy cruiser by torpedo before his own ship went down. The Japanese turned back when actually within sight of their prey. In all the Japanese lost 3 battleships, 4 large carriers and 6 heavy cruisers; the Americans lost 1 light carrier and 2 escort cruisers. This was the virtual end of the Japanese navy. At Pearl Harbor the Japanese had demonstrated the superiority of air power over battleships, but the Americans, not the Japanese, learned the lesson. Yamamoto might have done better.

MacArthur was now free to complete the liberation of the Philippines. He prepared plans for landing an army of five million men on the mainland of China. Then nothing happened. No response came from the Chinese. The great war on the mainland never took place. Instead MacArthur, the predestined conqueror of Japan, sat impotently in Manila while the American navy and air force completed the defeat of Japan.

Below and right **The Battle of Leyte Gulf**

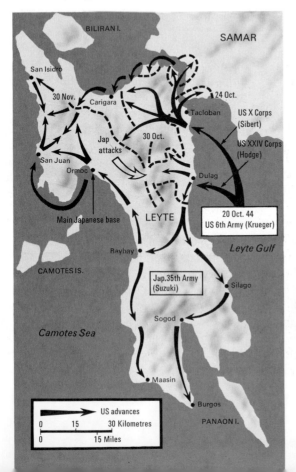

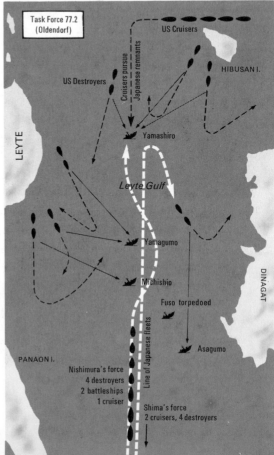

American bombers returning from attacks on Japanese islands

With the ripening of Allied plans for victory, meetings between the great leaders became less necessary, and none was held in 1944 until September when Churchill and Roosevelt met at Quebec. Churchill would have liked a coordination of political strategy against the Russians. Roosevelt turned a deaf ear. In any case Chur-

chill had a more pressing concern. Great Britain was at the end of the road: her currency reserves had run down and two-thirds of her exports had been lost. For her the end of the war and so of lend-lease would be a catastrophe. Churchill therefore offered full British participation in the Pacific once the European war was over. The American admirals wished to turn down the offer. Roosevelt overruled them. In this curious way Great Britain became involved in the Pacific war in order to keep her home economy going.

The only strategical decision made at Quebec was that the Allied air forces should revert to independent bombing and perhaps bring Germany to surrender without further fighting on land. There was also a startling, though short-lived, political decision. Churchill and Roosevelt were talked into a plan for destroying Germany's industry and reducing her to 'a country primarily agricultural and pastoral in character'. The British War Cabinet objected. Back in Washington Roosevelt, too, had second thoughts and forbade all speculation on the future of Germany. The 'pastoralizing' plan was discarded.

Churchill, having failed to rouse Roosevelt against the Russians, decided to tackle Stalin himself and went to Moscow in October. Stalin welcomed a definition of spheres of interest, a principle that had always been the basis of his policy. Churchill wrote on a scrap of paper: 'Romania 90% Russian; Greece 90% British; Yugoslavia and Hungary 50–50; Bulgaria 75% Russian.' Stalin read the paper and added a large tick in blue pencil. There was a pause. Then Churchill said, 'Might it not be thought rather cynical if we seemed to have disposed of these issues, so fateful to millions of people, in such an off-hand manner? Let us burn the paper.' Stalin replied, 'No, you keep it.' Next day Molotov insisted on changing the numbers to 80 per cent Russian in Hungary and Bulgaria. The precise figures had no significance anyway. Churchill returned home radiant. On 27 October he told the House of Commons: 'Our relations with Soviet Russia were never more close, intimate and cordial than they are at the present time.'

Churchill soon cashed Stalin's cheque. In Greece there was a Resistance force of 75,000 men, armed by the British, which had inflicted heavy losses on the Germans. Far from being Communist, the Greek Resistance ignored Communist promptings to cooperate with the former Greek authorities and prepared to set up a radical republic when the Germans withdrew in October. Churchill ignored the true nature of the Greek Resistance. In his eyes any radical movement was automatically Communist and a threat to British predominance in the Mediterranean as well. British troops were sent to Athens. Churchill wrote to their commander, 'Do not hesitate to act as if you were in a conquered city where a local rebellion is in progress.' Athens was, however, not a conquered city. The Resistance was stronger than the British forces. In England there was uproar. This seemed to be a new Darlan operation, compounding with the forces of Fascism against radical democracy.

Churchill was not deterred. On Christmas Day he went to Athens himself and imposed a provisional government under Archbishop Damaskinos, whom he described with a private chuckle as 'a scheming medieval prelate'. The Resistance agreed to disarm, though this did not prevent a civil war later. It cannot be said that postwar Greece has been a shining example of democracy. Soviet oppression in eastern Europe has been often condemned. But only the British followed the German example and took armed action against a popular national movement while the war was actually on.

Greece was not the only Allied worry at Christmastide 1944. At sea the position decisively improved when *Tirpitz*, the only remaining German battleship, was finally sunk in November by British aircraft attacking from Swedish airspace. By the end of the war the German surface fleet was down to 3 cruisers and 15 destroyers. The new schnorkels posed a threat to Allied shipping. But they were slow to come into production, and the American bombing crippled them for lack of oil. On land, however, all seemed well. On 15 December Montgomery told Eisenhower that he would like to go home for Christmas, and the next day he announced to his troops: 'The enemy is at present fighting a defensive campaign on all fronts; his situation is such that he cannot stage major offensive operations.' Montgomery was mistaken. That very morning the Germans began an offensive which threatened to disrupt the entire Allied front. This December offensive was Hitler's last stroke of strategic inspiration. Physically he had the appearance of a man already dead. His left side was paralysed, his eyes were glazed, he moved with a slow shuffling walk and was kept going only by increasing doses of drugs. All that remained was his indomitable will. Those who entered his presence gloomy came out uplifted. He was still the man of daring expedients, confident that his ingenuity could overcome material inferiority.

The generals told Hitler that an offensive was beyond Germany's strength. He replied, 'A defensive struggle could only postpone the decision and not change the general situation.... If Germany can deal a few heavy blows, this artificial coalition will collapse with a tremendous thunderclap. We shall master our fate all right.' For the field of the offensive Hitler chose again the Ardennes where four years earlier he had achieved the conquest of the west in a single afternoon. Once more the German forces would break through. This time they would turn north and take Antwerp. The British army would be cut off. There would be a new Dunkirk, and the British, perhaps even the Americans, would give up in despair.

The Americans had neglected the Ardennes as the French had done before them. On 16 December they had only 4 weak divisions to set against 28 German, 10 of them armoured. When the German offensive began, Eisenhower was out playing golf. Bradley dismissed it as a mere 'spoiling attack'. The Germans had the advantage of mist, which made air operations

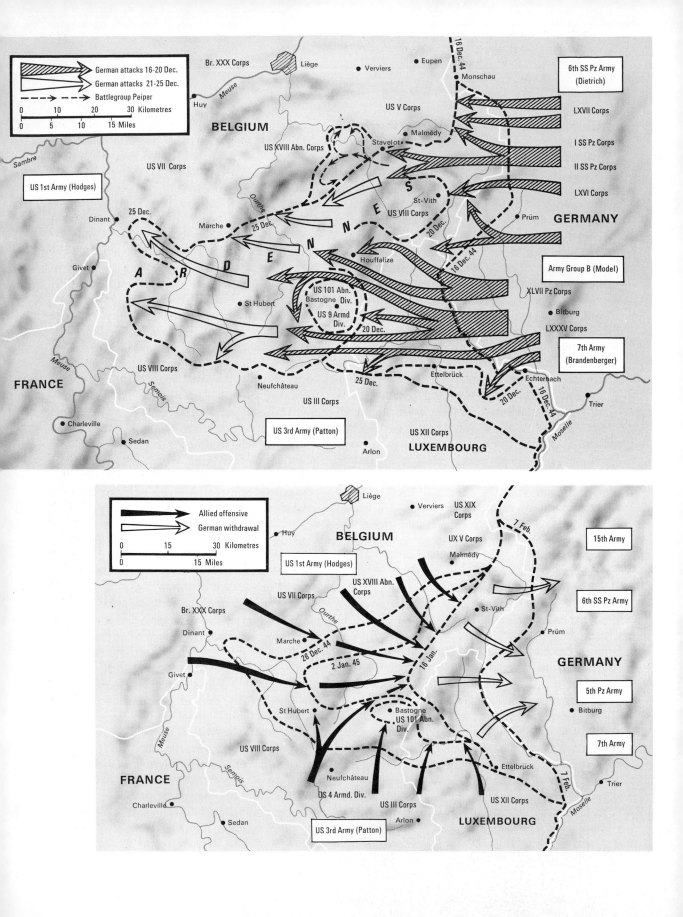

impossible for over a week. The breakthrough was accomplished, and the German advance swept forward. But from the start the operation went awry. It was one thing to smash forward with fully trained troops on a fine May morning; quite another for troops hastily assembled to contend with mist and snow. The American soldiers, unlike the French, continued to resist when their lines of communication had been overrun. The two shoulders held firm. The Germans were forced into a narrow lengthening corridor. They failed to take Bastogne and had to bypass it on secondary roads. Its American commander, McAuliffe, when called upon to surrender, replied: 'Nuts.'

The Germans were short of oil, and the Allied dumps were fired before the Germans could reach them. Their advanced forces came within six miles of the Meuse. They got no further.

German soldiers bypass a burning American halftrack in the Ardennes

Even so there was something like panic on the Allied side. Hundreds of miles behind the lines headquarters' staffs were packing up for evacuation. Gradually Allied counter-action stiffened. In the south Patton turned his army through ninety degrees and moved 133,000 vehicles seventy-five miles to the relief of Bastogne. Eisenhower feared that Bradley could not adequately control the American forces north and south of the Bulge, as the Germans spearhead came to be called. He therefore gave Montgomery overall command in the north. This provoked some hard feelings. On 20 December Montgomery strode into the headquarters of Hodges, the American general, like Christ come to cleanse the Temple. Afterwards he made things worse by claiming all the credit for victory at a press conference.

Montgomery certainly pulled the battle together and gave it effective shape. But what followed was an American victory, in which British troops played little part. On 24 December the weather cleared, and Allied aircraft took heavy toll of the German tanks. Two days later Patton relieved Bastogne. With this all chance of German success had vanished. Thanks to Hitler's insistence, the fighting dragged on for another fortnight. The Germans lost practically all their tanks. The Americans lost more, but they could replace their losses; the Germans could not. This was Hitler's last gamble – brilliant in conception, impossible to execute. The God of War does not love cleverness; he loves the Big Battalions.

There was a side effect to the Ardennes offensive. As a diversionary operation the Germans launched an attack towards Strasbourg in the first days of January 1945. Eisenhower, who needed his forces for the Ardennes, gave orders to abandon the city. De Gaulle rose up in wrath and ordered the French commander not to withdraw. Strasbourg was successfully held. The quarrel between Eisenhower and de Gaulle was somehow patched up. But it was a warning that rifts between the Allies would be among the troubles in the final year of victory.

10

The end of the war 1945

The year 1945 opened with an ironical display of Allied solidarity. The Anglo-American landings in France had provided a second front and so taken some of the strain off the Russians. In January 1945 the Western Allies appealed for a Soviet second front in order to take the strain off them. With the German offensives in the Ardennes and at Strasbourg not yet defeated, Eisenhower sent his deputy Tedder to Moscow with an appeal for help. Churchill telegraphed to Stalin: 'The battle in the West is very heavy. I regard the matter as urgent.' Stalin responded loyally and promised to advance the date for the projected Soviet offensive. Churchill was 'most grateful for [the] thrilling message' and wrote later: 'It was a fine deed of the Russians to hasten their vast offensive, no doubt at a heavy cost in life.'

Stalin wasted no time. The Soviet offensive, planned for 20 January, began on 12 January. The Russians were faced by 170 enemy divisions, as against 70 on the Western Front. But 30 of these were holding part of the Baltic coast where Hitler still hoped to train his new U-boats, and 28 were fighting to protect the oil and bauxite of Hungary. Only 75 guarded the long front from the Nemen to the San. The Russians had a local superiority of 5·5 to 1 in men, 7·8 to 1 in guns, 5·7 to 1 in tanks and 17·6 to 1 in aircraft. Even so it was not an easy operation. The air was thick with falling snow. The tanks could be distinguished only because they moved. The Russians went forward at a tremendous rate. In the centre Zhukov took Warsaw on 17 January. Further south Koniev broke into Silesia, Germany's

second-greatest industrial zone, hitherto virtually immune from bombing. The Russian armies advanced over 300 miles within eighteen days, roughly from the Vistula to the Oder. There, near Küstrin, their spearheads were only forty miles from Berlin.

Zhukov ordered his troops to consolidate their successes and then 'to take Berlin on 15–16

Warsaw, January 1945: liberation at last

February with a lightning thrust'. On 6 February Stalin rang him up from Yalta. He asked, 'Where are you, what are you doing?' Zhukov replied, 'We are planning the Berlin operation.' Stalin said, 'You are wasting your time' and called off the offensive. In all probability the halt was made for strictly military reasons. Stalin was a cautious commander. The Russians always halted their offensives after they had come two or three hundred miles. Now they had outrun their supplies. Poznań and Breslau, both untaken, hampered their communications. The law of overstretch, as Liddell Hart called it, had come into play.

Moreover Zhukov's advanced forces were now in an awkward salient with German armies of unknown strength on each side, and Stalin did not mean to repeat Hitler's mistake at Stalingrad or his own in February 1943 when the Germans retook Kharkov. His apprehensions were not unfounded. Guderian, now the German Chief of Staff, had seen the opportunity for a counter-offensive and, after prolonged wrangles with Hitler, attempted one from 10 to 14 February. This offensive was unsuccessful, but it was a warning of what might have happened if Zhukov had pushed further west.

Stalin's decision became later a matter of some controversy. In 1964 Chuikov, who had commanded one of the Soviet armies, declared that Berlin could have been taken within ten days: 'it would have been the end of the war'. Stalin's order to stop the offensive was presented as a supreme blunder, comparable to Hitler's order to halt the German tanks outside Dunkirk in 1940. Similar criticisms were made of Eisenhower's conduct of affairs in the west, particularly by Montgomery. It seems that the

Soviet troops on their way to Vienna

Allied armies were well supplied with generals who could have run the campaigns better than Stalin and Eisenhower did. Fortunately historians do not have to decide such questions.

Stalin may have been overcautious. There is not a scrap of evidence that he acted from any political motive, certainly not from any idea of avoiding an alarm by the Western Allies if he took Berlin. As might be expected, when halted in the centre, he resumed his offensive further south. On 11 February the Russians at last took Budapest. The German resistance was still tough. In mid-March a German offensive – the last on any front – pushed the Russians back from the frontiers of Austria. Soon they went forward once more. They cleared Slovakia and on 13 April took Vienna. When they launched their final offensive against Berlin three days later, all central Europe and part of Austria were under their control.

Behind the glittering façade of the Grand Alliance there was certainly mutual suspicion. East and West both feared a too great victory by the other. Both feared, too, that the other might make a separate peace with the Germans or even enlist German aid. Of these mutual fears the Soviet one was the better founded. There was no chance of a Soviet compromise with the Germans. As Beaverbrook said in 1943, 'The Russian dead stand in the way. You don't cross over that graveyard with ease.' In the West Churchill was already sounding an alarm against the Communist danger. A little later he actually ordered Montgomery to keep German arms intact in case they had to be used against the Russians. However, this is to interpret events in the light of what happened months or even years later. The great F. W. Maitland admonished other historians: 'It is difficult to remember that events now far in the past were once in the future.'

Whatever the future had in store, there was no flaw in Allied unity when the three great leaders met for the last time at Yalta from 4 to 11 February. Roosevelt and Stalin established close relations, much to Churchill's annoyance. For once there was serious negotiation and successful cooperation. Stalin agreed to Roosevelt's plans for the United Nations and to Churchill's proposal that France should be given a zone of occupation in Germany. Churchill and Roosevelt agreed to Soviet arrangements for Poland, though not to her western frontier. Roosevelt agreed that Russia should take reparations in kind from Germany, though he did not agree how much. The most important agreement was over the Far East. The Americans anticipated a hard struggle against Japan and were enraptured when Stalin promised to enter the Far Eastern war within three months of the end of the war in Europe. They were equally delighted with his assurance that he fully recognized Chiang Kai-shek and had no desire to promote the victory of the Chinese Communists – an assurance which was indeed true, though not for the reasons that the Americans supposed.

Yalta was, in Metternich's phrase, 'a very pretty little Congress', seemingly full of promise that Allied unity would for once survive victory. Stettinius, the American Secretary of State, wrote, 'The Soviet Union made greater concessions at Yalta to the United States and Great Britain than were made to the Soviets.' Harry Hopkins, Roosevelt's confidential adviser, was even more enthusiastic:

We really believed in our hearts that this was the dawn of the new day we had all been praying for. . . . The Russians had proved that they could be reasonable and farseeing and there wasn't any doubt in the mind of the President or any of us that we could live with them and get along with them peacefully for as far into the future as any of us could imagine.

Churchill endorsed this conclusion. On 19 February he told the War Cabinet that he had a very strong feeling that the Russians were anxious to work harmoniously with the two English-speaking democracies. Premier Stalin was a person of great power in whom he had every confidence.

The Yalta conference later acquired a bad reputation. The Western Powers, it was said, had been duped by Stalin. It would be truer to say that they duped themselves. They imagined that Soviet Russia would defeat the Germans for them and then withdraw within her own borders – at worst those of 1941 instead of 1939. This was not the Soviet intention. As German power crumbled in eastern Europe, Soviet power moved into the vacuum as the inevitable consequence of victory. The Russians behaved politically in eastern Europe much as the British and Americans had done in the west. They alone concluded armistices with the defeated satellites as the British and Americans had done in Italy. They excluded anti-Communists from power as the British and Americans took precautions against the Communists in Italy and France. In Romania Vyshinsky enforced a change of government by the same means as Lord Killearn had used in Egypt: he, too, surrounded the royal palace with tanks.

Poland was a special case. The British had an obligation towards Poland both as their original ally and because of the Polish forces fighting with them in the west. They continued to insist on free elections. But here there was an inescapable dilemma. Given the previous history of Polish-Soviet relations, there was no way in which free elections could produce a Polish government friendly to Soviet Russia. The Russians did not want domination. They did not want to spread Communism. They wanted security and only Communists or fellow travellers could provide it. However, this was not the basic cause of Yalta's subsequent discredit. In February 1945 the Western Allies still anticipated hard and bloody combats with the Germans – the British Chiefs of Staff even thought that the European war might drag on until November – and put unity first. Later, when victory proved unexpectedly easy, the British and Americans regretted that they had treated Soviet Russia as an equal. Allied cooperation did not break down because of the Yalta agreements; it broke down because the British and Americans repudiated them.

The apprehensions of February were shown in the renewal of Allied bombing. The Americans again concentrated on the synthetic-oil plants. Sir Arthur Harris dismissed these attacks as 'panaceas' and insisted on area bombing. He got his way. One more onslaught, Thunderclap would cause the collapse of German morale. If the attack also aided the Russians, so much the better. Harris chose as his target Dresden, a town not attacked before. On 13 and 14 February it was bombed by over a thousand aircraft. There was no opposition. The city was crowded with refugees fleeing from the Russians, and the Germans alleged that up to a quarter of a million people had been killed. Twenty years later the city authorities ascertained that the correct figure was 25,000.

The attack on Dresden was no different from countless others and less heavy than many. But when the war ended only three months later, it came to appear pointless, and everyone then forgot that in February German resistance was still regarded as formidable. The civilian leaders from Churchill downwards hastily repudiated responsibility for the raid on Dresden which they had in fact endorsed. Bomber Command was consigned to obscurity. Churchill did not mention it in his victory broadcast. No campaign medal was struck for it. Alone among the successful war leaders, Sir Arthur Harris was not elevated to the House of Lords. Yet indiscriminate bombing had been for four years the British achievement most prized by both public opinion and statesmen.

Victory in the west was not won without further wrangles between British and Americans. At Malta on the way to Yalta the Combined Chiefs of Staff disputed so fiercely that their debate had to be shrouded 'in the decent obscurity of a closed session'. Eisenhower clung to his strategy of advance on a broad front or, as it has been called, an elephant leaning on a house. Montgomery wanted a single powerful advance in the north, sweeping up to the Baltic coast or even to Berlin. It is curious that Montgomery, master in practice of the methodical approach, should repeatedly have cast himself as the leader of a lightning advance. In Sicily and again in Normandy he claimed that he was about to break out, when his real role was to pin down the bulk of the German forces while the Americans under Patton broke out elsewhere. Now events once more imposed the decision and the old pattern was repeated. While Montgomery battled towards the Rhine for a fortnight, further south the Americans discovered a bridge at Remagen that had not been blown up and were across the Rhine by 7 March with only fourteen casualties. Montgomery's forces did not cross the Rhine until 23 March. By then Patton's tanks were clearing the east bank of the Rhine ahead of them.

Eisenhower's next step followed inevitably from the existing situation. The American armies, which made up the greater part of his forces, were in central Germany. Montgomery had to advance in the north with British and Canadian troops alone. Churchill urged Eisenhower to go for Berlin and take it before the Russians did so. Eisenhower refused to pursue what he dismissed as a purely political objective. Even the political objective was futile. Berlin had already ceased to be the effective capital of Germany, and its capture would have been no more decisive than that of Rome had been. Besides it was irrevocably committed to the Soviet zone by long-standing agreement. Why then should the Americans sustain the three hundred thousand casualties which it cost the Russians to take Berlin? Eisenhower had a more urgent aim in mind. It was universally believed that the Germans had prepared a National Redoubt in Bavaria where they would make a last stand. The redoubt was in fact imaginary, the creation of some journalist's fantasy. But it determined Eisenhower's strategy in the last weeks.

During the first fortnight in April there was a pause before the final assaults began. On 12 April President Roosevelt, who had been failing for some time, died suddenly. Perhaps fate intervened to spare him the disappointment of his hopes. His successor, Truman, was not only inexperienced but much less willing to cooperate with the Russians, as his previous utterances had shown. In Berlin Hitler believed that Roosevelt's death was a miracle, comparable to that of Tsarina Elizabeth which had saved Frederick II in 1762. He was soon disillusioned. No suggestion for a compromise peace came from the Western Powers. On 20 April Hitler celebrated his birthday. It was the funeral feast of the Third Reich. Two days later Hitler dismissed his followers. Keitel and Jodl departed to direct the war as best they could, Goering to make peace with the Allies, or so he hoped. Hitler told Jodl, 'I shall fight as long as the faithful fight next to me and then I shall shoot myself.' Only Goebbels and his family remained with Hitler in the bunker.

And now all the armies were on the move. In Italy SS General Wolff had been negotiating with Allied representatives for some time and aroused Stalin's suspicions by so doing. When in mid-April the Allied armies at last advanced, they encountered little resistance. On 23 April they crossed the Po. Brazilian troops took Turin, no doubt somewhat puzzled about why they were there. Japanese Americans, debarred from service in the Pacific, were the first Allied troops to reach the French frontier. Italian partisans took over Milan, Genoa and Venice. In Venice Popski – the irregular leader of a private army – drove his jeep into the Piazza San Marco. Mussolini emerged from his obscurity. He tried to negotiate with the partisans in Milan. Then, taking fright, he joined a German convoy retreating through the Alpine passes. At Dongo on Lake Como partisans stopped the convoy and took Mussolini off the lorry where he was concealed. Bewildered what to do with him, the partisans consigned him and his mistress Clara Petacci, who had joined him, to a farmhouse.

The next day a Communist partisan colonel arrived. Mussolini said, 'You have come to save me? I will give you an Empire.' Petacci fumbled under the bedclothes. When asked what she was doing, she said, 'I am looking for my knickers.' The colonel took them a few hundred yards down the road, stood Mussolini against a wall and, when Petacci tried to protect him, shot them both. A few hours later their bodies were taken to Milan and hanged upside down outside a garage. Mussolini had carried with him letters with which he hoped to prove his innocence. He may also have had with him a large sum in foreign currency and other valuables. This 'treasure of Dongo' has disappeared, and those who sought for it paid with their lives. Mussolini was a small-scale dictator who tried to play above his class. Perhaps Count Dino Grandi, a veteran Fascist, passed the best verdict on him: 'Poor Mussolini.'

On 29 April the German forces in Italy capitulated, and their unconditional surrender came into force on 2 May. By this time the Allied Command was more concerned to forestall the partisans, both Italian and Yugoslav, than to defeat the Germans who were indeed ordered to retain their arms until Allied authority was consolidated. The Italian partisans proved unexpectedly docile. On Communist orders they handed over their arms. The Resistance organization formally dissolved itself. By the beginning of June 150,000 armed men had disappeared as though they had never been. Tito caused more trouble. His partisans entered Trieste just ahead of the New Zealanders and thus set the stage for the first, though as it proved premature, act of the Cold War.

In Germany, too, the Western Allies encountered little serious fighting. Some twenty German divisions had been moved to the Eastern Front. The main German force left was in the Ruhr. It was encircled and blockaded. On 18 April 300,000 men surrendered. Model, the Commander-in-Chief, shot himself. After that the Allied advance was a victory procession. Montgomery took Hamburg and reached the Baltic coast, thus securing Denmark from the Russians. On 25 April American and Soviet troops met at Torgau on the Elbe – a dramatic, though shortlived, demonstration of their comradeship in arms. Further south one French force took Stuttgart, and another penetrated into Tirol. Patton crossed the Czechoslovak frontier and hoped to liberate Prague.

The Russians had long timed their offensive against Berlin for the middle of April. Maybe they hurried up because of their mistaken apprehension that the Western Allies would get there before them. At any rate Stalin is reputed to have said, 'The little allies [soyuznichki] intend to get to Berlin ahead of the Red Army.' Stalin organized his own race: Zhukov was to attack from the east, Koniev from the south, and good luck to whoever won. This last campaign was no easy matter. All that remained of the German army stood at bay. The Russians deployed two million men, 41,000 guns, 6300 tanks and 5000 aircraft.

The Russian offensive began on 16 April. From the bunker Hitler directed imaginary armies and still wielded dictatorial power. He dismissed Guderian as Chief of Staff and appointed the sycophantic Krebs, who had once been embraced by Stalin on a railway platform. He dismissed first Goering and then Himmler on reports that they were seeking to negotiate surrender. On 29 April, with small-arms fire already audible in the bunker, Hitler realized that the end had come. He married his longtime mistress Eva Braun, wrote his testament, and appointed Admiral Doenitz as his successor – a snub for the generals who, he believed, had lost the war for him. The last sentence of his testament read:

Above all I charge the leaders of the nation and those under them to scrupulous observance of the laws of race and to merciless opposition to the universal poisoner of all peoples, international Jewry.

On 30 April Hitler said farewell to his few remaining followers. He and Eva Braun withdrew to their own room. She took poison; Hitler shot himself. Their bodies were taken out into the garden. Petrol was poured over them and they were set alight. The guards gave a last salute and returned to the shelter. What happened to the ashes will never be known. The Russians claim to have recovered the bodies

Above The end of the road: Soviet troops reach the Elbe
Right Soviet aircraft over Berlin

which they later destroyed. The identification has been disputed, and it is probable that Hitler's remains have disappeared for ever. It is, however, certain that he shot himself and that the Third Reich did not long survive him.

On the following morning Krebs attempted to negotiate a partial surrender. The Russian general he encountered was Chuikov, the hero of Stalingrad. Krebs told Chuikov that Hitler was dead and then said ingratiatingly, 'Today is the first of May, a great holiday for our two nations.' Chuikov replied, '*We* have a great holiday today. How things are with you over there it is less easy to say.' The overture from Krebs was rejected. Goebbels shot all his family and himself. The next day the commander of the Berlin garrison surrendered with 70,000 men. There was no organized capitulation of the city. The last German stand, it is said, was at an air-raid shelter in the zoo.

Doenitz attempted to discharge his functions as the new head of the Reich. He tried to secure a surrender in the west while continuing the war in the east. Eisenhower refused this suggestion. There were piecemeal surrenders. On 4 May the German forces in the north surrendered to Montgomery on Lüneburg Heath. In all, the Western Allies took three and a half million prisoners – one million in Italy and two and a half million in Germany, many of the latter no doubt fleeing from the Russians on the Eastern

The Reichs chancellery, May 1945

Officers and men of the Berlin garrison after surrender

Front. On 7 May Jodl signed an unconditional surrender at Eisenhower's headquarters in Rheims. The following day the signature was repeated at Zhukov's headquarters in Berlin. The formal ending of the war was a muddle. Stalin wished to hold back the news until after the ratification in Berlin. An American reporter broke the ban, not to Churchill's regret, and the Western Allies celebrated V-E day (Victory in Europe) on 8 May, the Russians on 9 May.

Some German surrenders were delayed until after the formal ending of the war. In Norway 350,000 German troops who had never seen fighting capitulated on 8 May. The garrison of the Channel Islands, 20,000 strong, capitulated on 9 May. The last Germans to surrender seem to have been in Heligoland which held out until 11 May. The last scene of fighting in Europe was strangely enough at Prague, a city that had hitherto escaped all scars of war. The Czech

Resistance rose in revolt on 5 May. Patton was already at Pilsen while the Russians were still far away. Eisenhower, who had already been told by Truman that he was loath to hazard American lives for political purposes, refused to allow Patton to move. The Czechs suffered heavy casualties – 8000 in all. They might have suffered many more. A German armoured division retreating from Slovakia moved towards Prague. It was arrested by the Vlasov Army, a force of Soviet renegades that had been formed to fight on the German side. Now, responding to an instinctive Slav solidarity, it barred the way to Prague. In this way Prague was saved by Russians – but by renegades, not by the Soviet army. Soviet forces entered Prague only on 12 May. Vlasov's tardy repentance did him no good. He was handed over to the Russians and hanged, along with many of his followers.

There came near to being another armed con-

The end of the war in Europe

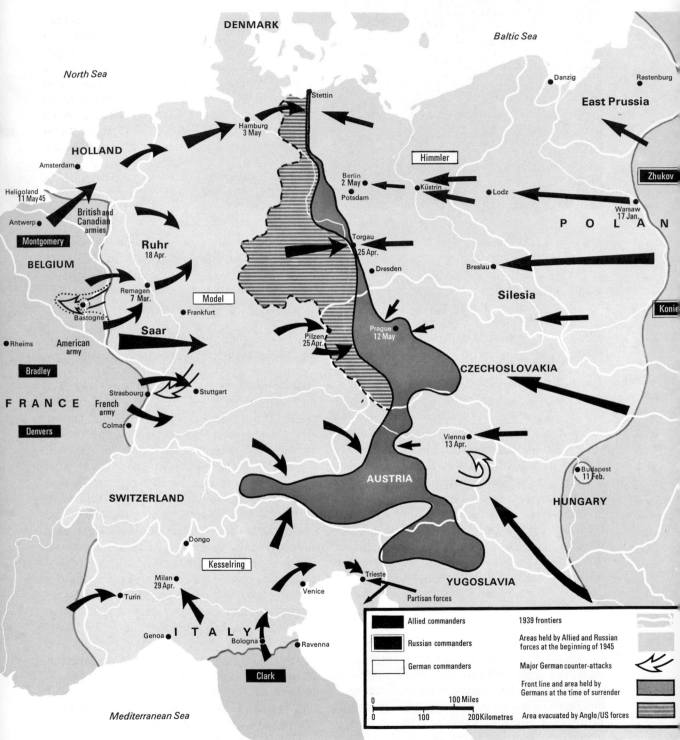

DENMARK

North Sea

Baltic Sea

Danzig

Rastenburg

East Prussia

Stettin

Hamburg
3 May

HOLLAND

Amsterdam

Himmler

Zhukov

Berlin
2 May

Küstrin

Lodz

Potsdam

Heligoland
11 May 45

British and
Canadian
armies

Warsaw
17 Jan.

Antwerp

P O L A N D

Montgomery

Ruhr
18 Apr.

Torgau
25 Apr.

BELGIUM

Dresden

Breslau

Remagen
7 Mar.

Model

Silesia

Bastogne

Frankfurt

Konie

Rheims

American
army

Saar

Pilzen
25 Apr.

Prague
12 May

Bradley

CZECHOSLOVAKIA

Strasbourg

Stuttgart

F R A N C E

French
army

Denvers

Colmar

Vienna
13 Apr.

Budapest
11 Feb.

AUSTRIA

HUNGARY

SWITZERLAND

Dongo

Kesselring

Milan
29 Apr.

Trieste

YUGOSLAVIA

Turin

Venice

Partisan forces

Genoa

I T A L Y

Bologna

Ravenna

Clark

Allied commanders	1939 frontiers	
Russian commanders	Areas held by Allied and Russian forces at the beginning of 1945	
German commanders	Major German counter-attacks	
	Front line and area held by Germans at the time of surrender	
0 100 Miles		
0 100 200 Kilometres	Area evacuated by Anglo/US forces	

Mediterranean Sea

Montgomery accepts the German surrender at Lüneburg Heath

flict when the war was officially over – sadly and paradoxically one between Tito's Yugoslavia and the Western Allies. In the last days of the war Yugoslav partisans occupied Istria which was indisputably Slav (Slovene and Croat) in population, and Trieste, which had a sizable Slav minority and was surrounded by Slav territory. Churchill was now disillusioned with Tito and regarded him as Stalin's agent, seeking to acquire a base on the Adriatic for some nefarious Soviet purpose. He was therefore eager to expel the Yugoslavs from Trieste, if necessary 'by force of arms'. Truman at first hesitated to go against an ally and then came to favour armed force in his turn. Stalin, who in fact already regarded Tito with some disfavour, pressed for a compromise. On 9 June Yugoslav forces withdrew from Trieste. Tito said, 'We were forced to submit to this great sacrifice with a heavy heart.' He did not forgive Stalin, and the Soviet failure to support Yugoslavia over Trieste started him on the road that led to his breach with Stalin in 1948.

In Germany and Austria there were also alarms that the zones under the control of the respective Allies would not be settled without conflict. Here, too, Churchill was in a combative mood. He contemplated the use of air power for 'striking at the communications of the Russian armies should they decide to advance further than is agreed' – though in fact it was the Western Allies, not the Russians, who had done

this – and Doenitz's rump government was kept in existence as a potential ally until 23 May. The Americans ignored these promptings. Public opinion could not be switched against Soviet Russia overnight. Besides, the Western Allies had in Europe less than half the strength of the Russians and were unlikely to succeed in an armed conflict even if they enlisted the shattered German forces on their side. The British and Americans gradually withdrew to the agreed boundaries, a withdrawal often of as much as 120 miles. Germany and Austria were each divided into four zones – France being included out of courtesy – with the four Allies sharing control of the two capitals, Berlin and Vienna. Allied Control Commissions were created to rule both countries. When agreements were reached on these matters, the war in Europe was truly over.

The Far Eastern war had yet to reach its climax. In the spring of 1945 British forces fought their way into Burma and took Rangoon on 2 May. This campaign was a dead end. The Americans had lost interest in enlisting the active cooperation of China, and the British recovered Burma only to relinquish it shortly afterwards. Indeed the entire British war in the Far East was fought to recover an empire which they would soon abandon – a somewhat pointless exercise. Still eager to count as a Far Eastern Power, the British pressed their naval assistance on the Americans who accepted it reluctantly and with scepticism. The Americans still had a long way to go or so they imagined. MacArthur anticipated the employment of five million men and casualties of a million before Japan was brought to surrender. Certainly Japanese resistance was as stiff as ever. In February the capture of the island of Iwo Jima cost the Americans 5500 dead. The battle for Okinawa, the next island to be invaded, lasted three months. The Japanese threw in *Yamato*, the largest battleship afloat. She was sunk by attack from 280 aircraft, a postscript to the battleship age. When Okinawa was taken in June, it had cost the Americans 12,500 dead.

American forces massed at Okinawa in April 1945

Despite this stubborn fighting Japan was nearing collapse. Two-thirds of her merchant shipping had been sunk. Factories were halted for lack of coal and raw materials. Food was down to an individual ration of 1200 calories a day – below that of the Germans in the worst time of the First World War. American aircraft attacked Japan almost without meeting opposition. In a single raid on Tokyo on 8 March 83,000 people were killed – 20,000 more than all the British deaths from air attack throughout the war.

In April Baron Suzuki, an aged admiral, became Prime Minister. He was a hero of the Russo-Japanese War and now, in his gentle way, a man of peace. The Japanese peacemakers moved cautiously. They feared a military revolt at any talk of peace; they even feared, not without cause, for their own lives. They wished to avoid the humiliation of unconditional surrender; especially they wished to secure the preservation of the Imperial dynasty. They sought to enlist Stalin as intermediary. Stalin, now resolved on intervention in the Far East, dismissed the Japanese approach as too vague. At the Potsdam conference in July the three war leaders issued a solemn warning calling upon Japan to surrender. Suzuki declared that he had

no public comment to make. This was translated, apparently wrongly, that he treated the summons with contempt. The Americans concluded that the war must go on.

American counsels were divided. The naval chiefs were convinced that blockade would bring Japan to an early surrender; the air chiefs were equally confident of the effects of bombing. Truman, like Roosevelt before him, remembered the warning of the army leaders that a military conquest of Japan would cost a million casualties. The Americans had already found a way out. This was Russian intervention in the Far Eastern war. Stalin had promised it with increasing firmness, and indeed it began on 8 August. But the earlier American enthusiasm for it had waned. With the ending of the European war, they were reluctant to be beholden to the Russians in the Far East. Moreover, already wrangling with the Russians over European questions, they began to resent Russian intrusion in the last stages of a war they had not fought. No doubt the Russians intervened for the same reason.

By the summer of 1945 the Americans had a fresh resource. For three years past they had been pushing on with the development of a controlled nuclear explosion, the technique of which they had learned from the British. Now three atomic bombs were ready. No one knew what their precise effect would be, but it was hoped that their devastating results would drive the Japanese to surrender with the added advantage that this would take place before Soviet Russia had time to intervene. Not all Americans were happy about this. On 18 June General Marshall judged that 'the impact of Russian entry on the already hopeless Japanese may well be the decisive action levering them into capitulation', and Eisenhower, when told of the intended use of the bomb during the Potsdam conference, believed that it was 'completely unnecessary' or, as he put it later, 'it wasn't necessary to hit them with that awful thing'. MacArthur, who was not consulted, said later that he agreed with Eisenhower.

Such opinions were irrelevant. Truman and

The end of the war in the Far East

U S S R

ALEUTIAN ISLANDS

ATTU   Mar.-May 43

MONGOLIA   SAKHALIN

Russian forces Aug. 45

HOKKAIDO

Peking

CHINA   Vladivostok

Hiroshima
6 Aug. 45   Tokyo

JAPAN

British armies   Chungking   Nagasaki   Osaka
                                            9 Aug. 45
DIA   HONSHU
        Mandalay   Shanghai
        Mar. 45

eiktila

Burma   Pacific Ocean

Rangoon   FRENCH   OKINAWA
3 May 45   Apr. 45   IWO JIMA
        SIAM   INDO-   Mar. 45   WAKE I.
Bangkok   CHINA
                        Hong Kong   TAIWAN

                        South China Sea   MARIANAS ISLANDS

                        LUZON   Manila   SAIPAN June 44
                                 Jan. 45   US victory
                        Philippines   June 44
                                        Leyte Gulf   Philippine   GUAM
                                        US victory   Sea   July 44   Feb. 44   MARSHALL
                                        Nov. 44   ISLANDS
Malaya   PALAU   CAROLINE ISLANDS   Feb. 44
                        June 45 Sept. 44
        Singapore   North   Nimitz
                       Borneo   May 45
                May 45   GILBERT IS.
                        CELEBES   Sept. 44   May 44   Feb. 44
Sumatra   Borneo
                                                New   Sept.   SOLOMON IS.
        DUTCH EAST INDIES   Guinea   43   Nov. 43
                                                                                GUADALCANAL
        Java   Timor   Port   NEW HEBRIDES
                                         Moresby Jan. 43   Aug. 42

                                        Darwin   Sept. 42   MacArthur

Indian Ocean   Halsey

                AUSTRALIA   NEW CALEDONIA

US task forces
US advances
Major sea battles
Air bases used by US for
raids on Japanese mainland
Fire bomb raid on Japan
Atom bomb raid on Japan
Areas still occupied by
Japan at surrender
0   300 Miles
0   500 Kilometres

a few men involved in producing the bombs made the decisions, and the views of the Chiefs of Staff were never sought. The desire to anticipate or to warn the Russians was a side issue. The decisive factor was that, once the bombs were there, they had to be used. As one high authority wrote:

The bomb simply had to be used – so much money had been expended on it. Had it failed, how would we have explained the huge expenditure? Think of the public outcry there would have been. . . . The relief to everyone concerned when the bomb was finished and dropped was enormous.

Few foresaw the enormous increase in potential

dropped on Hiroshima, he exclaimed, 'This is the biggest thing in history.' The Americans used the atomic bombs against Japan with peculiar satisfaction. They had no fierce moral indignation or desire for revenge against either Italy or Germany. But with the humiliation of Pearl Harbor behind them, they were ruthlessly determined to exact unconditional surrender from Japan.

The Americans had three bombs. The first was successfully exploded as a test at Alamogordo in New Mexico on 16 July. The second was dropped on Hiroshima on 6 August. The aircraft bearing it was blessed by a Roman

Hiroshima, after the atom bomb

nuclear destruction which followed within a few years. Practically no one imagined that any country except the United States would be able to develop nuclear weapons in the near future. No one reflected on the contaminated fallout that would follow a nuclear explosion. Nuclear weapons were 'just another bomb'. When Truman learned that an atomic bomb had been

Catholic priest. Seventy-one thousand people were killed instantaneously. Those who died later from wounds, burns or leukemia have never been counted.

The Japanese military chiefs still insisted that continued resistance might secure 'honourable conditions'. On 9 August the third and, though the Japanese did not know it, the last remaining atomic bomb was dropped on Nagasaki. Eighty thousand people were killed. This, together with the news of Soviet intervention in Manchuria, provoked the decision. Emperor Hirohito, faced with deadlock at the council of ministers, took the first independent action of his life and announced: 'The unendurable must be endured.' On 14 August Japan agreed to unconditional surrender – in fact with the condition that the Emperor's position should be preserved.

There was a last alarm. Hirohito had recorded a radio address which would tell the Japanese people of his decision. Young extremist officers broke into the palace and killed the general in command. They failed to find the record which was hidden in a cellar and hesitated to lay hands on the Emperor's sacred person. On the morning of 15 August the recording went out. Hirohito spoke the language of the court, flowery with a strange lilt. Most Japanese, it is said, did not understand what he was saying.

It took the Americans some time to arrange a ceremony of capitulation. MacArthur, the predestined ruler of Japan, was far away in the Philippines. He needed over a fortnight to reach Japan. On 2 September he received the formal surrender of Japan on the deck of the battleship *Missouri* in Tokyo Bay. By Truman's decree this marked V-J day (Victory over Japan). With MacArthur's permission Mountbatten received the surrender of the Japanese forces in southeast Asia at Singapore on 12 September. The Russians did not get a look in and had to be content with recovering what they had lost to Japan in 1905. Chiang Kai-shek seemed to have achieved his aim of victory without fighting and now turned his arms against the Chinese Communists, an enterprise in which he was less successful.

Counting from the German invasion of Poland to V-J day, the Second World War lasted precisely six years. Only Great Britain and the British Dominions other than Eire went through it from beginning to end. At the opposite extreme, some countries such as Turkey entered the war only in March 1945 – a belated gesture which qualified them as members of the United Nations.

Seventy million men were engaged as combatants at one time or another. Seventeen million of them were killed: one out of every 22 Russians, of 25 Germans, of 46 Japanese, of 150 Italians, of 150 British, of 200 Frenchmen, and of 500 Americans. In contrast to previous wars of modern times, more civilians were killed than soldiers – some by aerial bombardment, others murdered by the Germans as partisans or hostages, many more murdered gratuitously in execution of Nazi racial doctrine, many perishing from hardship and starvation while carrying out forced labour in Germany or when besieged at Leningrad and elsewhere.

Poland suffered most in proportion to her population: 300,000 soldiers killed and 5·8 million civilians murdered by the Germans, a third of them Jews – a total loss of 15 per cent. Soviet Russia lost 10 per cent of her population: 6 million soldiers killed, and 14 million soldiers and civilians murdered by the Germans. Yugoslavia had 1·5 million dead, only 500,000 of them combatants. Four and a half million Germans were killed in battle, three-quarters of them on the Eastern Front; 593,000 German civilians were killed by air bombardment. Japan lost over a million combatants in battle and 600,000 civilians from air bombardment. Between 3 and 13 million people died in China, more from general hardship than in actual fighting.

In the West, France lost 200,000 soldiers and 400,000 others – some killed in the Resistance, others dying in the German deportation camps. Three hundred thousand Italians were killed – half of them fighting as regular soldiers on the German side, half fighting as partisans on the side of the Allies. Great Britain lost 300,000 combatants, 62,000 civilians killed by air bombardment, and 35,000 members of the merchant navy. The United States came off lightest: 300,000 military dead, divided almost equally between the European and Asiatic theatres of operations, and no civilians.

Ashes and bones: 200,000 victims of the Maidanek extermination camp

The worst fate was reserved for two helpless innocent peoples. Out of Europe's 9 million Jews, between 5 and 6 million were murdered by the Germans in the gas chambers. The Gypsies of eastern Europe were virtually exterminated by the same means.

Material destruction was also enormous. In Soviet Russia 1710 towns, 70,000 villages, 6 million houses and 31,850 factories were destroyed; 5 million horses and 17 million cattle were stolen by the Germans. The industrial resources of Poland were halved, those of Yugoslavia reduced by two-thirds. French resources, too, were halved – more from air bombardment by the Allies than from looting and destruction by the Germans. Italy suffered less, mainly because there was no heavy fighting in northern Italy: her resources were only down 20 per cent. The Germans lost 2·5 million houses, and Hamburg alone suffered more than the whole of

Great Britain. But thanks to wartime dispersal, German industrial resources were less affected – heavy industry, the principal target of Allied bombing, least of all. Japan had lost her entire merchant marine and most of her cities were in ruins. Great Britain had lost half her merchant marine. Half a million homes were destroyed and 4 million damaged. The British foreign debt had increased sixfold. Of all the belligerents, only the United States came out of the war markedly richer than she entered it.

In 1919, after the First World War, there was a great peace conference at Paris. The victorious Powers failed to solve the problem of Soviet Russia. But they managed to make peace with all their former enemies, though not successfully with Turkey until 1923. The sequel to the Second World War was untidier. Peace was concluded with the lesser European enemies – Bulgaria, Finland, Hungary, Italy and Romania – on 10 February 1947. It was signed in the Salle de l'Horloge of the French Foreign Ministry, and the table used for the ceremony was the one on which the wounded Robespierre lay before he was guillotined. Japan caused more trouble. The Russians wanted a settlement dictated by the four Great Asiatic Powers – China, Great Britain, the Soviet Union and the United States. The Americans insisted on a wider body. Only they and their associates signed the peace treaty with Japan in 1952. Soviet Russia and her two satellites, Poland and Czechoslovakia, refused to sign and made their own settlement with Japan later.

Austria, like Germany, was partitioned between the four Great European Powers, France being substituted for China. The four remained in occupation for precisely ten years. Then, in a unique return to the former Allied solidarity, agreement was reached. By the State Treaty of 5 May 1955, the occupying Powers agreed to withdraw. Austria became independent and accepted permanent neutrality as its condition.

No agreement was reached over Germany. At the end of the war the four Great Powers assumed that their Control Commission would administer

Ruins of Stalingrad

a united Germany until the Germans had been 'de-Nazified' and somehow educated into democracy and that they would then withdraw. This assumption was already breaking down when the war leaders, somewhat changed – Truman in place of Roosevelt and, in the later stages, Attlee in place of Churchill – met at Potsdam in July 1945. The two principal stumbling blocks were Poland's frontier with Germany and reparations. At Yalta Great Britain and the United States had agreed that Poland should be compensated with German territory for the territory she had taken from Russia in 1921 and which Soviet Russia now reclaimed. No agreement had been reached over the exact extent. At the end of the war the Russians simply handed over to Poland all the German territory east of the Oder and the western Neisse, except for part of East Prussia which they took for themselves – Russia's only direct territorial gain from the war.

The Western Powers protested in vain. The German-Polish frontier had only a *de facto* validity until 1973, when it was finally acknowledged by the West German State.

Reparations were a more serious problem. Here again Roosevelt had vaguely promised reparations in kind from Germany to the Russians, though he had not agreed the exact figure. The Americans soon thought better of this, particularly when they were having to subsidize the western zones of Germany. Undeterred the Russians took reparations from their own zones. The Western Allies gradually closed their zonal frontiers against the Russians. In time two separate Germanies emerged: the German Democratic Republic controlled by the Russians and the German Federal State closely linked with the Western Powers. In this unplanned way the partition of Germany was effectively achieved. It was perhaps the end of the German problem.

In 1919 the maps of Europe, the Near East and Africa had been decisively changed. The Habsburg and Ottoman Empires disappeared. New national states came into existence. Germany lost her colonies. There were no great changes after the Second World War except as regards the frontiers of Poland. No old states perished and no new ones were born. Countries recovered more or less their prewar frontiers, though in the case of Russia these were the frontiers of 1941, not of 1939 – much to the indignation of the Western Powers. Czechoslovakia handed over Ruthenia to Russia, as President Masaryk had intended from the first. Italy lost Istria to Yugoslavia. Trieste became a Free City and returned to Italian sovereignty in 1955. The French also took a few Alpine passes from Italy. The British and French, though not the Dutch, recovered their empires in the Far East – not, however, as it turned out, for long. Russia recovered the rights in Port Arthur and Dairen which she had lost after the Russo-Japanese War and also the control of the Manchurian railway which she had sold to Japan in 1935. To everyone's surprise these gains, too, proved temporary. The United States established trusteeship over strategic islands which in fact gave her mastery of the Pacific. Only these gains have endured.

All the same there were great changes beneath the surface. People were moved instead of frontiers. This had started during the war. Hitler called home the *Volksdeutsche* – Germans living outside Germany – and settled a million and a half Germans in conquered Poland. Stalin moved the German settlers of the Volga and the Tartars of the Crimea to Siberia. Even the Americans followed Stalin's example: 250,000 American citizens of Japanese origin were taken from their homes on the Californian coast at a moment's notice and transferred to camps inland. The shifts which followed the war were more permanent. Before the war there were 7 million Germans in Silesia, the two Prussian provinces and Pomerania. Many of them were killed during the war; many more fled before the advancing Russian armies. The remainder, between 2 and 4 million, were expelled by the Poles. Three million Germans were expelled from Czechoslovakia. There were lesser expulsions disguised as exchanges of population – Hungarians from Czechoslovakia and Yugoslavia, Greeks from Bulgarian Macedonia, and German minorities from wherever they still

The roads of war

The world after the war

existed. In this brutal way the problem of national minorities was eliminated. Some peoples never returned home, most of the Poles for instance who fought on the British side throughout the war. Indeed there is still an anti-Communist Polish government in exile.

The victors of the Second World War pursued, they hoped more successfully, two aims that had caused much stir at the end of the First World War: the punishment of war criminals and the establishment of a worldwide organization for the maintenance of peace. An International Tribunal, in fact a tribunal of the four great victors, was set up at Nuremberg. Twenty-one leading Germans, headed by Goering, were charged with war crimes. Eleven were sentenced to death, three to life imprisonment, and four to various terms of imprisonment. Goering took poison an hour before he was due to go to the gallows; the other ten were hanged under brutal circumstances. In Japan seven leaders were hanged after a similar trial.

The immutable principles of justice were supposed to have been vindicated. Many of the charges were real crimes in either war or peace – the mass murders of prisoners of war and hostages, the extermination of the Jews. But what were the crimes against peace – preparing for aggressive war or waging it? All the Powers

had prepared for war, and it was a common complaint against the Allied governments that they had not prepared for it adequately or even that they had failed to launch a preventive or aggressive war themselves. Aggressive war, it seemed, was defined by the victors as a war against one of themselves, and Churchill passed a wise verdict on the proceedings at Nuremberg when he said to Ismay, 'You and I must take care not to lose the next war.'

The United Nations Organization was the most prized achievement of the Second World War: an organization truly world wide and with effective powers for maintaining peace. But its strength depended on the continuing unity of the five Great Powers, who became permanent members of the Security Council and each of whom held a veto over its proceedings. This unity did not outlive the end of the war. There was a rift between Soviet Russia and the United States, with the other three Great Powers more or less completely on the American side. The rift deepened until it became an antagonism so sharp as almost to resemble war, and it was indeed called the Cold War – war without fighting.

This outcome was not surprising. The two worlds of Communism and Capitalist democracies had been forced together by the common dangers from Germany and Japan. When these

Right V-E day in Leicester Square

Right, below Homeless German families

dangers were removed, the rival worlds returned to the mutual suspicions which they had harboured ever since the Bolshevik Revolution of 1917. At the time this charitable explanation was accepted by few. According to one view, Soviet Russia was set on the worldwide establishment of Communism. According to the other the United States wished to dominate the world and to impose the rules of liberal Capitalism.

The first view was certainly wrong. All Stalin's acts during the war, for instance in France, Italy and China, showed that any extension of Communism beyond Soviet Russia's sphere of influence was highly repugnant to him. The establishment of Communist rule in the states bordering on Russia came as consequence of the Cold War and did not cause it. As has been well said, the alarm over Russian aggression was a self-fulfilling prophecy: if you expected the worst from the Russians, you got it. Even so, Stalin tolerated liberal democracy in two border states, Finland and Austria, when it was coupled with a genuine popular support.

So far as Soviet policy was assertive, if not aggressive, this had nothing to do with Communism. It was the old Russian claim to be treated as an equal, a claim that the Western Powers did not acknowledge during the war except at Yalta, and still less after it. The Mediterranean provides a clear example. Soviet Russia was nearer to the Mediterranean than were either Great Britain or the United States, and more dependent on it as an outlet to the world. Yet the British and Americans were indignant at Russia's intrusion into the Mediterranean, while maintaining large fleets there themselves. The Russians were constantly urged to 'compromise'. What the Western Powers meant by this was 'unconditional surrender' – an abandonment of the Communist way of life. They would have been stuck for an answer if the Russians had offered to compromise by abolishing, say, the secret police and the one-party state on condition the Western Powers abolished the private ownership of land and the means of production.

The charge of American aggressiveness had more substance. Most Americans did not want a third world war, but many believed that their preponderance of power would bring Russian withdrawals of itself. Truman conveniently forgot the promises of a reconstruction loan to Russia that Roosevelt had made. At successive international meetings the Americans sought to impose their own way instead of securing a compromise. Some Americans even talked of 'rolling back' Russia from Europe and the Far East. Any such projects gradually died away, partly because the Russians soon discovered the nuclear secrets for themselves and partly because it came to be realized that atomic bombs were solely weapons of destruction, unsuited for a war of liberation. Maybe, too, the emergence of Communist China as a Power independent of both Soviet Russia and the United States tempered the rivalry of the two original World Powers. By the 1970s it was generally agreed in the West that the Cold War had been a false alarm, a mistaken enterprise, from the start, and, though the Russians never admit that they have been wrong, they probably think so too.

Mankind has been disappointed that the Second World War was not immediately followed by the outbreak of universal peace. But this was not its object. The Second World War was fought to liberate peoples from Nazi, and to a lesser extent Japanese, tyranny. In this it succeeded, at however high a price. No one can contemplate the present state of things without acknowledging that people everywhere are happier, freer and more prosperous than they would have been if Nazi Germany and Japan had won, and this applies as much to the countries under Communist control as it does to the world of Capitalist democracy. Future generations may dismiss the Second World War as 'just another war'. Those who experienced it know that it was a war justified in its aims and successful in accomplishing them. Despite all the killing and destruction that accompanied it, the Second World War was a good war.

Index

179; visits Hitler, 201; flight and death of, 220–1
Mustang aircraft, 179, 188–9

Nagasaki, 228
Namsos, 48
Nanking, 29
Naples, 84, 176
Napoleon, Emperor, 63, 66, 98, 101–2, 171
Narvik, 45, 47–8
Nazi-Soviet Pact, 34, 41, 205
Neisse, western, 231
Nemen, the, 216
Nenni, 175
New Guinea, 168
New Mexico, 106
New Zealand, 66, 83, 104
Nimitz, Admiral Chester W., at Midway, 136, 139; strategy of, 151, 168, 185
Nomonhan, Battle of, 29
Non-Aggression Pact (German-Polish), 32, 33
Normandy, 59, 130; campaign in, 173, 195, 201–2, 220
North Africa, French, landings in, 150, 153–4; 159, 168
Norway, campaign in, 45–8, 58, 153; Germans rule in, 63; 84, 97; Hitler's fears for, 141; Germans in, surrender, 222
Noyelles, 55
Nuremberg, International Tribunal at, 233

Oahu, 124
O'Connor, General Sir Richard, 85, 86–7, 88–9, 119
Oder, 216, 231
Okinawa, 226
Oppenheimer, J. R., 148
Oradour-sur-Glane, 63
Oran, 49, 62
Oslo, 47–8
Oświęcim (Auschwitz), 21, 149
Overlord, Operation, 186

PQ 17, 141
Pacific, war in, 10–11, 29, 81, 126–7; Japanese advance in, 135–6; American advance in, 169; British in, 212; American gains in, 232
Pact of Steel, 33
Palestine, 84
Papua, 136
Paris, Churchill in, 54–5; occupied, 59; SS in, arrested, 201–2; liberated, 204–5
Pas de Calais, 195, 201
Passchendaele, Battle of, 130
Patton, General George, in Sicily, 173; in Brittany, 202–3; and Montgomery, 205; at Bastogne, 215; crosses Rhine, 220; does not reach Prague, 221, 223
Paulus, Field Marshal Friedrich, and Stalingrad, 146–7, 160; surrenders, 166
Pearl Harbor, Japanese attack on, 10–11, 17, 121–7, 130, 136, 210–11, 228
Peking, 29
Persia, 80, 82, 84, 104, 128
Petacci, Clara, 220–1
Pétain, Marshal H. P., 56, 60, 80, 92
Peter, King, 89
Philippine Sea, Battle of the, 210
Philippines, 121, 130, 210–11, 228
Phillips, Admiral Tom, 220–1
Pilsen, 223
Placentia Bay, meeting at, 105
Ploesti, 177
Po, the, 192, 201

Poland, Hitler and, 32–3; Nazi-Soviet Pact and, 34–5; German invasion of, 11, 35–6, 97, 229; partition of, 41; 63, 65; exiled government of, 66; Jews in, 138; question of, at Teheran, 186–7; Russians enter, 189; Home Army of, 206; question of, at Yalta, 218–19; war losses of, 229–30; question of, at Potsdam, 231; new frontier of, 232
Pomerania, 232
Port Arthur, 232
Port Darwin, 135
Port Moresby, 125
Portugal, 64, 175
Potsdam, conference at, 226, 231
Pound, Admiral D., 83, 141
Poznań, 217
Prague, 32, 221, 223
Prince of Wales, 120; sunk, 131–2, 141

Quebec, meetings at, 175, 212
Quisling, V., 63

Raeder, Grand Admiral Erich, 32, 68, 79, 142
Rangoon, 135, 225
Rastenburg (Kętrzyn), 147
Ravenna, 192
Remagen, 220
Reparations, 13; at Yalta, 218, 230; at Potsdam, 231
Repulse, 120; sunk, 131–2, 141
Resistance, 21; Czech, 223; French, 170, 193, 202, 205, 229; German, 170, 201; Greek, 213; Italian, 176–7, 192, 221; Yugoslav, 178
Rethondes, armistice signed at, 60
Reynaud, P., 46, 54, 56, 59–60
Rhine, the, 205, 220
Rhone, the, 204
Ribbentrop, J., 33; in Moscow, 34, 41; and Molotov, 82; and Japan, 120
Ritchie, General N., 143
Robertson, General Sir W., 157
Robespierre, M., 230
Romania, and Hitler, 32, 44, 64, 83, 98–9; armies of, broken, 167, 177; Russians reach, 189; surrenders, 207; 212; Vyshinsky in, 219; peace with, 230
Rome, 172; bombed, 175; not taken, 176; taken, 190–2; 220
Rommel, Field Marshal Erwin, 22; on Meuse, 53; at Arras, 56; in North Africa, 88, 92–3, 96, 142; at El Alamein, 143–4; 157; in Tunisia, 159, 171; on Italians, 173; in Italy, 175; in Normandy, 195; suicide of, 201
Roosevelt, President F. D., and Depression, 16; position of, 22, 24–5; and Japan, 20, 27, 81–2, 119–20; appeal to, 60; and Battle of Atlantic, 80; and lend-lease, 86; and Soviet Russia, 104, 116; at Placentia Bay, 105; and Pearl Harbor, 121; at war, 128; and Second Front, 150; and North Africa, 151; and Darlan, 160; at Casablanca, 169–70; and fall of Mussolini, 171; and Badoglio, 175–6; at Teheran, 180; and Italian campaign, 192; and France, 193; at Quebec, 212; at Yalta, 218–19; death of, 220; and reparations, 231, 232
Rosenberg, A., 102
Rostov, 118
Rotterdam, 51
Royal Air Force, 12, 29, 70, 129, 206
Royal Oak, sunk, 43
Ruhr, the, 51, 179, 181, 205, 221

Rundstedt, Field Marshal C. R. G., in France, 50, 56, 68; in Soviet Russia, 100–1, 106–7, 144; in Normandy, 195, 201
Russia, 11; (*see also* Soviet Russia)
Ruthenia, 231

Saar, the, 205
Saint-Lô, 202
Saint-Nazaire, 203
Saipan, 210
Salo, 177
Salonika, 44, 80, 89, 91, 93
San, the, 216
Sardinia, 173
Scharnhorst, 141
Schelde, the, 50, 55
Schmid, Anton, 149
Schnorkel, 188, 213
Sea Lion, Operation, 68, 72
Second Front, 128–30, 150, 153, 169, 186, 191, 193; Soviet, asked for, 216
Sedan, 17, 50, 53, 123
Seine, the, 193, 201–4
Serbia, 89
Shanghai, 29
Siam, 119, 131
Sicily, 10, 88; landing in, 169, 172–3, 176, 220
Sidi Barrani, 80
Singapore, 87, 100; fears for, 104–5, 120–1; fall of, 131–2, 141, 144; recovery of, 229
Slapstick, Operation, 176
Slovakia, 64, 209, 218
Slovenia, 89, 209
Smolensk, 102, 180
Smuts, Field Marshal J., 89
Solomon Islands, 168
Somerville, Admiral Sir J., at Oran, 62; in Ceylon, 135
Somme, Battle of the, 17, 130; 55, 59–60
Sorge, R., 117
South America, 81
Soviet Russia, grievances of, 13; and Depression, 17; and League of Nations, 18; isolated, 20; conflict of, with Japan, 29; excluded at Munich, 31; Anglo-French negotiations with, 33–4; and Polish war, 41; supplies Germany, 43, 65; and Finland, 45–6; Hitler and, 22, 68, 81–2; invaded, 96, 102; losses of, 107; and Far East, 124; strategy of, 126; lend-lease to, 128; convoys to, 140–1; winter campaign of, 144; and Stalingrad offensive, 146; wants share in Italy, 177; army of, 180; breach of, with Poland, 187; German strength in, 188; Churchill and, 212; concessions by, 218; enters Far Eastern war, 226; war losses of, 229–30; makes peace with Japan, 230; East Prussia only gain, 231; rift of, with United States, 233–4
Spaatz, General K., 193
Spain, Fascist, 64
Spanish Blue Division, 99
Spanish Civil War, 20, 189
Stagg, Group Captain, 195
Stalin, J., position of, 22–5; on alliance negotiations, 34; and Poland, 41; and Finland, 45; remains neutral, 83; Hitler on, 98; and German invasion, 99, 103–4; demands of, 106; remains in Moscow, 117; thinks war won, 144; insists on offensive, 146; Churchill meets, 152–3; not at Casablanca, 169–70; and Sicily landing, 172; and Tito, 178; and Battle